Abhidhammā

The Buddhist Analysis of Consciousness

Part Three

Abhidhammā Categories

Published for free distribution

Abhidhammā:
The Buddhist Analysis of Consciousness
(Part Three: Abhidhammā Categories)

Author: Las Vegas Sayādaw
Edited by: Upāsaka Chaan
Cover photo: Buddha of Hawaii (Marilyn Tam)

Chaiya Meditation Monastery
7925 Virtue Ct., Las Vegas, NV 89113
Tel.: 702-456-3838 Cell: 702-219-0377
www.ChaiyaCMM.org
Email: Chaiya@ChaiyaCMM.org

ISBN 9798336114409

Namo tassa bhagavato arahato sammā-sambuddhassa
Namo tassa bhagavato arahato sammā-sambuddhassa
Namo tassa bhagavato arahato sammā-sambuddhassa

Contents

Foreword *11*

Abhidhammā Categories *13*

Akusalasaṅgaha 16

Āsavā (The 4 Intoxicants) 16

Oghā (The 4 Floods) 21

Yogā (The 4 Bonds) 23

Ganthā (The 4 Bodily Ties) 24

Upādānā (The 4 Graspings) 27

Nīvaraṇā (The 6 Hindrances) 31

Anusaya (The 7 Latent Defilements) 40

Saṃyojana (The 10 Fetters) 51

Kilesa (The 10 Mental Defilements) 63

Missakasaṅgaha 89

Hetu (The 6 Roots) 89

Jhānaṅga (The 7 Factors of Jhāna) 91

Maggaṅga (The 12 Constituents of the Path) 92

Indriya (The 22 Controlling Faculties) 107

Bala (The 9 Powers) 118

Adhipati (The 4 Dominating Factors) 122

Āhāra (The 4 Nutriment) 125

Bodhipakkhiyasaṅgaha 138

The Four Satipaṭṭhāna 138

The Four Sammappadhānā 153

The Four Iddhipādā 155

The Five Indriya 157

The Five Bala 160

The Seven Bojjhaṅga 170

The Eight Maggaṅga 176

Sabbasaṅgaha 184

The Five Khandha 184

The Five Upādānakkhandhā 189

The 12 Āyatana 192

The 18 Dhātu 195

The Four Sacca 198

Foreword

In May 2021, Las Vegas Sayādaw asked me to transcribe his recorded talks on *Abhidhammā*—the Buddhist analysis of consciousness—and compile them into a series of free books for his students and temple visitors. He handed me a large stack of CD's, containing some 100 hours of lectures he'd given on the topic in the English language.

I was intimidated.

Abhidhammā is a daunting and microscopically-detailed body of teachings. Known as the "higher doctrine," it explains *every* aspect of consciousness.

I felt in no way qualified to handle this undertaking.

And yet the master had asked me to do it.

Step-by-step, I began to pore through dozens upon dozens of long talks that Sayādaw had given to students in the late 1990s, shortly after the opening of Chaiya Meditation Monastery at its original location in a residential structure at Tropicana and Buffalo. As I did, I encountered fascinating lectures on mental states, the processes of death and rebirth, different beings and their various planes of existence, and the multi-faceted mechanics of *kamma*.

I was riveted.

But the project was also an exercise in patience, in creativity, and in exploring my own understanding of the Buddha's teachings—"higher" or otherwise.

I sometimes encountered garbled audio, missing files, and frankly, subject matter that I failed to understand. I often needed to consult other *Abhidhammā* publications and Sayādaw himself to help fill in the blanks. As I crafted these books, I often paraphrased and/or dramatically edited Sayādaw's words to facilitate ease of reading or narrative flow. And although I tried to limit doing so, I occasionally employed my own words to convey aspects of the teachings when I felt that the transcription of spoken word to written word just wasn't getting the point across.

Please forgive any poor judgments I may have made in the course of putting these books together.

My hope—and I believe Sayadaw's as well—is that this guide to *Abhidhammā* will provide its readers a tremendous opportunity to understand more deeply their own practice of this Dhamma.

Upāsaka Chaan
Santa Barbara, January 2023

Abhidhammā Categories

In *Pāli*, this chapter of Abhidhammā is called *Samuccaya*. Here, we will classify the subject matter into four sections, or four groups:

1) *Akusalasaṅgaha*

You're already familiar with the word *akusala*, right? It means unwholesome, or immoral. *Saṅgaha* means compendium. So this first group is the compendium of immoral categories. We will discuss unwholesome consciousness and unwholesome mental factors in this first section.

2) *Missakasaṅgaha*

The second section is the compendium of mixed categories. It covers unwholesome and wholesome mixed together.

3) *Bodhipakkhiyasaṅgaha*

The third section is the compendium of the factors of enlightenment. This is very important, right? We'll study the 37 *bodhipakkhiya*.

4) *Sabbasaṅgaha*

The fourth section talks about the compendium of the whole. This refers to miscellaneous mind and matter.

We'll be studying these four sections next, starting with the compendium of immoral categories.

Akusalasaṅgaha

Akusala means immoral or unwholesome, and *saṅgaha* means compendium, right? Here, we'll first be talking about the four *āsavā*. If you read books about this subject, you'll repeatedly encounter the words *āsavā*, *oghā*, *yogā*, *ganthā* and *upādānā*. After we study these terms, it will be very useful for our understanding. When we understand the meanings, we will find it very useful for our meditation.

Āsavā

Okay, so there are four *āsavā*, which we can also call the four defilements, or the four intoxicants. These *āsavā* are like fermented liquor. We might put liquor in a pot for a long time and then drink it. Why? Because once it ferments it can strongly intoxicate a man and make him drunk. We call this fermented liquor. In the same way, these four *āsavā* (intoxicants, or defilements) have been fermenting in our mind and body for a long, long time.

The four *āsavā* include:

1) *Kāmāsava* (sense-desires)

2) *Bhavāsava* (attachment to *jhāna* or existence in *rūpa* or *arūpa* planes)

3) *Diṭṭhāsava* (false view, or wrong view)
4) *Avijjāsava* (ignorance)

These four kinds of *āsavā* make a man drunk and forgetful of his liberation. Why is he forgetful? Because he's drunk. It's like he's been drunk on fermented liquor for many, many lives.

Kāmāsava

Kāma refers to visible objects, sounds, smells, tastes, and tangible objects. We call these *kāma*, or sense objects. We're talking here about attachment to the sense-sphere.

Where can we see *kāmāsava* nowadays?

To what sorts of things does the eye get attached? The television, right? Or attached to movies. We can watch television the whole night but find it difficult to sit in meditation for an hour. These are examples of attachment to visible objects.

When you drive from Las Vegas to Los Angeles, it takes about four hours. During that time, you can listen to music the whole time, right? But what about this lecture? After one hour of listening, you get bored. Right? This is an example of attachment to sound.

What about smell? One time I saw a small bottle of perfume that cost $5,000. People are attached to pretty smells.

How about taste? What about your tongue? Have we ever gone to a restaurant or a party and spent an incredible amount of money on a single meal? Couldn't that money have been used to benefit our meditation center? It's not just one time that people spend this kind of money on meals. People do this a lot, right? We have to go shopping a lot so that we can fill our kitchens with food. Why? For the love of the taste of good food.

What about tangible objects, like your clothing? How many sets of clothes do you have at home? In different colors too, right? You probably have many, many outfits. But you only need one, right? Instead, you might have a few dozen. What about your shoes? How many do you have at home?

What do all these examples illustrate? Attachment to sense desires.

Why are you attached so much? Because the attachment has been there for longer than just this one life. It's like fermented liquor. For so many years, so many lives, you've been attached to these things. That's why it's very hard to get away from the sense-sphere.

Q: I once knew a man from Africa who said that if you go to the refrigerator and can't decide what to eat, you're not really hungry.

It's true.

What we're talking about here is why the Buddha said that some have mental suffering and some have physical suffering. Where's it come from? It comes from sense-desire. It's because of your desire. Desire causes us suffering.

So this is *kāmāsava*, or sense-desire.

Bhavāsava

This is attachment to *jhāna*. It includes both *rūpajhāna* and *arūpajhāna*. If you're attached to your *jhāna*, then it's not wholesome. No, it's unwholesome. Also, when we sit in meditation we might experience auras, a feeling of lightness in the body, rapture, quietude or a number of other special things. If we attach to these special feelings or experiences, our *vipassanā* knowledge cannot grow. Instead, it will stop right there.

These are all illustrations of *bhavāsava*. In reality, it is *lobha*. It is still *lobha*, or attachment.

We can also be attached to existence in the *rūpa* or *arūpa* planes. Some people practice meditation or do some other meritorious thing and wish to be reborn in the *Brahma* world. This is *bhavāsava*. It is attachment to the *Brahma* world.

The Buddha said that we should not attach to anything–no plane, no person. When you do something meritorious, it would be better to think: "By the power of my meritorious deed, may I attain *nibbāna* and escape from all kinds of suffering." But if you want or wish to be reborn in any existence, this is *bhavāsava*, or attachment.

Why are you attached to *jhāna*, or to the *rūpa* or *arūpa* planes? Because we have been attached to these in many, many previous lives. This is *āsavā*.

Diṭṭhāsava

This is false views. We have 62 kinds of false views, but briefly, there are just two: *sassatadiṭṭhi* (eternalism) and *ucchediṭṭhi* (annihilation). So, *diṭṭhi* means wrong view.

You might have this wrong view: you think your body is an entity–a person, a man or a woman. You think you're I or you. This is false view. Really, there is no me, I, person, no entity, no individual, no man and no woman.

What do we really have? Realities, which we've studied. Your body is matter, right? Your mind is consciousness. Where is man or woman? Not to be found.

We have studied this, and now we know. Now we have right thoughts and good views.

When we call someone a man or a woman, a mister or a missus, we are using concepts (*paññatti*). But, really, that's all it is. There is only the reality of mind and matter–*citta*, *cetasika* and *rūpa*. That's all we have.

Avijjāsava

This is ignorance.

It is ignorance with regard to past lives. In other words, you don't know your past life and where you came from. If you don't understand *Abhidhammā*, you won't know where you were in the previous life. You might think, "Maybe this is my first life" or "Maybe I just ended up here in this human world." You don't understand your past life.

Avijjāsava is also ignorance regarding your future life after you die. "Where will I have to be reborn again?" You don't know.

Avijjāsava also includes ignorance with regard to both past life and future life, as well as the Four Noble Truths.

You know the Four Noble Truths, right? The first is suffering, the second is the cause of suffering, the third is the cessation of suffering, and the fourth is the path leading to the cessation of suffering, or the Noble Eightfold Path.

And *avijjāsava* is also ignorance regarding the law of dependent origination, or *paṭiccasamuppāda*.

So, *avijjāsava* is ignorance (*moha*) with regard to these eight things: past life, future life, both past and future lives, the Four Noble Truths, and the law of dependent origination.

We'll study the Four Noble Truths and *paṭiccasamuppāda* in detail later, but for now, I'll just briefly talk a bit about the law of dependent origination. These topics are very interesting.

Because of our ignorance, there is *saṅkhāra*. In other words, mental formations (volition) arises. Because of *saṅkhāra*, *viññāṇa* (consciousness) arises. Because of consciousness, mind and matter arises. Because of mind and matter, and so on. We call this dependent origination.

With *avijjāsava*, you don't understand this. If you don't understand about the past, the future, both the past and the future, suffering or its cause (i.e., you don't know why you suffer), this is *moha*, or ignorance.

Where does suffering come from? It's craving, or attachment. When you understand that, you'll know cessation and the way leading to its cessation. You will know that because of A and B there is C. In other words, you'll begin to understand cause and effect.

This is dependent origination.

But, because of *avijjāsava*, we don't know about these eight things.

With these four kinds of *āsavā*, how many realities are there?

Kāmāsava is *lobha*. *Bhavāsava* is also *lobha*. *Diṭṭhāsava* is *diṭṭhi cetasika*. Among the 52 kinds of mental factors, one is *diṭṭhi cetasika* (wrong view), right? And *avijjāsava* is *moha*.

So the names are fourfold but the realities are just these three–*lobha*, *diṭṭhi* and *moha*.

See that?

Lobha is attachment, *diṭṭhi* is wrong view, and *moha* is ignorance. These look like fermented liquor. They make a man drunk and forgetful of his liberation.

"I don't have time to practice meditation."

Because of what? Sense-desire, right?

"I have to go to a party...a restaurant...watch TV...follow the news..."

Sense-desire.

Or maybe there's *bhavāsava*, which includes attachment to things like "spending time with my family...my husband...my boyfriend...my girlfriend." This is *bhavāsava*. You don't have time to practice meditation and have become forgetful of liberation.

What about *diṭṭhāsava*?

"I don't want to sit in meditation. It's a waste of time."

We sometimes don't even know that we have ignorance, or *moha*. We don't know why we're in the situation we are in, where we came from or where we have to be reborn again. We don't know about cause and effect. We don't know anything.

These *āsavā* make a person drunk. And then, he cannot attain *nibbāna*.

This is because of *āsavā*.

After we do good things together here, I guide the people to say, "By the power of my meritorious deeds, may I be free from *āsavā*." We do this because we want to gain enlightenment, or *nibbāna*.

How many *abhiñña* (super-intellect) are there? Six, right? For a normal person, there are five: celestial eye, celestial ear, and so on. But the sixth one is for *arahants*. It is called *āsavakkhaya-ñaṇa*, or the extinction of *āsavā*. This means no *āsavā*.

When the Buddha gained enlightenment, there was the extinction of *āsavā*. And then he became the Buddha. He had eradicated all sense-desire, all attachment to *jhāna* or to existence in the *rūpa* or *arūpa* planes, false views and ignorance.

I would like to stop here for today. We'll continue next week. Thank you.

...

Today is June 20, 1998. Last week, we discussed the four *āsavās* (the four defilements, or the four intoxicants). Today, we will start by studying *oghā*. The name is different but the realities are the same. Their natures are also the same.

Oghā

We have four *oghās*, or four floods. The word *oghā* translates as flood. The word *oghā* is used because the four *oghās* look like the current of a great flood. If something or someone comes upon a flood, it might sweep them away, right? It flows directly to the ocean. In the same way, the four *oghās* can drag any being into the states of misery, or the woeful states. This is why the four *oghās* are compared to the current of a great flood.

1) *Kāmoghā*

This is *kāma-oghā*. *Oghā* is flood, and *kāma* is sensual desire. So, *kāmoghā* is the flood of sensual desire.

See? It's the same as *āsavā*.

2) *Bhāvoghā*

This is *bhāva-oghā*, or the flood of attachment to *jhāna* or existence in *rūpa* or *arūpa* planes.

After you understand the four *āsavās*, you see that the four *oghās* are very similar.

3) *Diṭṭhoghā*

This is *diṭṭhi-oghā*. *Diṭṭhi* is false view, right? So this is the flood of false views.

4) *Avijjoghā*

This is *avijjā-oghā*, or the flood of ignorance.

All of these are *akusala*, or unwholesome. They are unwholesome mental factors. The reality, the essential element, of *kāmoghā* is *lobha*, or attachment. For *bhāvoghā*, the essential element is also *lobha*. With *diṭṭhoghā*, false view is *diṭṭhi*, right? So the reality is *diṭṭhi*. And *avijjoghā* is ignorance, or *moha*.

So, every day, people are swept away because of these four floods.

Kāmoghā

We are in the current of this great flood. We enjoy our lives, we enjoy sensual objects. We want physical objects, sounds, smells, tastes, tangible objects. We want this every day. And because of this, we mostly don't have time to do good things with our lives.

Why is this? Because of the flood of sensual desire. We want to see this or that, hear this or that, eat this or that. We just follow sensual desires. And it looks like a flood.

Q: Does this mean that oghā is overwhelming us more than āsavā? Is it more powerful?

Oghā overwhelms us. But to the same degree as *āsavā* does. The only difference between the two is the technique that the Buddha was using to teach. He used *āsavā* as an illustration because some people were able to understand it right away, whereas others were able to understand it better when he described it as a flood. He just used these as different ways to help people understand the same thing.

If someone uses the term "one quarter," you might immediately understand what he means, right? But someone else might understand better if you used the term "25 cents." This is why the Buddha explained this in different ways. But, the realities are the same.

What do we call that part of a river that pulls you down? A whirlpool, right? If something gets stuck in a whirlpool, they get pulled down. *Oghā* is like this.

Human beings are mostly in this flood every day. It pulls us down to hell or the animal kingdom. Otherwise, everyone could attain enlightenment, right? But these floods prevent that.

We call this sensual desire.

Bhāvoghā

You're attached to your *jhāna* or to existence in *rūpa* or *arūpa* planes. Or even to this world. You're attached to your possessions. Or perhaps you're a teacher and you're attached to your job. Maybe you're a woman and you're attached to being a woman.

We call all of these *bhāvoghā*.

Diṭṭhoghā

This is wrong view. This is when your view is not correct but you're attached to it.

Avijjoghā

Ignorance. This is not knowing realities.

The four *āsavās* and the four *oghās*. They're the same, right? Their realities are just threefold: *lobha*, *diṭṭhi* and *moha*.

Let's look at *yogā* now.

Yogā

Yogā is the same as the other two. These are also four. They are described as bonds or yokes.

1) *Kāmayogā*
2) *Bhāvayogā*
3) *Diṭṭhiyogā*
4) *Avijjayogā*

These four yokes bind us to the round of existence, just as oxen are yoked to a cart. They cannot get away from the cart, right? Beings who have these four *yogās* cannot get away from these 31 planes of existence. They just continue to be reborn as human beings or *devas* or *brahmās* or animals or hell beings. It's because they are yoked to these worlds. These four kinds of *yogās* yoke beings to the round of existence. That's why *yogā* is translated as yoke or bond.

The realities for these four *yogās* as the same as for *āsavā* and *oghā*. *Kāmayogā* is *lobha*, *bhāvayogā* is *lobha*, *diṭṭhiyogā* is *diṭṭhi* and *avijjayogā* is *moha*.

Ganthā

Next, let's look at the four *ganthās*. These are different from *yogā*. *Ganthā* means bind, or tie. These are the four bodily ties.

What do they tie or bind? They bind the mind with the body, or they bind the present body with the bodies of future existences. It's because of these *ganthās* that we have mind and body when we are reborn again. They bind mind and body together, and they bind this present body and future bodies in future existences. After we die in this present life, we have to be reborn again, right? We take another body in another existence. So, these four bodily ties combine this present life and the future life.

1) *Abhijjhā kāyaganthā*

This is covetousness. *Ganthā* means bind, or tie. *Kāya*, here, doesn't mean body. In this context, it means group. It refers to grouping the mental and the physical. *Kāya* means grouping of mind and matter. What's *abhijjhā*? It is the intention to possess another person's property unlawfully. If we see someone's property and want to take it unlawfully, it's called *abhijjhā*. It's a mental action. Its reality is *lobha cetasika*.

2) *Vyāpāda kāyaganthā*

Vyāpāda is also a mental action. It's ill will. That's what *vyā* means. It intends to bring about the death or destruction of a person. Perhaps you want someone to die or lose their business. This is ill will. It's one kind of *ganthā*.

3) *Sīlabbataparāmāsa kāyaganthā*

Here, *sīlabbata* refers to rites and ceremonies, or rites and rituals. *Parāmāsa* means adherence. So the term means adherence to rites and ceremonies. Although this is how we usually see it translated into English, the meaning is actually deeper than that.

Let me give you an example of *sīlabbata*:

In the time of the Buddha, there were people who practiced as if they were a dog or a cow. They believed that if they practiced like a dog or a cow, they could purify their mind. And they thought that after death they would then go to heaven, so they practiced in this way. These people wouldn't wear clothes–they'd go around naked. And when they went somewhere, they'd walk about on four legs. When they saw people, they'd greet them like a dog or a cow might.

These people felt that practicing in this way would make them pure and be liberated and therefore gain *nibbāna*. But this is wrong view. It's one kind of *diṭṭhi*. We can call this bovine morality, practicing like a cow. Practicing like a dog is called canine morality. It is *sīlabbataparāmāsa kāyaganthā*.

This sort of practice is not found in Buddhism.

There's a story about *sīlabbataparāmāsa kāyaganthā* from the time of the Buddha that I'd like to share with you:

There were these two men. They practiced bovine and canine moralities for a long, long time. They did this because they thought they would become pure and be liberated by this practice.

When the two men saw the Buddha, they asked him questions. They told him that they practiced in this way for many years, and then asked, "After we die, what will happen to us? Can we go to heaven?"

The Buddha replied, "Don't ask me about that."

The men repeated their question to the Buddha, who again declined to answer.

After the men asked a third time, the Buddha said, "I asked you to stop asking me these questions. I don't want to answer you. But since you asked me three times, I have to answer you." He then explained, "Those who practice bovine conduct or dog conduct, after death will be reborn as a cow or a dog. If you think that practicing this way will lead you to purify your mind so that you can be reborn in heaven, after death you will instead be reborn in hell because this is wrong view."

The two men started to cry. They cried because they realized that they'd practiced this way because they thought that it was the best way to purify their mind and to be liberated. But the Buddha had explained that it was not; in fact, it was the opposite of how they should have been thinking.

The older of the two men became a Buddhist and changed his views to align with the Buddha, the Dhamma and the Saṅgha. He requested the Buddha ordain him as a monk. Once he was a monk, he practiced meditation and gained enlightenment.

Of the two men, this man–the one who practiced like a dog but then ordained as a monk–attained enlightenment, but the other man did not.

Q: To me, that sounds like people nowadays who think that in order to practice spirituality, you have to be natural. To them, this means that they don't think and don't study. Instead, they just react spontaneously to everything that happens. This sounds to me like a rather animal-like approach to spirituality.

This is one kind of *sīlabbataparāmasā*.

Today in India there are still people who practice in this way. They don't wear clothes, going about trying to be natural. When they eat, they put the food in their palm and lap it up.

There are people who have high respect for these practitioners. They think, "They're not attached to anything." But the Buddha said this is *sīlabbataparāmāsa*, or wrong view. The reality is *diṭṭhi*.

4) *Idaṃsaccābhinivesa kāyaganthā*

This is also a kind of wrong view, or dogmatic belief. Although these people practice incorrectly, they believe that their way alone is the truth. They believe that the way of others is not true or correct. This is also one kind of *diṭṭhi*.

If we still have wrong view, we cannot gain enlightenment in this life. This is why the Buddha said that we need to study, or *pariyatti*. But we also need to practice, or *paṭipatti*. And we also need *paṭivedha*. In Buddhism, we have what is called *pariyatti sāsana*. This is studying or learning. We also have *paṭipatti sāsana*, or practicing. And we have *paṭivedha sāsana*, or realization.

If we study but don't practice, there will be no realization. If we practice but don't study or know the correct way, we will not get realization. So we need both studying and practicing in order to clear our views.

So, among these four *ganthās*, how many realities do we have? The first one is *lobha*, the second one is *dosa*, and the third and fourth *ganthās* are *diṭṭhi*. These threefold realities–*lobha, dosa* and *diṭṭhi*–bind mind with body, and this present body and the future body. We have to be reborn again and again because of these *ganthās*.

Upādānā

We also have four *upādānās*. This is grasping, or clinging. It's stronger than attachment. It is strong attachment. If you're very attached to something, we call it *upādānā*.

1) *Kāmupādānā*

This is sense-desire. There is *kāma upādānā*, which we shorten into the word *kāmupādānā*. This is clinging to five-sense-objects.

Some people have to watch TV every day, right? Without TV, they are really unhappy. They're very attached to the TV and it's very important to them. Other people watch movies every day. They are attached to five-sense-objects.

Other people like food very, very much. They say, "I love curry...pork...beef." Or they say, "I like to drink." Maybe they can't appreciate a meal without drinking. They're attached and clinging, right? These are examples of *kāmupādānā*. Some people are very attached to tangible objects, like their clothing or personal effects. They attach so much.

This strong attachment is *kāmupādānā*.

Think about most people nowadays. Except for those who practice meditation, people have just *kāmupādānā*–clinging to five-sense-objects–all day, every day. They spend their time immersed in these five-sense-objects. Many, many hours each day, right?

Q: Isn't the whole point of a lot of advertising to encourage this?

Oh yes. But the people who watch ads don't understand themselves.

Particularly in America, there are 6- or 7-year-old kids who sit close to the TV and watch it all day, every day. I think it's not good. If we start doing this when we're six years old, we can probably guess how attached we'll still be when we're 60 years old.

But what about those of us who go to pray, chant or sit in meditation? Why is that? It's because we have changed our mind.

Most people don't understand this. They just go on enjoying their lives, watching TV and playing games, right?

How about you? Are you lost in these things every day? How many hours a day?

We're not talking about normal attachment here. This is strong attachment.

Good luck trying to invite someone to come sit with you in meditation for 15 minutes. They'll likely say they don't have time. Why? Because of these five-sense-objects. They are clinging to these. It's not only kids either. Even old people are attached so much to these five-sense-objects.

2) *Diṭṭhupādānā*

This is false view. This is *diṭṭhi*.

Whatever you try to explain to them, they don't listen. Their ideas are so strong, but they are false views, wrong views. Even if you say, "Let's go do chanting and sit in meditation" or "We should go to the temple or church," maybe they don't think it's a good thing to do.

This is *diṭṭhi*, or wrong view.

3) *Sīlabbatupādānā*

This is the same as *ganthā*, right? This is adherence to rites and ceremonies, or adherence to bovine and canine conduct. Because of this, since the time of the Buddha until now–that's more than 2,500 years–we still have people practicing like this. This is why. How strong is their view? You can guess, right?

4) *Attavādupādāna*

Soul theory. This is having wrong view regarding soul theory.

These people believe that a soul exists. They might think that a soul exists inside their body, and after they die, the soul doesn't die. In other words, they believe that they have an immortal soul. After death, the soul goes into another body and continues. They think this soul is immortal.

In the context of the five aggregates, there are 20 kinds of soul theories:

a) soul is identical with the body

This means they regard the physical body as *atta*, or as a soul. When you do something–you stand, you sit, you move your hand, you stretch or bend–you think the person, you yourself, moves. This is what is meant by soul being identical with the body. It is you yourself who performs the movement.

For example, if you're writing a note, you think that it is you yourself doing the writing. Really, though, it's not you. The writing occurs because your mind wants to write. Because of the *vāyo* (air) element, your body is positioned so that you can write. But it's not actually you.

So, this is soul being identical with the body.

b) soul is possessed of (belongs to) the body

This means that when your hand or head (as examples) are moving, the moving occurs in accordance with the desire of *atta*. It is because of your *atta* that your body moves.

This is a kind of wrong view.

Q: This sounds like what some Western philosophers have called "the ghost in the machine." The soul is the ghost driving the body, which is the machine.

Yes, like this. They think the movement is in accordance with the desire of *atta*. Because *atta* wants to move, you have to move. *Atta* wants to sit, so you sit. If *atta* wants to get up, then you get up. If you think like this, we call this soul possessed of the body.

This is one kind of wrong view too. This regards the body.

c) soul is in the body

Some say that soul pervades the whole body. They believe this. They think that the soul lies quietly in the cavity of the heart. Then, if you want to see something, this *atta* (soul) comes into your eye and then you see it. See? *Atta* is a soul in your body. If you want to hear, the soul comes to your ear and listens.

This is another kind of wrong view.

d) body is in the soul

This means that the soul is bigger than the body. Body is in the soul.

All of these ideas are wrong view.

So, for the body, we have these four kinds of wrong view.

We have five aggregates, right? For the body, there are these four. For feeling (*vedanā*), we also have four:

e) soul is identical with feeling
f) soul is possessed of feeling
g) soul is in feeling
h) feeling is in the soul

For perception, there are also four. For mental formations, there are four. And for consciousness, there are four.

So we have five aggregates, right? In brief, these are the 20 kinds of wrong view concerning soul theory.

I don't know about America, but some people in the world still have these wrong views concerning *attavādupādāna*. They say, "We have a soul." Even some people in certain Buddhist countries hold these beliefs.

I don't know if you're aware of this, but in some places they put money in a dead person's mouth. The relatives say, "Maybe they will need this money to pay for passage over the bridge or across the river." This is why they put money in the dead person's mouth.

Q: They did this in the West too, until very recently. They used to put pennies on the eyelids of corpses.

See? It's the same.

Q: Sometimes, they'll also put the dead person's possessions in the casket with the body before they bury it. They might put the person's watch in there with them.

Yes, it's the same. In certain parts of China, they'll bury the person's car, his TV, his radio, thinking that he'll then be able to take these things with him. But, in reality, he can't.

Q: A good example of that is the ancient Egyptians. They'd put all sorts of wonderful things, like gold and very valuable jewels, in the tombs with the mummies.

Some people think, "After we die, for seven days our soul will stay in our house. And after seven days, it will go away."

This is a kind of *attavādupādāna*. Mostly, they think that soul doesn't die, right? They think it's immortal. We're talking about *diṭṭhi*, right?

In the *upādāna* group, there are only two realities. The first one is *lobha*, the second is *diṭṭhi*, the third is *diṭṭhi*, and the fourth is also *diṭṭhi*. There are only these two realities. Even if we say that there are four *upādānas* (grasping or clinging), there are only two realities.

Now, let's go to *nīvaraṇā*. This is very important, especially for meditators.

Nīvaraṇā

There are six *nīvaraṇā*. These are hindrances, or obstacles. There are actually eight, individually, but we will talk first about the six *nīvaraṇā*. These are obstacles to the way to celestial and supreme bliss. If you have these six hindrances, you cannot go to the celestial world and you cannot gain enlightenment. They prevent the arising of good thoughts and obstruct the eye of wisdom.

What are they? I'll tell you what they are and then I'll explain how they obstruct our way.

1) *Kāmacchandanīvaraṇā* (sense-desire)
2) *Vyāpādanīvaraṇā* (ill will, or aversion)
3) *Thīnamiddhanīvaraṇā* (sloth and torpor)
4) *Uddhaccakukkuccanīvaraṇā* (restlessness or remorse)
5) *Vicikicchānīvaraṇā* (skeptical doubt or perplexity)
6) *Avijjānīvaraṇā* (ignorance)

How can we go to heaven if we have these six hindrances? These hindrances stop, block and obstruct our way to the celestial world. Why? Well, what do we need to go to the celestial world? We need generosity and morality. We need good conduct.

When you have sense-desire, you are attached to the five-sense-objects. When you are attached to your body and to your property, you don't want to donate or share your belongings with others. This is because you are attached to these five-sense-objects. Perhaps you lack morality too. Then, after you die, you can't be reborn as a celestial being. Your way has been blocked.

If you have ill will, you get angry with someone. Or maybe you feel depressed. Your mind is not pure. Then, how can you practice meditation and gain concentration? Ill will prevents it.

If you have drowsiness or sleepiness, you try to sit in meditation but it stops about five or 10 minutes later. You feel sleepy, right? Sloth and torpor stop the meditation. They are very dangerous. We call these hindrances.

With *uddhacca*, your mind wanders. You think about this and that. This is distraction. You cannot gain concentration and you cannot gain wisdom because of this distraction, this restlessness. With *kukkucca*, you have this remorse and so you feel sorrow and think about something you've done. You feel unhappy. These things obstruct your way.

And with doubt, you doubt the virtues of the Buddha. You doubt whether he was a great and supreme teacher. You doubt whether his teachings are right, and whether his disciples were good people. You also doubt the way you practice meditation. "Is it right or not?" In other words, you doubt your way of practice. And you also doubt *kamma*–cause and effect, previous *kamma*, and present *kamma*. If you have doubt, you cannot gain concentration. You can't gain wisdom. It obstructs your way to the celestial world or to gain enlightenment.

It's the same with ignorance. Here, you don't understand reality.

These six kinds of hindrances obstruct the way to celestial and *nibbānic* bliss, and prevent the arising of good thoughts. They do not allow you to gain *jhāna* or *magga-phala* (enlightenment). Not only that, but you can't even be successful in worldly affairs—such as your business—if you have these six kinds of hindrances.

Let's think about these hindrances one-by-one. I would like to explain why *thīna* and *middha* are two kinds of realities grouped as one. Sloth is one reality, and torpor is another, right? Likewise, *uddhacca* and *kukkucca* are also two kinds of mental factors grouped as one.

I said that there are six *nīvaraṇās* but eight individually, right? *Kāmacchandanīvaraṇā* is *lobha*, *vyāpādanīvaraṇā* is *dosa*, *thīna* is a mental factor, and *middha* is a mental factor. That's a total of four, so far. *Uddhacca* is a mental factor, *kukkucca* is a mental factor, *vicikicchā* is a mental factor, and so is *avijjā* (*moha*). That's a total of eight mental factors.

So why are *thīna* and *middha* grouped together, as are *uddhacca* and *kukkucca*? It is because their functions, their causes and opposing factors are similar. That's how eight mental factors become six *nīvaraṇās*.

What is the function of sloth and torpor? Mental inactivity. We cannot do anything, right? We're just drowsy and sleepy. What about their cause? Laziness. We're very lazy, right? Laziness becomes sloth and torpor. Laziness is the cause. And what are their opposing factors? Energy. If you had energy, you wouldn't feel sleepy. But because of your lack of energy, you have *thīna* and *middha*.

With regard to *uddhacca* and *kukkucca*, their function is disquietude. *Uddhacca* is distraction, and *kukkucca* is remorse. Their cause is vexation. It is vexation about loss of property, for example. Their opposing factor is tranquility.

So, because their functions, causes and opposing factors are the same, we put them into groups. That's the reason.

In the Buddhist scriptures, especially in the Commentaries, it mentions the hindrances. It talks about what these hindrances look like. Sense-desire is compared to water mixed with various colors. If we have a glass of water with various colors in it, the water is not clear, right? If it's not clear, then we can't see our reflection in the water.

Why do the scriptures compare sense-desire to water mixed with various colors? In those days, people were very poor. When they could not have a mirror but wanted to see a reflection of their face, they put water in a container and then looked at it to see their face. This is why the Buddha explained that sense-desire looks like water mixed with various colors. If there are many colors, you can't see your face, right?

In the same way, what happens when sense-desire arises while you're practicing meditation? You want this or that, or you're attached to someone or something. If sense-desire arises, you cannot see realities in your body or your mind. You cannot see your sensations when they occur. You cannot see the arising and disappearing of these realities. Why? Because it's like water that is not clear.

So, sense-desire is compared to water mixed with various colors.

When you have ill will, you get angry with someone, right? It is also a feeling of aversion or unsatisfactoriness. This is compared to boiling water. When water is boiling, you can't clearly see your reflection in it. When you get angry or you're unsatisfied, you can't gain concentration. And then, you cannot see your primary object of meditation very clearly. As such, you can't see realities. You can't see what is occurring in your body or mind. This is because of your ill will, your aversion, your *dosa*. It looks like boiling water.

Sloth and torpor is compared to water covered by moss. When you see a pool of water that is full of weeds, the water is very unclear. But if the water is very clear, you can see your reflection in the water, right? If you have sloth and torpor while you're sitting in meditation, you feel sleepy all the time. How can you see what's arising and disappearing in your mind and body? You can't see these realities. You can't see what is mind, what is body. You can't see the air-element or the fire-element. You can't see anything when there is sloth and torpor.

Restlessness and remorse are compared to perturbed water caused by wind. When wind blows over water, it shakes and perturbs the water, right? When that happens, you cannot see your reflection in the water. In the same way, when your mind wanders you cannot see what happens in your mind and body. This is why restlessness and remorse are compared to perturbed water caused by wind.

When skeptical doubt about something arises, it's compared to turbid and muddy water. This water is not clear or clean, right? Because the water is not clear, you cannot see your reflection in it. Likewise, if you have doubt about the Buddha, his teachings, his disciples, about your meditation technique, or about *kamma*, your mind cannot gain concentration. And then, you can't see realities. That's why we call these hindrances.

Whenever a hindrance occurs in your mind, you cannot see realities. If many hindrances occur, believe me that it obstructs your way. You cannot gain concentration, you cannot gain wisdom. Even those who are not meditators find that they don't accomplish anything when the six hindrances occur in their minds. Because they doubt about *kamma*, they don't want to donate or help people. As such, they can't gain any merit. When you get angry, you don't want to help the person who made you mad, right?

So, briefly, how many hindrances are there? Six. These six hindrances can be temporarily inhibited when we gain *jhāna*. But they can return when we lose *jhāna*.

To completely eradicate all hindrances, what do we need to do?

If you gain the first stage of enlightenment and become a stream-enterer, which hindrances do you eradicate? Doubt. Only that one. You'll no longer have doubt about *kamma* or about your meditation technique. You will have eradicated the hindrance of doubt.

When you gain the third stage of enlightenment and become a non-returner, you will eradicate sense-desire, ill will and remorse. You will eradicate these three kinds of hindrances.

And when you become an *arahant* and gain the fourth stage of enlightenment, you will completely destroy and eradicate all the remaining hindrances, including sloth and torpor and restlessness.

Please remember this last point for knowledge. Only an *arahant* can completely eradicate sloth and torpor. Even those who have attained the first three stages of enlightenment can experience drowsiness. That's why we may experience sleepiness almost every time we practice meditation, right? Only an *arahant* can completely eradicate it. When you gain *jhāna*, it's temporarily inhibited.

We try to fight with these hindrances every day.

We sit in meditation, and sense-desire arises. We make a mental note, sense-desire disappears and then we try to concentrate our mind on our primary object. Then, if we get angry with someone and aversion arises, we try to realize it and make a mental note. The anger goes away–arising and disappearing. Then we go back to our primary object. When we feel drowsiness, we try to make it stop and then concentrate on our primary object. When the mind wanders, we make a mental note–"wandering, wandering, wandering"—and the wandering stops. We then concentrate on our primary object again. If we feel remorse or sorrow about something we've done, we just note it–"sorrow, sorrow, sorrow." We know this experience for ourselves, the remorse stops, and we then return to our primary object.

This is how we try to fight with these six hindrances.

If you only make an effort one time, you won't be successful. You have to do this many, many times. We are trying to train our minds. To get concentration, whatever comes to your mind, just make a mental note and it'll go away. Eventually, you'll be successful. No mental hindrances will occur in your mind, and then you'll get peace of mind and gain deep concentration. Then, the wisdom-eye will occur to you.

This is why we need to practice meditation. No one can eradicate all of these hindrances without meditation. Please consider this.

Q: Some people believe that there are two or three ways of gaining enlightenment. They think that you can gain enlightenment by doing a lot of prayers or studying scriptures and praying. They think that is a way to enlightenment besides meditation.

Meditation is the proximate cause of gaining enlightenment. Without meditation, you cannot gain enlightenment. Praying and generosity support our minds and help us gain concentration, but they don't lead directly to enlightenment. By only practicing generosity, you can't reach directly to *nibbāna*. In the same way, prayer only does not lead directly to enlightenment.

The Buddha said that we need *dāna* (generosity) and *sīla* (morality). Even if you practice meditation, if you don't fulfill the five precepts, you cannot gain concentration. And without concentration, you cannot gain wisdom.

We still need these things. But the proximate cause of enlightenment is meditation.

We have two kinds of meditation. If you only practice praying and chanting, this is *samatha* (tranquility) meditation. With tranquility meditation, your mind gains concentration. But you cannot realize realities with just concentration. You also need to practice *vipassanā* (insight) meditation to know and understand the realities of impermanence, suffering and selflessness.

This is very important.

Q: So many religions are based on samatha.

Oh yes, mostly *samatha*. Even Buddhism has this as a foundation.

Samatha is tranquility, right? Buddhism teaches morality, tranquility and wisdom. These are the essence of Buddhism. We need these three kinds of things. If we have no *sīla* (morality), then we cannot gain tranquility. If we can't gain tranquility, then we cannot gain wisdom.

Some people do chanting and praying. This is tranquility. It's a kind of meditation.

We have 40 kinds of meditation, right? Forty subjects. This is one of them. But the important one is *vipassanā*.

Q: Is samatha the same as samādhi?

Yes, calmness, tranquility. The same. Some people use the term *samādhi*, while others use the term *samatha*. It's one-pointedness.

In *Pāli*, our practice consists of *sīla*, *samādhi* and *paññā*. This is very important. If someone fulfills *sīla*, *samādhi* and *paññā* then they are following the correct way. But if they have *sīla* and *samādhi* but no *paññā*, then it's not the correct way.

We observe five or eight precepts, right? This is morality. And we try to gain concentration by observing our mind. This is tranquility, or *samādhi*. And then, wisdom (*paññā*) will arise. When it does, we will know softness or hardness (earth-element) or whether something is cold (fire-element), right? Pressure, pushing, moving or motion is the air-element.

You will see these realities. You'll see your mind. If you want something, you'll know it's not you, it's not soul, it's not ego. What wants something? Desire, *lobha*, attachment. You'll know these realities.

"I'm angry." It's not you who is angry. What's angry? It's aversion, or *dosa*. You'll know right away that it's *dosa*. That's the reality of it.

You'll know whatever happens to your body, whatever sensations occur. "I feel pain...or numb...or itching." You'll know that all sensations arise and disappear. You'll see the impermanence.

This is *paññā*. You'll know it right away.

You won't see this as your body. "It's not my body." It's just mind and matter. We studied mind, right? Our mind just arises. There is just mind and body–only these two. Every bodily and mental activity just arises and disappears, all the time.

But we won't see these things if we don't have concentration. Even though mind and body have arisen and disappeared many millions of times, you won't see it. This is why we have to try to concentrate our mind to see this in every moment. In this way, we develop our wisdom.

So, let's stop here for today. We usually meet for two hours but I think that's enough for today.

Any questions?

Q: I work 60 hours a week but still try to get up every morning at 4 AM to practice sitting meditation. I get very drowsy while I meditate. Is that still sloth and torpor?

Yes. Sloth and torpor obstruct concentration. If there's no concentration, then there's no *jhāna*, no *magga*, no *phala*, no attainment.

Q: I acknowledge that I'm overworking and don't get enough sleep at night. Although there's sloth and torpor, is there such a thing as just being tired?

Yes, it's sloth and torpor.

Q: If a person sleeps one hour a night for five straight nights, is it still considered sloth and torpor?

Sleeping is *bhavaṅga*.

The Buddha said we should work on the Middle Way, which is a path of no extremes.

Q: In the West, sloth and torpor have a strong moral connotation. If you're guilty of sloth and torpor, it's like there's something morally wrong with you. It's as if it's something you've caused. But as I've gotten older, I've found that I sometimes get very sleepy in the afternoons. I don't want to waste time napping but I'm not sure how to handle it. Is it appropriate to take a nap? Perhaps my meditation will be better if I take a nap first. Or should I ignore the nap and force myself to do the meditation?

I gave you a method for dealing with sloth and torpor.

Q: When we're older, sleepiness is more prominent than when we're younger. We have to try a little harder.

Oh yes, maybe sometimes you'll need to nap for 10 or 15 minutes. If you're that tired, you should take a nap. Even though our mind is so strong, our body is not so strong.

Q: So the Middle Path is to not become a slave to your body, but also to not ignore it completely?

Yes, right. If you just follow desire and don't want to get up–"It's my day off, so maybe I'll sleep seven or eight hours"—that's not good. You can't allow yourself to be like that.

Q: If it's okay, I'd like to ask some questions about things we've talked about before. First, is the reality of fear dosa cetasika?

Yes.

Q: Thank you. Also, in talking about various beings, you talked about moisture-born, spontaneous-born and womb-born. I don't think you really talked about egg-born beings. Am I right in thinking that they are similar to womb-born beings in terms of realities?

That's right.

Q: I remember reading where Shwe Taung Gone Sayādaw [Sayādaw U Paṇḍita] said that mindfulness was the proximate cause of mindfulness. But Abhidhammā seems to say that with kusala citta ñāna sampayutta as a cause, the result in this lifetime is kusala ahetuka, and the result in the next life is mahāvipāka. So how does being mindful now lead to more mindfulness, in terms of cause and effect? I'm a bit confused.

Can you please also help me understand when and how kusala citta gives results, especially as it relates to the development of mindfulness?

Mindfulness is always associated with *kusala citta*. They are working together. Previous *kusala* is the cause; subsequent *kusala* is the result—*kusalodhamma kusalassa dhammassa*. *Kusala citta* can give the result in this lifetime as well as the next life.

Q: So, for example, somanassa sahagata ñāna sampayutta asankhārika as a cause could yield both kusala vipāka ahetuka and sobhaṇa vipāka citta as results in this life and/or the next life?

Yes.

Q: Since ahetuka is the only akusala vipāka, does that mean that the results of the 12 akusala cittas can only be akusala ahetuka?

Right!

Q: I typically seem to dream very little, if at all. When I do dream, they are very seldom bad or unpleasant. For the last few nights, though, I've had several anxious dreams each night. It's really unusual for me. I'm curious if you have any ideas about why I'm suddenly experiencing unpleasant dreams several times a night. There doesn't seem to be anything in my daily life that is triggering them. If it's the result of old kamma, why now?

Please practice loving-kindness meditation from the time you go to bed until you fall asleep. Then you will not have bad dreams anymore.

Okay, let's stop here. *Sādhu, sādhu, sādhu*. Thank you.

...

Today is January 17, 1999. It has been many months since our *Abhidhammā* class last met. Last year, we studied six chapters and began the seventh chapter. Today, we'll pick up where we left off and continue with the seventh chapter. I hope to finish all of the chapters of this *Abhidhammā* class over the course of the next 20 weeks.

Unlike the earlier chapters we studied, this and the next two chapters are not so difficult. But, moving forward, we will need to refer to what we've already learned. You will need to review the chapters on consciousness, mental states, thought processes and the 28 kinds of material properties. If you refer to the previous chapters, this new material will not be so difficult.

All of this discussion of our mind and meditation is especially useful for meditators. Even if we don't have a lot of deep knowledge about *Abhidhammā*, by studying the next three chapters I hope that most of you will still understand about 70-80% of the material. The hardest chapters were the first and the second, which we really should try to remember.

So, today, we will begin by studying the seven kinds of *anusaya*. *Anusaya* means latent.

Anusaya

Anusaya is like a tree. A tree has the potential to bear fruit. We don't know when, but it has that potential, right? Well, *anusaya* here refers to defilements, which we can classify into three groups or by three levels, by the intensity of the defilement.

1) Transgressive defilement

This is the grossest kind of mental defilement. It's very gross and rough.

2) Obsessive defilement

3) Latent defilement

Transgressive defilement means the grossest defilement. When these arise in our mind, we can break our precepts. We might kill someone, steal someone's belongings, commit sexual misconduct, lie or use drugs. We break our five precepts and disturb the rights of others. It's like committing a crime, in that it doesn't merely happen in the mind. We commit these deeds physically or verbally. As such, we call it transgressive defilement, or grossest defilement. In daily life, this happens to practically everyone who is not aware of their mind and body, or those who are not practicing meditation. This is the grossest defilement.

Obsessive defilement arises on the mental level. It's sometimes called medium-gross defilement. It just occurs on the mental level and does not manifest in physical action or speech. Even if you want to kill someone, you don't actually do it. It just arises on the mental level. Or if you want someone's property but don't actually make an effort to steal it, it is obsessive defilement. It occurs only on the mental level.

The third level of defilement is subtle defilement. It is the most subtle defilement, which lies latent and sleeps deep in your heart. When conditions are favorable, these latent defilements arise. These potentialities wait until conditions are favorable to arise.

Today, we will start by studying latent defilements, which are called *anusaya* in *Pāli*.

Latent defilements can arise within the continuity of a being's existence in *saṃsāra*. This means that they can arise in not just this life, but even in future lives if we have not yet attained enlightenment. If we have not yet attained enlightenment, we still have these defilements, which can arise anytime during the continuity of our existence as beings.

There is greed, hatred and delusion, right? If we don't attain enlightenment in this life–that is, we remain an ordinary worldling–all these *anusaya* sleeping deeply in our minds will stay with us after death and continue on into another existence. This is *anusaya*.

When a clear object of mind and body appears to our eyes, ears, nose, tongue, body or mind, latent defilement will arise. This can happen anytime. Like, right now, perhaps none of you feel greed or hatred–you're not angry with anyone right now, right? But anger is still deep in your heart. You still have it. Everyone has it. So if the object is clear and comes to attach to one of your six sense-doors, then your anger will arise. This means that its arising is dependent upon conditions. When conditions are favorable, someone does something to make you angry, and then your anger occurs.

Normally, you don't have that, right?

So we have three intensities of defilement. Everyone who is not a noble person will fully have all *anusaya* latent in their minds. These *anusaya* sleep deeply inside of us.

Some people see or hear something that is desirable. Then, *lobha* occurs. Or, if the object is undesirable and they dislike it, then anger occurs. This happens on a mental level. We call it medium-gross or obsessive defilement. This is when you get angry in your mind or you mentally want to have something that isn't yours. Here, we don't do anything physical or verbal–it's just inside. Then, when your medium-gross defilement has more intensity, you will commit a deed bodily. Or perhaps you'll say something bad. This is transgressive defilement.

These are the three intensities of defilement.

Now, let's explore some examples:

You have a glass and you fill it halfway with water. If the water in the glass is not shaking, then it's like latent. When you take the glass, put it in the microwave and hit *START*, in a few minutes the water is boiling, right? It's still in the glass, but it's boiling. This is like obsessive. If you continue heating the water for five or 10 minutes, it gets so hot that it spills out of the glass. This is like transgressive.

In the same way, the three levels of defilements intensify, step by step.

A stream-enterer has no wrong view or doubt, right? These two kinds of defilement have been uprooted or expelled. These latent defilements inside of them have been eradicated. When there's no *anusaya*, no obsessive defilement can arise in their mind. This is because obsessive defilements are dependent upon latent defilements. As such, stream-enterers do not break precepts.

We can also take a cat as an example.

Normally, a cat stays with us and is very polite. But when the cat sees a rat running in front of him, what happens to him? The nails come out right away. This is how *anusaya* operates. Normally, the cat is very good and polite, right? But when conditions are favorable–that is, if something happens to trigger the cat–then *anusaya* will arise in their minds. Then, the nails come out but they don't really do anything. What do you call that? Obsessive defilement. Then, they'll run after the rat and catch it. This is transgressive defilement.

Soon, we will talk about how to abandon these three levels of defilement.

First, though, I would like to tell you about the seven latent defilements. Really, we should be studying these in our minds. In every daily activity, with every thought, these defilements occur. What are these latent defilements arising in our mind? We should try to know them right away when they occur. When we know a defilement has arisen, it will stop. This is especially so when we use our meditation technique, our mindfulness, our awareness.

1) *Kāmarāgānusaya* (attachment to sensual pleasure)
2) *Bhavarāgānusaya* (attachment to existence)
3) *Paṭighānusaya* (hatred)
4) *Mānānusaya* (pride)
5) *Diṭṭhānusaya* (false views)
6) *Vicikicchānusaya* (doubt)
7) *Avijjānusaya* (ignorance)

So, we've talked about *āsavā, yogā, ganthā*–so many different names–but their realities are just the 14 unwholesome mental states. We should understand these realities.

Kāmarāgānusaya

The reality is *lobha*. This is attachment to sensual pleasure.

Normally, we might say, "I don't have attachment. I don't want anything." You don't take anything because in your mind you don't want to. But this latent defilement is deep in your mind. Nothing happens now because an object, a condition, is not very desirable for you. "I don't want anything."

But suppose you decide to leave the temple today, and as you're leaving, you notice $1,000 sitting on the platform. What arises? Attachment to sensual pleasure. "Oh!" When you stay at the temple, you normally don't feel any attachment or greed, right? But when you see all that money–"Ah!"—you might look around and see if anyone is nearby. If you see no one, you might take it.

This is *anusaya*. This *lobha* is sleeping deeply in your mind. Then, you want it. And then, you take it. Step by step, right? Latent defilement becomes obsessive defilement, which becomes transgressive defilement.

Or maybe you know a lady who seems to have a very good heart and never gets angry. She says, "Oh, I don't get angry." But if the person is not an *anāgāmī* or an *arahant*, this latent defilement is still in their mind. If you say or do something they don't like, they will get angry. Their face will change, right? This means that their latent defilement has become obsessive defilement. It arises on the mental level. And then, maybe she'll use her hand to slap the person who made her mad or perhaps she'll say something harsh.

We have to know that *anusaya* is a latent disposition sleeping deeply in our mind. It can occur anytime–and not only in this life, even in the next existence–if we are not an *ariya*, or a noble one.

Bhavarāgānusaya

This is attachment to existence. Everyone is attached to their position in life. As human beings, we are attached to *bhava*–existence, our life. The reality of this is *lobha*.

Everyone–not just human beings, but animals too–are attached to their existence, their life. According to the scriptures, the angels or gods living in heaven have much more happiness than we do as human beings. Their lives are better than ours. People will often do good deeds and assert that they want to be reborn in heaven because they think that heaven is better than the human realm.

But imagine if someone came to you and said, "As human beings, we suffer so many miseries. You're a good person. Knowing that you'll be reborn in heaven if you die right now, do you want to die right now?"

Your answer would be no. Even if you believe that the *Brahma* realm is a million times better than the human realm, you'll still want to stay here because you're attached to your life.

This is attachment to existence.

It doesn't only apply to humans. It applies to animals too. Some animals are very pitiful. They are in poor health with ugly bodies and many diseases. But if someone comes at them to beat them, they will run away because they're afraid to die. Why? They are attached to their life.

These are just examples. We can take many examples for *bhavarāgānusaya* because everyone has it.

Someone might say, "I'm not attached to my life. I'm ready to die anytime."

These are just words. It's another story deep in the mind.

If someone asks them, "Do you want to die right now? You can go to heaven today," what do you think their answer would be?

"Let me think about that." Right?

Paṭighānusaya

This is hatred. What is the reality? *Dosa*.

As I've mentioned, for the most part, most people think they don't have anger or aversion. But when they are confronted with something or someone that is undesirable, they get angry. Right? This means we still have this *anusaya*, or latent defilement.

Mānānusaya

Pride, or conceit. *Māṇa* is conceit.

Perhaps you think, "I'm the best...I'm better than others...I'm richer than him...I'm more clever than her." In other words, you make a comparison with others. This is pride. It's a kind of *māṇa*.

But it's not only handsome or wealthy people who have pride. Although the levels may differ, everyone has pride, or *māṇa*.

Even a beggar or a homeless person has pride. Even though they have nothing, there are homeless people who have pride over their ability to gather income without having to work all day like most people. This is *māṇa*.

So-called "normal" people have pride too. They have their homes, their cars, their jobs, their food. They might have pride that they can survive without having to ask other people for assistance. This is also *māṇa*.

And, of course, rich people may think, "Oh, I'm the richest person in this city." This is *māṇa*.

So, although the levels may differ, everyone has pride. But, normally, there is this *anusaya* (latent defilement) and we just think, "I'm a very humble person." But that's just because the conditions are favorable at that time. When something happens, you make a comparison with others. This is *māṇa*.

Do you understand what I'm talking about? This is the nature of *māṇa*. It's pride or conceit.

If you say, "This person knows everything. But other people know it too. I know this," then you're making a comparison. This is *māṇa*. It's pride.

Diṭṭhānusaya

This is false view. There are many types of wrong view. In detail, there are 62 types. We've talked about this many times since the first chapter, but I'd like to talk about it a bit more.

There is wrong view about eternalism. This view might be that when a human being dies, he will be reborn as a human being in the next life. Or he might think that our body will change but our mind will not. He might think that there is an unchanging soul that continues into the next existence. In *Pāli*, we call this *sassatadiṭṭhi*, or eternalism. It is wrong view.

There is also wrong view about annihilation. This view might be that our life ends after death. He might think that there is no further existence, no rebirth. This is annihilation, which is also wrong view.

And there is wrong view about self-theory. You might see something and think, "I see." Or you might hear something and think, "I hear." In reality, you cannot see or hear. A person, a man, a woman, cannot see or hear. Who sees? Seeing-consciousness sees. We already studied this, right?

Every ordinary worldling can have these latent defilements. Even those who practice meditation but don't understand the realities of mind and matter might hold a view like, "After we die, our spirit stays inside our home for seven days before being reborn again." This is wrong view.

Normally, though, we might not hold wrong views. But if we come across something that changes our mind, we could shift from right view to wrong view. Of course, this can only happen if we are not a noble person (*ariya*).

Vicikicchānusaya

This is skeptical doubt. We doubt about *kamma*, we doubt about everything.

Someone might say, "For this person's business, they kill animals and they sell alcohol. Why is their business making them so rich?" A person with skeptical doubt thinks like this.

Others might say, "That's a good person with a good heart and good livelihood. Why is their business unsuccessful?" Why might they wonder about that?

These people doubt *kamma* because they don't understand the law of cause and effect. As we studied in the second chapter of the second book, our lives depend on our previous *kamma* too. Even though we may try so hard to be good in our present life, about 50% of our life situation is conditioned by our previous *kamma*.

We may be in the exact same line of business and have the exact same business model as another person but one of us may be more successful than the other. Why? It depends on our previous *kamma*.

There are also those who have doubt about the Buddha. Is he really the Enlightened One? Is his teaching correct? Do his disciples practice correctly? Are we, as meditators, practicing correctly? In other words, we doubt the virtues of the Buddha, his teachings, his disciples, about the way of practice, about meditation, about *kamma*. This is *vicikicchā*.

Avijjānusaya

This is ignorance. We don't know the truth. We don't know what suffering is, we don't know the cause of suffering, the cessation of suffering or the way leading to the cessation of suffering. We don't know these things. We don't know about the past, about the future, or about the past and the future. We don't know about dependent origination. We call this ignorance.

Because of this *anusaya*–this latent defilement–we have to suffer. We have to be reborn again and again.

The reality for *diṭṭhānusaya* (false view) is diṭṭhi, *vicikicchānusaya* is the mental state of doubt, and *avijjānusaya* is *moha*, right?

So, these are the seven *anusaya*, or latent dispositions.

How do we abandon the three intensity levels of defilement?

The Buddha taught us to use our virtue, our precepts, our good conduct, to overcome and abandon transgressive defilement. Before we practice meditation, we take the five or the eight precepts. If we're following these precepts, we can't commit transgressive defilement, right? Even if these defilements arise in your mind, because of your *sīla*, your virtues, your precepts, you don't kill, don't steal, don't commit sexual misconduct, don't lie and don't use drugs or alcohol. This is *sīla*.

The Buddha explained that we have to take this kind of medication to treat this kind of disease. For this poison, we use this antidote. The Buddha explained this to us.

So we should understand that we can overcome transgressive (grossest) defilement through our virtue, our *sīla*, our morality, our good conduct. Just observe our precepts. If we do, we don't have to worry about transgressive defilements.

What do we have to do about those obsessive defilements that occur on the mental level? We develop concentration. This is why we need to practice meditation, even *samatha* (tranquility) meditation. Through this concentration, we can abandon obsessive defilement.

Greed and hatred occur on the mental level. If we have good concentration and try to practice meditation–just observing our present meditation object–then no greed and no hatred arise in the mind.

So, to overcome obsessive defilement, we use our concentration. This means that concentration allows us to overcome or abandon obsessive (medium-gross) defilement. Normally, we might have greed or hatred, right? But when we sit in meditation with good concentration, these do not arise in the mind.

What do we have to do to overcome or abandon latent defilement? We need *paññā*, or wisdom. In order to attain the wisdom to uproot all latent defilements, we need to become a noble one, or *ariya*. But even if one has not yet reached nobility through enlightenment, the latent tendencies can be temporarily abandoned by mindfulness and insight.

The Noble Eightfold Path consists of eight factors. Three of them are *sammāvācā* (right speech), *sammākammanta* (right action) and *sammājīva* (right livelihood). These three factors of the Noble Path comprise *sīla*. When we have right speech, right action and right livelihood, we do not commit transgressive defilement. This is because of our *sīla*. We have overcome these defilements because of our *sīla*.

Sammāvāyāma (right effort), *sammāsati* (right mindfulness) and *sammāsamādhi* (right concentration) comprise *samādhi*, or concentration–the second of the three components of the Noble Eightfold Path. When we practice meditation and try to observe our meditation object with constant awareness, we utilize right effort, right mindfulness and right concentration to fix our mind one-pointedly. This is *samādhi*, or concentration. When we have concentration, no obsessive defilements occur on the mental level. It's quiet.

The third component of the Noble Eightfold Path consists of *sammādiṭṭhi* (right understanding) and *sammāsaṅkappa* (right thinking). These two are wisdom. Even if we haven't gained enlightenment yet, if we have wisdom through our practice of meditation we can temporarily abandon all three levels of intensity of defilement.

If we sit in meditation for five minutes, we try to concentrate our mind and focus it on our meditation object. In that moment, we aren't doing anything physically or verbally, right? This means that we have fulfilled our good conduct, our precepts, our virtue. We are not committing any wrongdoing.

Then, we try to observe our object with *viriya*, or right effort. Whatever arises, we make a mental note and be aware of the object. This is mindfulness. As our mind does not go anywhere else, it is one-pointed. At that time, we have good concentration. As we have good concentration, there are no medium-gross (obsessive) defilements.

Although we haven't totally uprooted latent defilements yet, with right understanding we see realities. No matter what happens in our body (our actions, our sensations) or our mind (and our mental states), we see that everything is just arising and disappearing, arising and disappearing. We see this. This is right understanding. We see the truth.

What do we call arising and disappearing? Suffering. Everything that is oppressed by arising and disappearing is suffering. See? Suffering is not just something like pain. Whatever is oppressed by arising and disappearing is by its very nature suffering.

So we see everything just arising and disappearing, arising and disappearing. We see the suffering. This means that we see the truth of suffering.

Q: Sometimes when I'm meditating, thoughts from way back come and rise to the surface.

In our mind, we think about this or that. It changes all the time. Your mind is just arising and disappearing in different kinds of consciousness. Maybe you get angry, or maybe you feel happy. Maybe you feel sorrow. A lot of things occur.

Even with sensations, sometimes you have very pleasant feelings and sometimes your feelings are unpleasant. Even pleasant feelings don't last long. They become unpleasant feelings, or perhaps neutral feelings.

Your feelings, your sensations, your whole body–your eyes, ears, nose, tongue, body, vibrations–just occur all the time. Your body is shaking, moving, vibrating all the time.

When we see these realities, we call it the truth of suffering.

When we see this truth, our latent defilement just sleeps. It just lies in our mind. It does not arise. This is how we can temporarily abandon it.

So it's very necessary to practice meditation. Without meditation, nothing can help us to abandon or eradicate all of these mental defilements. Think about these modern times when scientists can make all of these high technologies. It's unbelievable what they're capable of making. But they can't produce anything to eradicate even one kind of defilement. They can't do it.

For the most part, technological products just lead to the arising of mental defilements. When you watch TV or read a newspaper or see advertising, it just induces you, right? "Ah, this is very interesting!" Or maybe you see a movie and get angry about something in the film. See how it just pushes you? Although we have all of this high technology, it just makes our defilements bigger and bigger. This technology is developed for the purpose of business.

To abandon these defilements step by step, we should use the technique of meditation. Just practice meditation. Use your mindfulness and insight. Without mindfulness, insight wisdom cannot occur. We have to be aware of every object when it occurs to the eye, ear, nose, tongue, body and mind. Be aware of these objects, make a mental note, label it, realize it, and then all defilements will stop right away.

What kinds of latent defilements can a stream-enterer eradicate? He cannot eradicate *kāmarāgānusaya*, *bhavarāgānusaya*, *paṭighānusaya* or *mānānusaya*. But what about *diṭṭhānusaya*, or false view? A stream-enterer can eradicate this defilement. He can abandon and uproot *diṭṭhānusaya*. He can also eradicate *vicikicchānusaya*, or doubt. He can only eradicate these two latent defilements.

What about a once-returner? A once-returner cannot eradicate any of the remaining latent defilements. Still, his attainment has allowed him to weaken them.

As for a non-returner, he eradicates *kāmarāgānusaya*, or attachment to sensual pleasure. But he still has *bhavarāgānusaya*, or attachment to existence. See? He eradicates the first one but still has the second one because attachment to existence does not include attachment to the sensuous state. *Bhavarāgānusaya* is attachment to the fine-material or immaterial realms. As such, non-returners are still attached to this existence.

A being may practice *samatha* meditation and gain *jhāna*. It's easy to feel very satisfied by *jhāna* and get attached to it. As such, they might think, "When I die, I won't have to be reborn as a human being again. I won't have to be reborn in heaven either. I will be reborn in a very peaceful realm that is higher than heaven." This is attachment to the *rūpa* or *arūpa* realms. So even non-returners still have this kind of latent defilement.

What about the third type of latent defilement–*paṭighānusaya*, or hatred? A non-returner no longer has anger. If someone claims to have reached the third stage of enlightenment but still has anger or hatred, they're not actually at that level. No matter what someone does to a non-returner, no anger will occur in his mind. This is because a non-returner has eradicated *paṭighānusaya*, or hatred.

What about pride, or *mānānusaya*? Even a non-returner still has this. As for the fifth and sixth types of latent defilements, stream-entry has already eradicated these. But a non-returner still has *avijjānusaya*, or ignorance. They still have *moha*. See? He still has attachment to the *Brahma* realms, believing that to be a happy life. This attachment is due to ignorance. The Buddha said that wherever we are born, there will be suffering. But we fail to understand this because of our ignorance. Ignorance does not understand the truth. A non-returner still has some ignorance remaining.

I would like all of you to know that a stream-enterer eradicates the fifth and sixth types (false views and doubt), a non-returner eradicates attachment to sensual pleasure and hatred, and an *arahant* eradicates the remaining latent defilements.

What about ordinary worldlings? We have all seven, right? Yes.

We've been talking about *anusaya*.

Saṃyojana

And now we go to *saṃyojana*. There are 10 of these *saṃyojana*, which we can call fetters. These *saṃyojana* mean that they bind beings to the round of existence. It binds beings from this present life to the next life. This is *saṃyojana*.

We have two methods that we can use to talk about *saṃyojana*. The first one looks at the ten *saṃyojana* by the *Suttanta* method. We have three kinds of teachings of the Buddha, right? We have the *Suttanta* (discourses), the *Vinaya* (discipline) and the *Abhidhammā* (highest teaching). By exploring the two methods, we can see how the realities differ a bit.

What are the 10 kinds of fetters?

1) *Kāmarāgasaṃyojana*

It's the same as the first *anusaya*, right? It's attachment to sensual pleasure. They are different in name and nature but they share the same reality. See, the Buddha thought of many ways to help people understand what he was trying to teach. With some people, he explained this in terms of *anusaya*, while he explained it in terms of *saṃyojana* with others.

So, according to the *Suttanta* method, we have these 10 fetters. The first is attachment to sensual pleasure.

2) *Rūparāgasaṃyojana*

We studied the 31 planes of existence, right? This fetter is attachment to *rūpa* realms, or *rūpajhāna*. How many *rūpajhānas* do we have? Among the 31 planes of existence, we have four woeful states, the human realm, six celestial realms, 16 *rūpa* realms and four *arūpa* realms. Although there are 16 *rūpa* realms, one is for mindless beings. Beings of the other 15 *rūpa* realms have both mind and matter. Beings of the four immaterial or *arūpa* realms have mind but no matter. Here, *rūparāgasaṃyojana* is attachment to the *rūpa* realm, or the realm of form.

3) *Arūparāgasaṃyojana*

This is attachment to the *arūpa* realm, or formless realm. See the difference? Can you see how the realities are the same, though? What are they? *Lobha*, craving or attachment.

A non-returner has no *kāmarāgasaṃyojana*, but still has attachment to *rūparāga* and *arūparāga*. They are still attached to these *jhānas*.

4) *Paṭighasaṃyojana*

This is hatred. It is *dosa*.

5) *Mānasaṃyojana* (pride)

6) *Diṭṭhisaṃyojana* (false views)
7) *Sīlabbataparāmāsasaṃyojana*

This is usually translated as adherence to rites and ceremonies. This isn't quite right, though. Fortunately, the Commentaries explained what this term means. It specifically has to do with wrong views regarding practicing like an ox or a dog, believing that such practice will lead to enlightenment or a rebirth in heaven after death.

So *sīlabbata* means wrong view about habits and exercise–the way of practice. Perhaps we don't see this so much nowadays but a lot of people practiced like this in the time of the Buddha. They did this because they thought it would lead to enlightenment or a heavenly rebirth.

Q: Is that like practicing austerities, like people in India holding their arms up in the air for years at a time?

No, that's mortification. *Sīlabbata* doesn't mean mortification. It refers to bovine or canine conduct. They might walk around on four limbs like a cow or use their tongue to lap up food like a dog. This is *sīlabbataparāmāsaṃyojana*.

Q: What about people who think that certain rituals will lead to enlightenment? Is that the same?

No, not the same. The scriptures specifically define what I'm talking about as practicing like a canine or a bovine. Other false ways of practice fall under false views.

Every society or religion has ceremonies, right? We chant every day, don't we? That's a ritual. But it's not *sīlabbataparāmāsasaṃyojana*. The Commentaries explained what this term refers to. It refers to practicing like a dog or a cow. That's how it's defined.

8) *Vicikicchāsaṃyojana* (doubt)
9) *Uddhaccasaṃyojana* (restlessness)
10) *Avijjāsaṃyojana* (ignorance)

There are these 10 *saṃyojana*, but there are only seven realities. This is by the *Suttanta* method.

What are the seven realities? The first, second and third kinds of *saṃyojana* imply craving, or *lobha*–that's one reality. The sixth and seventh are *diṭṭhi*. That's another reality. This is why there are altogether seven realities according to the *Suttanta* method of evaluating *saṃyojana*. What are the seven realities? *Lobha, dosa, māna, diṭṭhi, vicikicchā, uddhacca* and *moha*.

The second method is the *Abhidhammā* method, wherein we have eight realities among 10 *saṃyojana*. How are the two methods different?

1) *Kāmarāgasaṃyojana* (attachment to sensual pleasure)

This is the same, right?

2) *Bhavarāgasaṃyojana*

This is attachment to existence. The *Suttanta* method breaks this into two *saṃyojana*: *rūpa* and *arūpa*. Here, *bhavarāga* means attachment to *rūpa* and *arūpa*.

3) *Paṭighasaṃyojana*
4) *Mānasaṃyojana*
5) *Diṭṭhisaṃyojana*
6) *Sīlabbataparāmāsasaṃyojana*
7) *Vicikicchāsaṃyojana*

These are all the same.

8) *Issāsaṃyojana* (envy)

This one is different, right? It means jealousy. It's one kind of *saṃyojana*.

9) *Macchariyasaṃyojana* (avarice, or stinginess)
10) *Avijjāsaṃyojana* (ignorance)

When we look at the realities, the first and second are *lobha*, the third is *dosa*, the fourth is *māna*, the fifth and sixth are *diṭṭhi*, the seventh is doubt, and the eighth is also a mental state, right? Do you remember which one? Jealousy arises when we have unwholesome consciousness rooted in ill will, or *dosa*.

Q: So the two methods are the Suttanta and Abhidhammā methods? Is it because they have different views?

Yes, these are the two methods but they don't have two different views. The methods are just a little different. I'll explain.

What is different? For *Suttanta*, there are seven realities. For *Abhidhammā*, there are eight realities. What is the different one? The *Suttanta* method doesn't recognize the eighth or nine *saṃyojanas*–no *issā* and no *macchariya*–of the *Abhidhammā* method. Although the *Suttanta* method still has *dosa*, we don't find these two listed as *saṃyojana*. And the ninth *saṃyojana* of the *Suttanta* method–*uddhacca*–can't be found in the *Abhidhammā* method.

That's the only difference.

If we combine these two methods, how many essential realities are there? Only nine. What are they? According to *Abhidhammā*, there are eight. If you add *uddhacca* from the *Suttanta* method, that's a total of nine realities.

Please remember that there are seven realities according to the *Suttanta* method and eight realities according to the *Abhidhammā* method. When we combine them, it becomes nine realities. What are they? *Lobha, dosa, māna, diṭṭhi, vicikicchā, uddhacca, moha, issā* and *macchariya*. That's nine. For the *Suttanta* method, *uddhacca* is different, and *issā* and *macchariya* are different for the *Abhidhammā* method.

This is *saṃyojana*. It binds beings to the round of existence.

Even if you're reborn in a higher plane–such as the highest realm, the *arūpa* realm–if you are still an ordinary worldling this *saṃyojana* will bind you and force you to be reborn later in the human or celestial worlds. And from the human or celestial worlds, that very binding can pull a being down to a woeful state. See that?

Why does it pull a being down like this? Why do *saṃyojanas* bind beings to the round of existence? You cannot escape from the field of existence, these 31 planes of existence. Why?

Because of *saṃyojana*. They bind you.

I'll give you some examples:

Even if you want to do good things–for example, go to the temple, to a meditation center, to do chanting, to go on a silent retreat, to gain *jhāna* or enlightenment–this *saṃyojana* binds you like a string, as a rope tied to a dog's neck binds the dog to the backyard. Even if the dog wants to go somewhere, the rope tied to its neck keeps pulling him back. He can only keep walking in circles. He can't leave the circle.

In the same way, even if we want to go out from this world, we can't. Why? Because of these 10 *saṃyojana*. These nine realities–craving, hatred, delusion, pride, wrong view, doubt, stinginess, envy and restlessness–pull us back. As such, we have to die and be reborn again and again and again. We can't get away from this field of existence because of these *saṃyojanas*.

Let's look at *kāmarāgasaṃyojana* for some examples of how this works:

Maybe you want to go to a meditation center to practice meditation. But what tends to happen? "I don't have time to go because I need to work and take care of my house." This is because of your attachment to sensual pleasures. See? You're attached to your house, your job, your belongings.

You're attached to your hobbies, too. You don't do good things because you'd rather spend time focusing on your hobbies, right? Perhaps you're attached to eating too. You might think, "When I go to the meditation center, I might have to eat vegetarian food. I don't like vegetarian food." Or maybe you're attached to the place where you normally sleep: "If I go to the meditation center, I might have to share a room with someone else. I want my own room." What about your clothing? "I wish I could wear my own clothes when I go for a retreat. I don't like wearing the traditional uniform." Or how about this: "If I go to the meditation center, I'll miss my favorite TV show on Wednesday."

You're attached to sights and sounds, right? You're attached to touches, tastes and smells too. This is attachment to sensual pleasures. This attachment prevents you from moving about with freedom.

These are examples of *kāmarāgasaṃyojana*. They pull on you and don't let you go. And even if you do go, you might get pulled right back again very soon.

See this? These are examples.

You can think of each of these *saṃyojanas* one-by-one and come up with your own examples. By doing so, you can see how they bind beings to the round of existence.

Even someone practicing meditation and gaining *jhāna* can find themselves attached to their *jhāna*. That attachment prevents them from wanting to practice insight meditation, which is what can allow us to escape from all existence. Instead, these attached meditators think, "Oh, I'm so peaceful." They're very satisfied by their *jhāna*. They think, "I won't have to worry about my next life because I'll be reborn in a very peaceful

Brahma realm." Can you see how they're attached to rebirth in a *Brahma* realm?

They still have *rūparāga* or *arūparāga*, which is really just *lobha* (attachment). And later on, they'll have to come back to the human world. Can you see how they can't escape the world? This *rāga* (attachment), *lobha* (craving) pulls you back.

What about *paṭighasaṃyojana*, or hatred? This is the opposite of *mettā*, or loving-kindness. Because you have *dosa* or are unsatisfied with something, you go places and don't like the people, the place or the food, right? Even if you go somewhere to practice meditation, you'll find reasons to complain about the place, the food or the people. And then maybe you'll quit, right? This is hatred too. Or maybe you're unsatisfied with yourself, which is also a kind of *paṭigha*, or hatred.

This *dosa* will not let you go out from this world.

There's also *māna*, or pride. And *diṭṭhi*, or false view. Maybe you think, "I'm going to do whatever I want to do with my life because it won't matter once I'm dead." This is false view. If you're unconcerned about rebirth then you won't bother doing anything good.

Think about all this *lobha, dosa, moha, māna, diṭṭhi, vicikicchā, issā* and avarice. These things bind you and pull you to be reborn again and again and again and again. We practice meditation for the purpose of getting rid of all these *saṃyojanas*, step-by-step, little-by-little, one-by-one. Once we become an *arahant*, we will have eradicated all *saṃyojana*. This is why an *arahant* will not have to be reborn again after he dies.

Let's stop here for today. Thank you. *Sādhu. Sādhu. Sādhu.*

Q: Can I ask a question? When you were talking about how impermanence is suffering, are you including dukkha in that also? I mean, is anicca itself suffering?

When a meditator sees impermanence, he also sees suffering. He will see *anattā* (selflessness) too. He will see that everything is beyond our control. He will see one of these three characteristics. If he sees one, he will know the remaining two as well.

Suffering to most people means, "Oh, I feel pain. I hurt." They just think of this as suffering. Everyone, even an animal, knows this kind of suffering. But the suffering that a meditator needs to understand is that whatever is oppressed by arising and disappearing, arising and disappearing, is itself suffering. We call that suffering.

Whenever we practice meditation, we will see vibration, shaking, arising, disappearing. Impermanence, right? This impermanence itself is what we call suffering.

Q: So we include anattā and dukkha in that too?

Yes, they are also suffering.

Who likes suffering? No one likes it. But you can't control it.

Even though you may want to have a steady and long-lasting pleasant experience, you have no control over that. It's *anattā*. It's the nature of mind and matter to just arise and disappear–impermanence. This is their nature.

So when we see impermanence, we see suffering. When we see suffering, we see impermanence. When we see impermanence and suffering, we see the lack of control.

Q: When you were talking before about non-returners, do you mean that he doesn't come back to the earth?

A non-returner cannot come back to the human or celestial worlds. It's not just the earth. He can't even return to heaven. These human and celestial worlds are called sensual realms. A non-returner cannot return to these.

Q: Even though a non-returner is not yet an arahant, can he become an arahant in a higher realm?

Oh, sure. Yes. Someone who becomes a non-returner will be reborn in the *rūpa* or *arūpa* realms. From there, he will become an *arahant*.

Q: Can he die in those upper realms and then be reborn in those upper realms, or is there just that one existence in the upper realms?

It depends. Let's look at the five Pure Abodes as an example.

After he dies from the first level, he can't be reborn on the same level; he has to go higher. Or perhaps he gains *arahant* first. But if he doesn't become an *arahant*, he will go to the second realm. When a being reaches the topmost Pure Abode, he can't go to another realm. Instead, he must become an *arahant*. This is an excellent realm, right?

...

Today is January 24, 1999. Last week, we discussed *saṃyojanas* (fetters) according to the *Suttanta* method and the *Abhidhammā* method. Today, I would like to talk about fetters a bit more.

As I told you, *saṃyojanas* bind beings to the round of existence. These 10 fetters do not allow beings to go beyond this world. By "this world" I mean the 31 planes of existence.

We have two levels of fetters, two groups of *saṃyojanas*. We have lower fetters, and higher fetters. Lower fetters bind beings to be reborn again and again in the lower states. This refers to the four woeful states, the human realm and the celestial realms. We call these the lower states. In contrast, the higher realms are the 20 *Brahma* realms.

What are the lower fetters?

1) *Kāmarāgasaṃyojana* (attachment to sensual pleasure)

People are attached to sensual pleasure. They attach to visible objects, sounds, smells, tastes and tangible objects. And they will do evil things based upon this attachment. In accordance with this attachment, when they commit these evil deeds after death they have to be reborn in the lower realms.

But even if we do something that is meritorious–like now, we practice generosity, perhaps observe five or eight or even 10 precepts, we sit in meditation and perhaps do some chanting–if we do these things because we hope to be reborn as a higher-class human or as an angel, this is attachment to the *kāma* realm, right? For that reason, a person who does this will have to be reborn again in the human or celestial realms. Again, in this context, we call these the lower realms.

What about *rūparāga* and *arūparāga*–attachment to the *rūpa* and *arūpa* realms? These are regarded as higher realms. For now, I'm talking about the lower fetters, though.

2) *Paṭighasaṃyojana* (hatred)

Your anger might cause you to kill someone, right? Some creature may die because you get angry. According to this evil action, you cannot go to heaven after you die. Instead, you go to a woeful state. This is why hatred is also called a lower fetter. It binds beings to be reborn in a lower existence.

Māna is higher, right?

3) *Diṭṭhisaṃyojana* (false or wrong view)
4) *Sīlabbataparāmāsasaṃyojana* (adherence to rites and rituals)

These two *saṃyojanas* are wrong view. Those who do demeritorious things based upon these *saṃyojanas* will be reborn in a woeful state. Even if they do meritorious things, their wrong view will cause them to be reborn in either the human or celestial realms. But these are still lower realms, right? That's why these two *diṭṭhi* are also called lower fetters.

5) *Vicikicchāsaṃyojana* (doubt)

Doubt refers to vexation due to perplexed thinking. In other words, this is the inability to make a decision. This is when a person has doubts about *kamma* or the consequences of *kamma*. What does a person who doubts these things tend to do? Mostly demeritorious things, right? As such, after he dies he cannot go beyond this world or to a higher plane. Mostly, he will just be reborn in the woeful states.

For these reasons, *lobha* (attachment), *paṭigha* (hatred), *diṭṭhi* (wrong view), *sīlabbataparāmāsasaṃyojana* (also wrong view) and *vicikicchā* (doubt)—these five fetters—are called lower fetters. I want you to remember that the first, fourth, sixth, seventh and eighth fetters are called lower fetters. These five fetters will bind beings to the lower existences.

Among the remaining five fetters, there is *rūparāgasaṃyojana* (attachment to the realm of form) and *arūparāgasaṃyojana* (attachment to the formless realm). Some people practice tranquility meditation and gain *jhāna*. Because this *jhāna* is so satisfying, they can get attached to it. They might think that it's a good thing to be reborn in the *Brahma* realms after death. The *Brahma* realms are higher realms. This is why *rūparāgasaṃyojana* and *arūparāgasaṃyojana* are called higher fetters. They bind beings to the *Brahma* realms, which are higher realms.

And also, we have *māna*, or pride—

Q: Can you please explain a bit about how saṃyojanas are uprooted once a being becomes enlightened?

Okay, let's look at the *Suttanta* method first.

A *sotāpanna*—or stream-enterer—has uprooted *diṭṭhisaṃyojana*, *sīlabbataparāmāsaṃyojana* and *vicikicchāsaṃyojana*. These three are uprooted. They no longer have false views or adherence to rites and ceremonies, right? As we already talked about, in the time of the Buddha people would practice like a cow or a dog. But someone who gains enlightenment has come to understand that following the Noble Eightfold Path is the only way to enlightenment. For that reason, a *sotāpanna* will not adhere to rites and ceremonies.

A once-returner cannot get rid of any *saṃyojanas*; they can just weaken them.

A non-returner gets rid of *kāmarāgasaṃyojana* (attachment to sensual pleasure). Also, a non-returner has no hatred at all. They still have *rūparāga*, *arūparāga*, *māna* and *avijjā*, though. Only an *arahant* can get rid of these. An *arahant* doesn't have to reborn again because he gets rid of all *saṃyojanas*.

Remember, these *saṃyojanas* bind beings to be reborn into the round of existence. When we get rid of these, we are free from the 31 planes of existence.

Now, let's look at the *Abhidhammā* method. It's a little different.

One who gains the first stage of enlightenment uproots *diṭṭhisaṃyojana* and *sīlabbataparāmāsaṃyojana*. There's also no *vicikicchāsaṃyojana*, *issāsaṃyojana* or *macchariyasaṃyojana*. In other words, there is no longer jealousy or stinginess once enlightenment is attained. If a person still has these qualities, he is not enlightened.

We're talking about a person's disposition, right? We're talking about their nature. If they still have jealousy or stinginess, they're not a *sotāpanna* yet. A *sotāpanna* has no *diṭṭhi*, no jealousy, no stinginess and no doubt. He has eradicated five *saṃyojanas*.

Let's not get too far ahead of ourselves.

Let's first continue by examining further the five higher fetters. They are *rūparāgasaṃyojana*, *arūparāgasaṃyojana*, *mānasaṃyojana*, *uddhaccasaṃyojana* and *avijjāsaṃyojana*. These five kinds of fetters are called higher fetters because they bind beings to the higher existences—to the *rūpa* and *arūpa* realms.

According to the *Abhidhammā* method, the lower fetters include the following: *kāmarāgasaṃyojana, paṭighasaṃyojana, diṭṭhisaṃyojana, sīlabbataparāmāsaṃyojana* and *vicikicchāsaṃyojana*. That is, *lobha, dosa*, the two *diṭṭhi* and *vicikicchā* are lower fetters. The remaining five by this reckoning–*bhavarāgasaṃyojana, mānasaṃyojana, issāsaṃyojana, macchariyasaṃyojana* and *avijjāsaṃyojana*–are called higher fetters. Those who still have *māna* (pride), jealousy, stinginess and ignorance are bound to the *Brahma* realms.

Now, let's look more closely at which kinds of fetters can be eradicated by noble ones.

Someone who has practiced *vipassanā* meditation and gained the first stage of enlightenment is a stream-enterer. What kind of *saṃyojanas* has a stream-enterer eradicated? Let's look at them one-by-one.

For the *Suttanta* method, he has eradicated *diṭṭhi* (false view), *sīlabbataparāmāsaṃyojana* and doubt. He has eradicated just these three fetters. For the *Abhidhammā* method, he has eradicated the same three.

A once-returner cannot uproot any fetters. We already talked about this, right?

What about a non-returner? What kinds of fetters does he uproot?

He has uprooted *kāmarāgasaṃyojana* (attachment to sensual pleasure) and *paṭigha* (hatred, ill will, aversion). There is no anger for a non-returner.

And, as I also shared a few minutes ago, *issāsaṃyojana* is part of the *Abhidhammā* method, right? This is envy or jealousy. A person who has gained the first stage of enlightenment no longer has envy or jealousy. He eradicates this, as he does avarice, stinginess or selfishness. There is no stinginess in a stream-enterer. If someone says that they attained stream-entry through their practice of insight meditation but they still display jealousy or stinginess, they are wrong. No jealousy or selfishness will exist in a noble person.

An *arahant* eradicates the remaining five *saṃyojanas*. What are they? For the *Suttanta* method, we're talking about five, right? They include *rūparāgasaṃyojana, arūparāgasaṃyojana, mānasaṃyojana, uddhaccasaṃyojana* and *avijjāsaṃyojana*.

With respect to restlessness, we probably know what it's like to practice meditation and have our mind distracted and wandering all over the world, thinking about the past or worrying about the future. Only an *arahant* can eradicate this restlessness. This is why we try to train our mind to focus on one object. Even a non-returner has to deal with restlessness.

Let's move on to the 10 kinds of *kilesa*.

Before we do, though, I want to make sure that you understand that these *saṃyojanas* are fetters. They bind beings to be reborn again and again in the round of existence. Just as a rope binds the neck of an ox, these fetters bind all beings and prevent them from running away or going anywhere. They can't go far, right?

Especially for ordinary worldlings, these 10 kinds of fetters bind us. That's why we can't go anywhere. Even in this life, our attachment, our anger or our doubt bind us to a very confining space. Can you see that? Even one rope prevents a creature from running away, but now, we have 10 ropes that bind us. That's why we can't go anywhere. And even when we die, we have to be reborn in the 31 planes of existence–mostly in the lower planes.

This is why we have to practice meditation. As we do, we can eradicate these fetters one-by-one, little-by-little. A stream-enterer eradicates the two kinds of *diṭṭhi* and doubt. A non-returner eradicates hatred and attachment to sensual pleasures. And when we gain *arahant*, we eradicate all the remaining fetters. This is why we need to practice meditation.

Now, let's go to *kilesa*.

Kilesa

We have 10 kinds of kilesa, briefly. Most people think that there is just *lobha, dosa* and *moha* but there are actually 10 mental defilements. That's what *kilesa* means–defilement. This is because *kilesas* defile our mind. They make our mind impure. They torment the mind.

What are they?

1) *Lobha* (greed)
2) *Dosa* (hatred)
3) *Moha* (delusion)
4) *Māna* (pride)
5) *Diṭṭhi* (false view)
6) *Vicikicchā* (doubt)
7) *Thīna* (sloth)
8) *Uddhacca* (restlessness)

9) *Ahirika* (moral shamelessness)

This is a lack of moral shame. We're not ashamed to carry out immoral actions. This is *ahirika*.

10) *Anottappa* (moral fearlessness)

So we have 10 kinds of *kilesas*, or impurities. Of these various kinds of immoral categories we've been talking about, *anusaya* is the strongest. This is why we separate *kilesa* and *anusaya*.

Q: Anusaya is stronger than kilesa?

Yes.

So, among the 14 unwholesome mental states, we have a number of categories we've been talking about. What are they?

1) *Āsavā*
2) *Oghā*
3) *Yogā*
4) *Ganthā*
5) *Upādānā*
6) *Nīvaraṇā*
7) *Anusaya*
8) *Saṃyojana*
9) *Kilesa*

That's nine different categories covering the 14 unwholesome *cetasika*. The Buddha would classify these 14 unwholesome *cetasika* into varying categories depending upon his audience when giving a talk. Sometimes he would talk in terms of *anusaya*, whereas other times he might talk about *kilesa* or *āsavā*. We have these different categories because his audiences differed.

But even though we have these nine groups, what are they concerned with? Just the 14 unwholesome mental states. These 14 can be classified into many groups. We can reclassify them based upon their nature in a given context.

Mostly, though, we talk in terms of *kilesas* or *nīvaraṇā*. When we hear a *Dhamma* talk, they don't usually talk about *āsavā* or *ganthā*, right? But we hear the word *kilesa* a lot.

These are all enemies for meditators. That's why we fight with them every day.

Q: When you were talking about thīna and middha, is it always akusala? I mean, is it still akusala when we're really tired?

Sometimes, there may be a little bit of *sasaṅkhārika*, but it's not so strong. It is *akusala citta*, but not strong. But, yes, *thīna* and *middha* are *akusala cetasika*.

Q: Should we try to reduce thīna and middha even when we're really tired and sleepy?

No, sometimes we are tired and sleepy because of the needs of our body. It's not *akusala* when that's the case. But when we say, "I want to sleep instead of practicing meditation," then it's *akusala*.

Sometimes we feel sleepy because the body needs sleep. Mainly, though, it's our mind that tells us that we're sleepy. But it is the nature of the body to sometimes require rest.

So, let's look more closely at the 10 *kilesas*:

1) *Lobha*

This is attachment. What is *lobha* attached to? Everything. It is attachment to visible objects, sounds, smells, tastes, touches and mental objects. It's attachment to existence too. Even if we gain *jhāna*, we attach to that as well. We attach to objects and to the world. It's all *lobha*, greed, craving, attachment.

What happens when a mental defilement such as *lobha* arises in the mind? Our mind becomes impure. Whenever they arise in our mind, our mind is not normal. Inevitably, we have to suffer. And it's all because of this *kilesa*. The more we are attached, the more we have to suffer. If we are attached a little, we suffer a little. If we are attached a lot, we have a lot of suffering. This is the nature of our mind. It's the nature of the law of *kamma*.

Most people aren't satisfied with what they have. They need more. This goes on for their entire lives. They never have enough and always want more. It's important that we study the books and the scriptures to understand this phenomenon, but more importantly, that we study the mind to address the problem. If we don't understand the consequences of mental defilement, then the problem continues.

Let's look at some examples of how *lobha* finds its way into our daily lives:

We're never satisfied with what we have, right? Maybe we have a good car, but it's old. So we decide that we need a new car. Although the old car was just fine, now we have to spend a lot of money on a new car. Do you think that makes us happy now? I don't think so.

Normally, you can buy a cheap old car and not worry much about its safety. But you worry constantly about a shiny, new and expensive car. Even at night, you might peek out the window to see if it's okay in the driveway. Or if you go somewhere with it, you're always worrying about whether someone scratches the paint.

It's not just the car itself that we worry about. We also worry about the payment, right?

What about our house? Our house might have a few bedrooms, and that's enough. Last year, a person I know bought a new house with seven bedrooms. It was just two people! I don't know why they bought such a big house.

Actually, it's because of *lobha*.

Now they've got this big house. But they can't go anywhere because they have to spend every day taking care of it. Every day, they have to take care of the house, the payment and the maintenance. Not only that! Some families need to have a television in each room. A big television too.

Why do they buy all this stuff? Attachment. They're never satisfied with what they have. They always want more, bigger and newer. This is because of attachment. And because of this *lobha*, they have to suffer. If something happens to their property, they suffer. Whenever they leave their property unattended, they have to worry and suffer about it. They probably lose sleep as they worry about their stuff.

Think about the debt that people build up because they never have enough. We have so many clothes and so much stuff. It's meaningless. This attachment binds them. How much income do they have? How much of it do they spend on stuff? Probably more than they make, so they have to use credit cards.

This is why people suffer all their lives. It's because of *lobha*, or craving. They don't know how to control their *lobha*. They see something and they just want to have it. They buy it, even on credit. It makes people suffer.

People often have to get a second job–thereby giving them less time to sleep–so they can earn more money to pay for their stuff. Why do they have to work so hard? They have to take care of house payments, car payments, television payments, and so on. If you buy a newer, bigger house, you might only get to spend four hours a day there because you're working the other 20 hours a day trying to pay for it.

We need to understand that attachment is the cause of suffering. It controls us. But we need to control *lobha*. *Lobha* is not our good friend. It is our enemy because it causes us to suffer. When we know this, we can control our mind. We need to be content with what we have. If we know our situation, know our income, know our spending, we won't have to suffer so much.

Every day, we are getting closer to leaving this world. A day passes so quickly. Eventually, we die. Just working all the time is not good. It's not good when it's all because of our *lobha*. And even when we're not working, we're up at night worrying about the stuff we're attached to.

This *lobha* defiles and impurifies the mind.

2) *Dosa*

This is hatred. This is anger, aversion. When you're not satisfied with something or someone, you get angry. When you get angry, the anger destroys you first and then perhaps others later. You get angry first, right? And then maybe you'll want to fight someone. See? Anger destroys you first. It's like a poison. Anger puts poison in your heart. It's very dangerous.

When *lobha* and *dosa* arise, they are associated with *moha*. Attachment and ill will are always associated with ignorance because *moha* doesn't understand realities, which is why *lobha* and *dosa* are allowed to arise.

Dosa is not just anger. If you worry about something, it's *dosa*. If you're not satisfied with something or someone, it's *dosa*. If you're depressed, it's *dosa*. That's why *dosa* destroys your mind, your body and your heart first, and then you destroy others.

Normally, how does *dosa* affect our face? Usually, you can see a person and get a sense of whether they're a good person. They might look pretty or handsome. But what happens when they get angry? The color of the face reddens. The whole body becomes stiff.

Can you see how the face changes right away, as soon as anger arises in the mind? Even if a person is normally pretty or handsome, how do they look when they are angry? Not good.

The Buddha taught us that those who get angry often will be reborn ugly in the next life. In other words, you'll be reborn with an ugly face. It's not good. It's not good in this life either.

When it comes to *lobha* and *dosa*, every day most people are mainly filled with greed and attachment. It just arises and arises all the time. How can we eradicate *lobha* and *dosa* and the others? We should have a method, right?

When we discussed *anusaya* (latent defilements), I explained that the grossest mental defilements (transgressive defilements) are overcome by way of virtue, or morality. Medium-gross mental defilements (obsessive defilements) can be eradicated by concentration. We talked about this, remember? Whatever arises on the mental level, these obsessive mental defilements can be temporarily eradicated when we have good concentration.

Latent defilements are eradicated by wisdom–by *magga ñāṇa*. When we gain enlightenment, we can uproot them. But it's very difficult to gain enlightenment. Until we do, what can we do to temporarily eradicate all kinds of *kilesas*? Well, even if we haven't gained enlightenment, by understanding our life, by understanding all kinds of mental defilements, by understanding the consequences of mental defilements, we can reduce their level and degree–we can make them lower and lower and lower. This is accomplished through our understanding.

With *lobha*, we are attached to everything and everyone. It's just greed. This occurs in our mind. If we have a lack of understanding of this, our *lobha* may just get bigger and bigger, right?

What do we need to understand about our life? We need to understand that the more we have attachment, the more we will suffer. We need to know the nature of attachment. We need to know the consequences of attachment.

We should reflect appropriately. "Why do I have to buy everything and be attached to everything?" We should think about how nothing is permanent. We can die anytime. We should think about this too. "Why do I have to attach to sensual pleasures? I don't need to attach so much because I can die at any time."

When you're attached to something, it doesn't just end with this life. Because of this craving and attachment, in the next life you'll become a hungry ghost. If someone buys a big house and a luxurious car and then dies with attachment to these things, they cannot go anywhere because of the attachment. Mostly, they stay around as hungry ghosts. This *lobha*, this craving and attachment causes them to stay close to those things they are attached to.

If you happen to have a lot of money in the bank, it's good to reflect that nothing is permanent and that you will one day have to part with that money. Even before death, you may have to part with it anyway–perhaps you'll gamble it away or loan it to someone who doesn't pay you back.

We might lose our property or lose our money. This means that our life, our property–and everything in the world–is impermanent. Why do we have to attach so much to impermanent things? If we think about impermanence in this way, we can reduce our craving.

As human beings, we have a duty to take care of our families–that's okay. But we don't have to work so hard to acquire the endless things we get attached to. We'll have a simple, happy and easy life if we can reduce our attachments.

We've been talking about ways to reduce *lobha*, right?

What about *dosa*?

Mostly, as ordinary worldlings, when we come across undesirable objects that appear to our eyes, ears, nose, tongue or body, we get angry right away. When we get angry, we destroy ourselves first and then treat others badly. We find it difficult to eat, sleep or enjoy anything whenever we have anger.

So what do we have to do to reduce anger, aversion, hatred, *dosa*? We need to use *mettā*, or loving-kindness. We need to cultivate love for everything.

But please remember that loving-kindness and attachment are quite different. Attachment to something or someone is *lobha*. It's craving. That is a mental state associated with unwholesome consciousness rooted in attachment. On the other hand, loving-kindness is a wholesome mental state associated with wholesome consciousness. The two are quite different.

There are two kinds of love, right? There is *lobha*, and there is *mettā*. The two are very different. We often say, "I love you." What kind of love are we talking about? Craving or *mettā*? To reduce *dosa*, use loving-kindness. This *mettā* is very useful in society. It is necessary to develop this quality.

How long will we be here on this earth? Maybe a long time, or perhaps just a short time. We don't know. I might go first, or you might go first. Who knows when we will depart? No one knows.

Try to look at this life experience as if we are traveling together. Maybe we are traveling together on a plane. But according to our ticket—our destination—perhaps we reach some city and then you get out. Maybe I transit and then continue on. In other words, consider that we are just travelers temporarily meeting each other for a short time. It's just temporary.

So we shouldn't fight each other, right? This meeting is only temporary. Even if we don't like the way a person acts or speaks, it's just temporary. It won't be long before they get up and exit the plane.

Think like this.

As human beings, we should help each other when we meet. What can we do for others? Try to use loving-kindness, help others, and then there are no problems. We can then spend our short time together without issues.

Couples often fight so much. Why? A lack of loving-kindness. We might say nasty things or use violence. A couple won't find happiness without loving-kindness. If everyone had loving-kindness in their hearts and minds, a group of 200 or 2,000 people could stay together like a happy family with no fighting.

I will do whatever I can for you. And if you have an opportunity to help me, that's wonderful too. After you help me, I will be happy. And I will be happy if I can help you.

See that, right? When you're helping someone, you feel very happy. And after you help them, you can think about the goodness of your deeds and feel happy. If we have loving-kindness and help each other mentally, verbally and physically every day, our world will be very peaceful and wonderful.

We need this. To reduce hatred, aversion, anger, use loving-kindness.

Also, I will encourage all of you to consider the Buddha's teaching that there is no one who has not been a member of your family before–perhaps a brother, a sister, a mother or a father. In the round of rebirth, this is not our first life. We have been born so many times that all beings–not just human beings, but animals too–used to be our brothers, sisters, mothers or fathers. There is no one who has not been a member of our family before.

We should think of everyone as being a part of our family.

"We used to be family." Think like this. "That was my mother in a previous life."

Think like this and you will feel happy. If you do something kind for someone, regard that person as your brother—you will feel happy. If we all had this attitude and understood life in this way, how wonderful would it be?

Instead, countries are at war because of mental defilements. We fight over attachments and hatred. So, please use your loving-kindness to reduce *dosa*, or hatred. Think about everyone you see as being a former member of your family, and then you won't get angry. It's good for you, and good for others.

3) *Moha*

Moha is ignorance. It's a kind of mental defilement. It clouds the mind and blinds the eye. It prevents us from seeing reality. It doesn't understand *kamma* (action), the consequences of actions, or the Four Noble Truths. It doesn't understand these things.

We call this *moha*, delusion or ignorance. Craving and hatred occur because of *moha*. *Moha* is like the leader. It associates with *lobha* and *dosa* all the time. Whenever you have attachment (craving) or hatred (anger), *moha* is always associated with it.

This is *moha*.

How do we temporarily eradicate *moha*? By understanding. If we don't understand action, the results of action, or the Four Noble Truths, what do we have to do? We have to study. That's why we're studying these things now. We're studying the consequences of actions. We're studying the Four Noble Truths.

What are the Four Noble Truths? Do you remember? Suffering, the cause of suffering, the cessation of suffering, and the way leading to the cessation of suffering.

But *moha* doesn't know that. To know the Four Noble Truths, we study them now.

What is suffering?

Briefly, birth, decay, disease and death are suffering. Associating with people you don't like is suffering. Disassociating with those you love is suffering. Not getting what you want is suffering. Like slaves, having to take care of this body—these five aggregates—is suffering.

Where does suffering come from? What's the cause?

Attachment. Suffering arises because we are attached to sensual pleasures and attached to existence. If someone tells you that life in heaven is better than human life and offers you the opportunity to head to heaven immediately, will you take it? No, you want to stay here because you're attached to your existence.

Because of our attachment, we have to be reborn again. Then, there is decay, disease and death again. This is suffering. The cause is attachment.

If you know this, you can reduce your attachment. The cause of suffering will then be reduced, right?

What is the cessation of suffering?

It is *nibbāna*. If there is no attachment, there is no suffering. This is *nibbāna*, the cessation of suffering. *Moha* doesn't understand this. But now we know that the cessation of suffering is *nibbāna*.

What is the way leading to the cessation of suffering?

It is the Middle Way of morality, concentration and wisdom. This is right understanding, right thinking, and so on. This is the way leading to the cessation of suffering.

When we understand suffering, its cause, its cessation, and the way leading to its cessation, *moha* becomes *amoha*, or non-delusion. *Moha* is delusion, right? Non-delusion is wisdom or knowledge. When we have understanding about *kamma*, the results of *kamma*, and the Four Noble Truths, our attachment, our hatred and our delusion are temporarily eradicated. This is because we are reducing *lobha*, *dosa* and *moha*.

So to eradicate *moha* (delusion), study. After we study, we practice. As we practice, we are walking the path leading to the cessation of suffering.

As we understand that we're not supposed to have craving or hatred—as we understand cause and effect—we will reduce our *lobha* and *dosa*. Then, our suffering will also be reduced.

So we need to study, and practice in line with our understanding, our knowledge.

4) *Māna*

Māna is pride, conceit or arrogance. Arrogance is thinking oneself to be superior to others.

If you think you are of a higher class, a higher family than others, this is conceit. If you think you are more wealthy than others, this is conceit. If you think you have greater power or position than others, this is conceit. If you think you are better educated than others, this is conceit. If you think you are more attractive than others, this too is conceit. This is *māna*.

We cannot be happy when *māna* arises in our mind. There will be no happiness in our mind. This is because *māna* is a mental defilement, or *kilesa*.

Those with pride or conceit walk, talk and act a certain way, right? It's because they think they are superior to others. They think that they are more clever and more knowledgeable than others, and so they look down on them. They think that they are better than other people. As such, they don't care so much for others.

How do we have to think to reduce our *māna*?

Firstly, if we are a clever or wealthy person, we should use that fortunate position to help others. That's how it should be. Also, though, we should not overestimate ourselves. However rich or clever we are, it's just temporary. Besides, most people don't want to associate with people who have arrogance. They avoid such people because of the way they act, talk and think. They tend to look down on others, so no one wants to be around them.

We should consider that life and our property are impermanent.

If someone says, "You're very pretty," you should consider what this means. What's pretty? It's only as deep as the skin. But what about below the skin? What about inside the body?

We have 32 impure parts of the body. The Buddha called these impurities.

If someone says, "Your hair is beautiful," you usually express appreciation and feel happy, right? But your hair is impure. If one of your hairs falls out and lands in your food, how do you feel about it?

"Your nails are so beautiful." If one of your nails landed in your soup, how would you feel? "Your teeth are beautiful." Pull out one of your teeth and put it on your dinner plate. Or perhaps sit there and watch someone clean their teeth with dental floss after a meal. Maybe that's not so pleasant to look at, right?

The Buddha called these impurities. Head hair, body hair, nails, teeth, bones, skin, lungs, kidneys, urine. There are a lot of impurities in our body. See that, right? These are all impurities.

"Your eyes are so pretty." You shouldn't think like that. They're not pretty.

Some people spend a lot of money on their hair and nails every week, right? They do this to try to look pretty. It costs time and money to beautify the face and the body.

But what we really have to do is develop insight. We need to develop our mind. We need to elevate the mind to be higher and more pure. This means that we need to try to eradicate *lobha* and *hatred*. We can purify and elevate our mind by thinking and understanding our life and by practicing meditation. This causes our mind to become pure.

We need to do this. And then, our conceit comes down too.

5) *Diṭṭhi*

This is wrong view, or misbelief. Misbelief means not believing in the right way. In detail, we have 62 kinds of *diṭṭhi*, some of which we've talked about before.

There are some people who don't believe in *kamma* and results, right? They don't believe that there are consequences of unskillful behavior. This is wrong view. There are some who don't think it makes a difference when we give alms or offer support to a church or a school or a hospital. This is also wrong view.

And there are those people who think that offering on a big scale—making a big contribution to a cause—is not meaningful. They say, "Don't do that. It doesn't matter anyway." Or perhaps they think that giving gifts—Christmas presents or maybe wedding presents—is useless. These are all examples of wrong view. The scriptures talk about this.

There are those who think that there are no consequences to our good or bad actions. They feel that we should just do whatever we want to do. But this is wrong view.

Others think that this world does not exist. This means a belief that beings living in other worlds—like angels in heaven—cannot be reborn in this world after they die. People who believe like this think that when a being dies in another world, it's the end of their life.

There's also the misbelief that there are no other worlds. This means that there are no other worlds to be reborn into after we die. They believe that everything ends at the end of this life. This is a kind of wrong view.

Some think that there is no mother and no father. They think that good or evil done to parents produces no result. In other words, they think that doing good things for our parents yields no results, just as they think that doing bad things to our parents yields no results. This is wrong view. These people don't respect their parents. Because of a wrong view like this, these people believe that they don't have to take care of their parents. Likewise, they think their parents don't do anything for them. This is based upon misbelief.

There are those who don't believe in spontaneously-born beings. We have four kinds of beings, right? There are beings born from moisture, like mosquitoes. There are also spontaneously-born beings, such as hell beings. When someone dies from this human world to be reborn in hell, he is reborn spontaneously. Or, according to our meritorious deeds, we may be reborn as an angel, god or *brahmā*. This also happens spontaneously.

It is wrong view to say that there are no spontaneously-born beings. If a person thinks that he will not be reborn in hell for doing evil things, this is a disbelief in hell...or heaven, for that matter, as the case may be. No gods, no hell beings. These people don't believe in these things.

On the other hand, those who believe in spontaneously-born beings like angels or gods will do good things. They do so believing that these good things might lead to rebirth as a human, an angel or a *brahmā*. We think like this, right? Or, if we do bad things, we might go to hell—so we avoid doing bad things. We believe like this.

This has to do with the existence of hell or heaven. But these people reject their existence, as they reject the existence of spontaneously-born beings.

There are also those who don't believe that there are noble ones who can expound on this or other worlds through true, direct knowledge in accordance with their own effort. A person like this does not believe that you can attain enlightenment through the practice of meditation. This is wrong view. They don't believe anything. This is false view.

What do we tend to do when we have false view? Demeritorious things, mostly. Even when we do meritorious things, they are associated with wrong view. And because of our wrong view, we have to go to a woeful state after we die.

What's eradicated by someone who practices insight (*vipassanā*) meditation and gains the first stage of enlightenment? *Diṭṭhi*, or wrong view. There is no more wrong view. There's also no doubt. Wrong view and doubt hold people to the woeful states. This is why the Buddha said that it's very important to eradicate wrong view and doubt. To illustrate the importance, the Buddha said that if someone were to have their hand set afire or a spear plunged into their chest, they should try to extinguish wrong view before they try to extinguish the fire or remove the spear. Extinguishing wrong view is the priority.

Remember this. It's very important.

Why is this so important? This knife, this spear, or someone stepping on our chest—we could die right away, right? Maybe we believe that this is our only life. Or maybe the fire on our hand burns us completely and we die. Then it's all over. If we hold the wrong view that there is no future life, we will do evil things in this life. In accordance with these wrong views, we will do these evil things and go to a woeful state in the next life. And when we end up in a woeful state, it's very hard to come back out. The way in is wide open but the way out is very narrow. It's very hard to exit.

The Buddha said that if you have wrong view, it will produce evil actions and you will end up going to a woeful state, then you will spend many, many lives in that state. Even if we don't go to hell, we could end up being an animal. And it's very hard for an animal to be reborn as a human being.

We try to do meritorious things, right? People practice generosity, they try to keep their precepts, they do chanting and practice meditation too. But we're not certain where they'll be reborn after they die, right? Some may be reborn as human beings again, while others may go to a woeful state. But animals are unable to practice generosity, keep precepts, or cultivate wisdom. This is why it's very difficult for an animal to be reborn as a human being again.

This is why the Buddha said that it should be our priority to first remove *diṭṭhi*, and then extinguish the fire that is burning our hand.

This is the nature of *diṭṭhi*.

Perhaps someone kills their parents. Why? Maybe they want the life insurance, money or property. The money they get might sustain them for 20 or 30 years before they die and go to hell. If the person knew that he would go to hell for a long, long time, maybe he wouldn't commit the crime. But the person in this example doesn't believe in hell. This is wrong view.

Because of our *diṭṭhi*, we believe that we can do whatever we want with our lives. We feel that there are no consequences of our good or bad actions. Whatever you want to do, just do it, right? No mother, no father, no this world, no other world. There is no existence after death. There is no rebirth.

This *diṭṭhi* is very dangerous. That's why the Buddha said that we should try to pull it out first. And those who practice meditation and gain the first stage of enlightenment eradicate both doubt and wrong view. When they do, the door to the woeful states is closed.

6) *Vicikicchā*

This is skeptical doubt. It is vexation due to perplexed thinking. We can't make a decision. It's doubt.

Those who have doubt don't know whether it's appropriate to be generous. They wonder whether it's beneficial or effective. Because they don't have a firm belief in something, they can't make a decision. As they can't make a decision, they don't do anything. As they don't do anything, they don't gain anything.

The reality of doubt is a mental state. It associates with unwholesome consciousness rooted in ignorance. You doubt and can't make a decision. This is because your mental state is associated with *moha*.

But, as I just shared, doubt is eradicated upon attaining the first stage of enlightenment.

What do we need to do to eradicate doubt temporarily? We need to study. When we study, we understand mind and matter, cause and effect. We will understand *kamma*, the consequences of *kamma*, and the Four Noble Truths. We will no longer doubt these things. This is why we need to study them.

7) *Thīna*

This is sloth. This is sickness of the mind. It is the morbid state of the mind.

The nature of *thīna* is of two varieties. The first is very easy to understand. When we listen to *Dhamma* or practice meditation, we may experience some drowsiness. In that moment, you can't control your body. This is sloth, or *thīna*. It's a kind of mental defilement.

Actually, time is up for today. Thank you. *Sādhu. Sādhu. Sādhu.*

...

Today is January 31, 1999. Last week, we discussed the 10 kinds of mental defilements from attachment through doubt. Today, we will continue with *thīna*.

As I started to say at the end of the last class, the nature of *thīna* should be understood as being of two kinds. The first kind is sloth, or drowsiness. Often, when we sit in meditation or listen to *Dhamma*, we start to get sleepy or drowsy. We call this *thīna*. It's very clear what this is, right?

The other nature is sickness of the mind. This is the morbid state of the mind. When this arises, you don't want to do anything. This is also *thīna*. You don't want to study, to read *Dhamma*, to do chanting, to practice generosity or to do anything else that is good. You don't want to keep your precepts. You don't want to sit in meditation. This is the nature of *thīna*.

Do you remember when we studied hindrances (*nīvaranā*)? *Thīna-middha* is one kind of hindrance. This *thīna* obstructs the way to the sensual blissful state, the *Brahma* realms, and *nibbāna*.

It also prevents the arising of good thoughts. When *thīna* arises in your mind, there are no good thoughts. You can't control your body either, right? You're sleepy. So how can you have good thoughts? *Thīna* prevents good thoughts. And when you read a book, you feel sleepy and don't understand what you're studying. *Thīna* obstructs the eye of wisdom. Wisdom cannot occur when there is *thīna*. It obstructs the way.

Thīna stands between us and all good things. It is our enemy.

It's not uncommon for us to sit in meditation for 30 minutes and start to feel sleepy. Then, meditation time is up, we get up, and *thīna* is gone. It just arises and obstructs our way, our good thoughts, and our wisdom-eye.

When we studied mental states, I told you about the remedies and antidotes to *thīna*. We talked about how to cure and eliminate it. It's good if we talk about it again because this is very important, especially for meditators. Otherwise, *thīna* obstructs our way and prevents us from doing good things. If *thīna* arises in our mind, we cannot see the nature of mind and matter. This is due to a lack of concentration. When we lack concentration, no wisdom can occur. This is why we should know the techniques to deal with *thīna*. We need to know what antidote we should employ to attack *thīna*—sickness of the mind—when it arises.

Remember that we have nine ways. I'll explain this to you again because it's so important for everyone. When you sit in meditation for five minutes, how often do you start to feel sleepy and lose control of your body? We should use the Buddha's methods and techniques to fight with drowsiness.

a) Firm resolution

When you sit in meditation or listen to a lecture, you often start to feel sleepy. If you just follow this drowsiness, you'll fall asleep and/or not learn anything. But with firm resolution, you change your mind or attitude: "I will not allow drowsiness to overtake my mind. I will sit in meditation for one hour. I will try to concentrate my mind on my primary object. I don't want to sleep."

This is firm resolution. It's necessary to have this.

b) Accurate application of the mind on the object

We have a primary object of our meditation, right? It might be our nostrils, our abdomen, or perhaps a sensation. Try to observe this object.

Here, our primary object is the movement of our abdomen. From the beginning of the rising, through the middle, and to the end, our noting mind should follow the movement. When the abdomen begins to rise—"rising." Note this movement from the beginning, through the middle, and to the end. Follow the movement. Follow the object.

This is what is meant by accurate application of the mind on the object. It is necessary to do this.

Sometimes, you may struggle with *thīna* (drowsiness) if you only concentrate your mind on the rising and falling. If so, you need to add an object. First, note "rising" and "falling"—that is, know that your abdomen is rising and falling—and also know (and note) that you are sitting. "Rising...falling...sitting...rising...falling...sitting." If you add one more object, drowsiness can go away. If drowsiness doesn't go away, go to recitation.

c) Recitation

You know some words from the chanting. Do the chanting again and again and again. When you recite some words, your drowsiness can go away.

If you are practicing meditation alone, perhaps you can recite "*Buddho. Buddho. Buddho*" or perhaps "*Namo tassa bhagavato...*" We can use any words.

Make a recitation and *thīna* may go away. If it doesn't go away, then use another technique that we call mental recollection.

d) Mental recollection

This refers to contemplating something we've studied. For example, we've studied unwholesome consciousness. In *Pāli*, this is called *akusala citta*. With this technique, you think about *akusala citta*. Reflect on what it is. *Citta* is consciousness. Why do we call it unwholesome? Think about the meaning of these words. If you do, your drowsiness may go away.

We call this mental recollection. If your drowsiness doesn't go away, then use another technique.

e) Pulling the ear or rubbing the body

When you pull your ear or rub your hand, face or body, you may become alert and your drowsiness may go away. This is another technique.

Or, despite using this technique, you may still feel sleepy. If so, what do we have to do?

f) Visualize light

Look at a light. If you're sitting in meditation, you may have a candle or other light in front of you. Look at it. Or, you can get up, go outside, and look at the moon, the sky or the stars. Your drowsiness may then go away.

This is called visualizing light.

g) Washing the face

Wash your face with cool water, or perhaps even warm water. Or take cold water and put it in your eyes. Your drowsiness may then go away. If not, use the next technique.

h) Brisk walking

This is quick walking meditation. It's brisk walking, noting "left, right, left, right, left, right." It's quick.

By using this quick walking meditation, your drowsiness may go away. But even though you've tried these eight different antidotes to drowsiness, you may still feel sleepy. If so, what do you have to do?

i) Graceful surrender

This means acknowledging, "Okay, I'm sleepy. I need to sleep." But when you do, you continue noting every movement involved in the process of taking a rest. As you stand, you note "standing." As you sit on the bed or lie down, you note these as well. You make a mental note of every movement, including such movements as "stretching," "bending," "sitting down," "touching," "moving," "changing" and closing the eyes. If your eyes feel heavy, note "heavy." Do this until you fall asleep. As you fall asleep, you should know "Now I have to take a rest. I need to sleep for a while. As soon as I wake up, I will resume my meditation practice."

This is graceful surrender.

As you wake up from your rest, note "waking, waking." Then return your awareness to the rising and falling movement of your abdomen—"rising...falling...rising...falling." Start to practice again. Start noting.

These techniques are antidotes to *thīna*, or drowsiness. Most people don't think of sleepiness as a mental defilement. Mostly, they think of mental defilements only in terms of *lobha* (craving), *dosa* (hatred) and *moha* (ignorance). Without studying *Abhidhammā*, we would never know that *thīna* is also a mental hindrance and a mental defilement.

8) Uddhacca

This is restlessness. This is our mind just wandering all the time. Our mind only stays with us when we practice meditation. Otherwise, we're just thinking about the past and the future. This is restlessness.

This is why we need to practice meditation to gain concentration. This concentration is peace of mind. If we don't practice meditation, the mind just keeps wandering all the time. It's restless and distracted.

If you want to confirm that this is how the mind operates, just sit still and observe your mind. You'll see that it's just thinking about something all the time. Even if we try to control our mind—to fix it on a present object—it's very difficult. It just runs away, right?

Our remedy to this is that we need to concentrate our mind on one object. We need to practice *samatha* or *vipassanā* meditation. If we don't, there is no way to keep the mind from being restless.

With respect to *thīna* and *uddhacca*, only *arahants* can eradicate these two mental defilements. Everyone but an *arahant* has to deal with drowsiness and restlessness. Even stream-enterers, once-returners and non-returners have this.

9) *Ahirika*

This is moral shamelessness. This means that a person is not ashamed to carry out evil actions.

If we are not ashamed to kill creatures, to steal someone's property or to commit sexual misconduct, these are evil physical actions. If we are not ashamed to lie, slander, use harsh speech or speak vainly, these are evil verbal actions. And if we are not ashamed to think in terms of covetousness, ill will or wrong view, these are evil mental actions.

This is what *ahirika* means. It's a lack of shame in carrying out these various evil actions.

So how should we think?

We should think: "I come from a good, high-class family. If I kill something or someone, steal, commit sexual misconduct or lie, this is shameful behavior." We should think like this. If we don't, we feel no shame in committing evil actions.

We should think: "I meditate every day. I'm not supposed to kill or steal." Think about your family or your teacher: "I'm the student of a great teacher. I am the child of good parents. I'm an educated person. I shouldn't do this. This is shameful." In other words, think about your family, your teacher, your parents, your education and your position in life.

"I'm the boss at work." If the boss kills, steals or commits sexual misconduct, it's not good, right? No, it's shameful.

When you think in a skillful way like this, you won't commit any evil actions. So, we should think like this.

10) Anottappa

This means that a person is not afraid to carry out evil actions. In other words, there's no consideration of how people will think about them if they kill something or someone, if they steal, if they commit sexual misconduct, and so on. These people fail to consider whether they will be punished in this life for their misdeeds. They don't think about the results of their immoral actions. Instead, if we recognize that sooner or later we will have to receive the consequences of our misdeeds, we'll be afraid to do evil things.

Even very smart or rich people still have to receive consequences. Sometimes in America, we hear about someone with a lot of money getting away with a serious crime. Money talks, right? They can perhaps escape from punishment in this life, but they cannot escape from the law of *kamma* in the next life. A person can run from the law now but they cannot escape the law of *kamma*. Whatever they did, they have to take responsibility for it in the next life. Mostly, these consequences are felt in the woeful states.

So it's important that we think about this. Otherwise, we are unafraid to carry out evil actions.

I remember a story about this. Whenever you do something, even if no one sees you do it, you know about it yourself, right? There may be holy ones who also know. This means that there are no secret places in the world.

Let me tell you this old story from the life of the Bodhisatta, or our Buddha-to-be:

The Bodhisatta was once a student at a very famous university where rich people sent their children. His chief professor had a daughter who was very pretty.

The professor thought: "My daughter is now 20 years old. I would like for her to marry one of my 500 students. I want her to marry the student who is most clever, sincere, and honest. I will need to test them."

The professor called his 500 students and said, "I have a very pretty, clever daughter. I would like to present her to one of you. To help me decide which of you is most deserving of my daughter, I would like all of you to go home and take something special from your family—maybe gold, diamonds, rubies or silver—and bring it to me as a gift. Don't tell anyone what you've done. I will allow whoever brings the best gift to marry my daughter."

Four hundred and ninety-nine of the students went home, stole suitable gifts from their parents, and happily returned later to present the gifts to the professor.

But one student was different from the others.

The Bodhisatta had reflected on the professor's words: "The teacher said that we are not to tell anyone that we are stealing, but I know what I will be doing." The Bodhisatta realized that, even if no one else knew about his dishonest deed, he knew about it himself. As such, he said to himself: "I cannot steal anything. There are no secrets in this world, because I will know what I have done."

When the Bodhisatta returned to the university, the professor asked, "How about you? What did you get for me?"

The Bodhisatta replied, "Well, you said that we need to take something from our family without telling anyone what we've done. But I cannot find a secret place. Even if no one else knows, I know what I've done. For that reason, I didn't take anything from anyone."

Upon hearing this, the chief professor said, "You're very clever and honest, very sincere. For this reason, my daughter deserves you. I present my daughter to you for marriage."

So, today, I would like all of you to bear in mind that there are no secrets in the world. This is true. You yourself will always know of your misdeeds. Perhaps holy people—or people who can read minds—might know as well. But, at minimum, you will know.

The professor praised the Bodhisatta, didn't he? He said, "You have good conduct. You're very clever. So I give my daughter to you."

I'm talking about *anottappa*, right? Even if you escape from the law, you cannot escape from the law of *kamma* in the next existence.

We've studied the 10 kinds of mental defilements. These mental defilements cause turmoil and conflict in society and the world. Why do we fight each other? Attachment and hatred, delusion, pride and wrong view. Because of wrong view, we become selfish people. Not only that, but because of mental defilements, we encounter difficulty eating, sleeping—no peace of mind. We have to worry and suffer about everything we're attached to or hate.

What starts as a latent defilement becomes obsessive, and what's obsessive becomes transgressive. Then, we commit crimes. When we commit crimes, we go to jail. Why? Because of mental defilement. It is because of attachment, hatred, and so on. We suffer because of this. Whenever you think about your misdeeds, you feel unhappy. And after you die, you go to hell or another woeful state.

We can compare these mental defilements to fire. They are fires burning all the time.

What do they burn?

They burn our eyes, ears, nose, tongue, body and mind. Just burning, burning. When you see something agreeable, there's *lobha* (attachment). The fire of greed and craving burns your eyes. You see this desirable thing and say, "I like that. I want it." Or maybe you see a man or a woman and say, "I like that person." Who knows, you might end up committing sexual misconduct. Or you see an expensive television, admire it, and decide to steal it.

Can you see how it can go from the eyes to committing a crime? This is *kilesa*. The fire of *lobha* burns our eyes.

In the same way, you get angry if you see something that is undesirable. Hatred, right? *Dosa*. It burns you. It's another kind of fire burning your eye.

The fires of craving and aversion burn the eyes and the ears. If you like or dislike something, it burns. The same applies for smells, tastes, touches and the mind. We constantly think: "I want this" or "I want that." We might get angry at a person and hold on to that anger even years after they've died. Emotions continue to arise, right? This is burning us.

When craving and aversion burn our eyes, ears, nose, tongue, body and mind, can we sleep well? No. "I can't sleep tonight"—because the fire is burning all the time. However rich you are, you're not a happy person if you still have mental defilements burning your eyes, ears, nose, tongue, body and mind. You'll suffer over it.

The fires of mental defilement burn your eyes, ears, nose, tongue, body and mind. If you don't extinguish these fires, they lead to the fires of hell. Do you believe that? What this means is that our inability to control our mind can lead us to such great anger that we might kill someone. Or maybe we steal something if we can't control our greedy mind, right? After you die, you'll go to hell for it. But, initially, these fires burn our six sense-doors. They lead to the fires of hell. And then, it's very hard to come back to the human world.

So what do we need to do?

For something like *dosa*, we need to use *mettā*. For all of these mental defilements to be eradicated, we need to practice meditation. We need to do what the Buddha taught, which is the Middle Way. What is the Middle Way? The Noble Eightfold Path.

The Noble Eightfold Path can be divided into three groups: morality, concentration and wisdom. Our method to cure and extinguish all mental defilements is to have good conduct (morality), concentration and wisdom. This is why we need to practice meditation every day. As we do, we are working to extinguish these fires. It's necessary to do this.

We've been talking in terms of 10 *kilesas*, right? But *lobha*, for example, can also be viewed in terms of 108 types. I'll explain.

There are three kinds of craving (*taṇhā*):

1) *Kāmataṇhā*

This is craving for sense objects: form, sound, smell, taste and touch. This concerns the sensual realm. This is very clear, right?

2) *Bhavataṇhā*

This is craving for existence. It means craving for the *rūpa* or *arūpa* realms. It is craving for *jhāna*. It is associated with the view of eternalism, believing that everything is permanent. This is eternalism. It is a belief that we have a soul that doesn't die when our body dies. It's a belief that this soul continues to the next life. It doesn't perish. If you think like that, it's called eternalism.

3) *Vibhavataṇhā*

This is craving for non-existence. This is thinking that everything perishes and is finished after death. It is a belief that there is no more rebirth. It does not believe in hell or heaven.

So, we have these three kinds of craving.

We also have six objects. This refers to craving for forms, sounds, smells, tastes, bodily impressions, and mental objects.

The three types of craving multiplied by the six objects becomes 18 types of craving.

These 18 kinds of craving can occur in the past, in the present, and in the future. So we need to multiply 18 by three, right? When you think about the past, this craving can occur. It's the same for the present, and if you think about the future, it occurs again. That's why we multiply by three. So, that's 54 types.

These 54 types can be internal or external.

Internal means thinking about yourself. What are you craving? "My eyes are very pretty," "I love my beautiful nose," "My face is good-looking," "I have such pretty hair." This is internal. It refers to your body or belongings, but especially your body. You have craving associated with your eyes, ears, nose, tongue, body, hair, fingers, nails, skin and so on and on.

External refers to craving about external objects. "Her hair is so pretty" or perhaps "His teeth are beautiful."

See how craving can be internal or external? For this reason, we multiply 54 by two. This gives us 108 kinds of craving.

This is for knowledge. We won't learn this in other books. Only in *Abhidhammā* will we learn how craving can go from one to 108 kinds. So, again, we have the three kinds of craving multiplied by the six sense objects. Those 18 kinds can occur in the past, present and future, so we multiply 18 by three. Those 54 kinds can be found both internally and externally, which becomes 108 kinds of craving.

The 10 kinds of *kilesas* can become 1,500 kinds of mental defilement. This is why we need to practice meditation every day—to fight with all of these mental defilements.

How do 10 kinds of *kilesas* become 1,500 kinds of mental defilement?

Citta means consciousness, right? Although we have 121 types of consciousness, their nature is awareness of the object. So there's just one nature. Therefore, let's consider *citta* as one.

We have 52 *cetasika*. We also have 18 types of *nipphanna rūpa*, which is concretely-produced matter, as well as four types of *lakkhaṇa rūpa*. *Lakkhaṇa rūpa* refers to characteristics of matter. Remember the 28 types of matter? The last four are the characteristics of matter: production, continuity, decay and impermanence.

Altogether, we have one *citta*, 52 *cetasika*, 18 *nipphanna rūpa* and four *lakkhaṇa rūpa*. That's 75 entities, right?

These 75 entities can exist both internally and externally. This means that we have mind, mental factors, *nipphanna rūpa* and characteristics internally—in our body. We can also find all of these in someone else's body—externally. This means that they exist internally and externally.

For this reason, we multiply 75 by two. This means that mental defilements can occur from our bodies (internally) and outside (living things and non-living things that are external). This is why we multiply 75 by two. This becomes 150, right?

These 150 entities are the object or operation for each mental defilement. They are the objects of mental defilement. That's why we multiply 150 by 10 (the 10 *kilesas*).

That's how 10 mental defilements becomes 1,500 mental defilements. The fires of these mental defilements can lead you to the fires of hell.

See that, right?

So what do we have to do about this?

How many types of craving are there? One hundred and eight. This craving is the chief root of suffering. Why do we suffer? Because of this craving we have to die and be reborn again and again continually in this round of *saṃsāra* until we can eliminate these mental defilements and extinguish all of these fires.

To accomplish this, the Buddha taught us a technique. It's called the Middle Way. We do this by observing good conduct (morality), by practicing meditation to gain peace of mind (concentration), and by eventually realizing the nature of mind and body for what they really are (via the practice of insight, or *vipassanā*, meditation). When we have fulfilled this, we become a noble person.

What kind of mental defilements do we eradicate when we become a stream-enterer? Doubt and wrong view, right? When we become a non-returner, we eradicate hatred and attachment to sensual pleasure. And when we become an *arahant*, we eradicate the remaining mental defilements.

We need to practice meditation to accomplish this.

...

Now, we have finished talking about unwholesome categories. How many do we have? How many groups? *Āsavā, oghā, yogā, ganthā, upādānā, nīvaraṇā, anusaya, saṃyojana* and *kilesa*. That's nine groups.

Although we can divide these unwholesome categories into a group of nine, their realities are the 14 unwholesome mental factors.

Now, having finished immoral categories, we go to what's called *missakasaṅgaha*, or mixed categories.

Missakasaṅgaha

When we studied immoral categories, we were just talking about unwholesome things. Here, "mixed" means that we will be discussing categories that are moral, immoral or indeterminate. Indeterminate means *vipāka* and *kiriyā*. In other words, indeterminate is not moral and not immoral but is resultant and functional.

So, we'll be talking about these mixed categories in this section.

We'll start with *hetu*.

Hetu

We already know some of these. What is *hetu*? It means root, cause or condition. When we do *Paṭṭhāna* chanting, we say *"hetu paccayo." Hetu* means root, cause or condition.

How many roots? Six.

1) *Lobha* root
2) *Dosa* root
3) *Moha* root
4) *Alobha* root
5) *Adosa* root
6) *Amoha* root

Paramattha dhamma is a *Pāli* term that refers to realities. We are talking here about essential elements.

So, what is *lobha*? *Lobha cetasika*. It's greed. *Dosa* is aversion, and *moha* is delusion.

Alobha is non-attachment, or non-craving. *Adosa* is goodwill, which is loving-kindness. It's non-aversion. And *amoha* is wisdom, or non-delusion.

Where do we find *lobha, dosa* and *moha*? These are immoral roots, right? It's because of these three roots that evil actions arise. Why do we do something bad? Because of *lobha* root, or perhaps aversion or delusion. Sometimes it's all three of them, sometimes it's two of them, and sometimes it's just one of them. And then, we do something bad.

Think about this. These are the roots of our evil mental, verbal and physical actions.

What's the cause of our meritorious actions? What's the root? What's the condition? *Alobha* (non-attachment), *adosa* (goodwill) and *amoha* (wisdom). *Alobha* is non-attachment, right? If you're attached to your money, will you make a donation? No. If you have *adosa* (*mettā*, or loving-kindness), you can do good things. And with *amoha* (wisdom), you know the consequences of your actions. Based upon that understanding, you choose to do good things, you speak well, and you have good thoughts.

Alobha, *adosa* and *amoha* are the roots of good mental, verbal and physical actions.

But these last three roots (*alobha*, *adosa* and *amoha*) can be moral roots or indeterminate roots. In *Pāli*, indeterminate is *abyākata*—it's neither moral nor immoral. It's an indeterminate root. Strictly speaking, it's *vipāka* (resultant) and *kiriyā* (functional). So, these three roots—*alobha*, *adosa* and *amoha*—are called moral or indeterminate roots.

Why do we call these roots? The roots of a tree make the tree firm, well-established and prosperous, right? In the same way, these six roots (mental factors) associate with consciousness and mental factors to make them firm, well-established and prosperous at the sense object.

Look at *lobha*. Where does *lobha* arise? *Lobha* associates with the eight types of *lobha mūla citta*. Whenever unwholesome consciousness rooted in attachment arises, *lobha* (greed) *cetasika* will always arise with it. *Lobha* associates with mind and other mental factors. It's not only *lobha cetasika* that arises with that consciousness. There are many mental factors that arise with *lobha* consciousness. This is why I say that *lobha* makes the mind (consciousness) and mental factors associated with it firm and well-established at the sense object.

Whether we're talking about *lobha*, *dosa*, *moha*, *alobha*, *adosa* or *amoha*, it's the same.

Let's look at *adosa*, or loving-kindness.

When you radiate your loving-kindness, *adosa* is one of the mental factors. *Adosa* associates with beautiful consciousness. What is beautiful consciousness? It is sense-sphere beautiful consciousness, resultant consciousness, functional consciousness, sublime consciousness and supramundane consciousness. If it's one of those, *adosa* will be associated with it all the time. When *mettā* arises, it makes the mind and other associated (concomitant) mental factors firm and well-established on the person or object to whom you are radiating your loving-kindness.

Now we know what *hetu* means. When we chant "*hetu paccayo*," we should know that it's talking about the six roots. Greed, aversion and delusion are the cause or condition of evil action. The remaining moral roots are the cause or condition of good mental, verbal or physical actions.

<u>*Jhānaṅga*</u>

This term consists of two words: *jhāna* and *aṅga*. *Aṅga* means constituents or factors. *Jhānaṅga* refers to constituents of *jhāna*.

When we studied *jhāna* before, how many factors or constituents were there? Five, right? Remember? They were *vitakka*, *vicāra*, *pīti*, *sukha* and *ekaggatā*. In this context, though, we have seven. Why? Because mixed categories mixes moral and immoral, thus making seven factors of *jhāna*.

What are the *paramattha dhammas* (realities, or essential elements)?

1) *Vitakka* (initial application, or *vitakka cetasika*)
2) *Vicāra* (sustained application)
3) *Pīti* (joy)
4) *Ekaggatā* (one-pointedness)
5) *Somanassa* (pleasure)
6) *Domanassa* (displeasure)
7) *Upekkhā* (equanimity, or indifference)

I talked about *jhāna* when we studied consciousness. Why do we call it *jhāna*? Because it burns up opposing conditions or hindrances. Another meaning of *jhāna* is that it closely perceives or observes the object, whether good or bad.

Can you see how the term *jhāna* doesn't refer only to meditative absorption? As we attempt to kill something, we're closely perceiving the object, right? This is also *jhāna*.

Q: Is it concentration?

Yes, if we want to kill someone, we won't hit our target if we lack concentration. We need concentration to do it. This concentration is *ekaggatā*, or one-pointedness.

Vitakka (initial application) could be good or bad, right? It could be either one. If your mind thinks about wanting someone's property, it's *vitakka*. In other words, the mind is directed toward the object. As you continue to think about that object, it's *vicāra*. If you feel joy about it, there's *pīti*. As your mind doesn't think about anything else in that moment, there is *ekaggatā*. With *somanassa*, you feel happy. If you're thinking about something you don't like, that's *domanassa*. And if the object is just normal—nothing special—there is *upekkhā*.

We should understand that *jhānaṅga* in the context of mixed categories becomes both moral and immoral. If we look at *domanassa*, we see that displeasure can only be immoral, right? But the remaining six factors can be moral, immoral or indeterminate.

The reality of *vitakka* is *vitakka cetasika*. *Vicāra* is *vicāra cetasika*, *pīti* is *pīti*, and *ekaggatā* is *ekaggatā*. They each have their own name, right? But what is *somanassa*? *Vedanā*. This is feeling. *Domanassa* is just feeling too. *Upekkhā* is also just feeling. These three kinds of feeling—pleasant, unpleasant or neutral—are treated as one: *vedanā*. For this reason, the seven constituents of *jhāna* have just five realities. What are they? *Vitakka, vicāra, pīti, ekaggatā* and *vedanā*.

Q: Is jhānaṅga referring to the same "jhāna" we talked about before? Is it absorption?

Yes, *jhāna* and absorption are the same. But, in that context, we were talking about sublime consciousness—the highest stage of mundane consciousness. We call this absorption.

But we can't call immoral jhānaṅga "absorption." This is why we should know the two meanings of *jhāna*. Immoral *jhānaṅga* takes the meaning of closely perceiving the object. This, too, is *jhāna*. When you go fishing, your mind closely perceives the object in order to catch a fish, right?

Can you see how *vitakka, vicāra, pīti, somanassa, domanassa* and *upekkhā* can arise even when we're doing demeritorious things? That's why we also call this *jhāna*.

Maggaṅga

This is the 12 *magga aṅga*. Usually, how many *magga* are there? This is the Noble Eightfold Path, right? So there are usually eight *magga*. Because *missakasaṅgaha* include both moral and immoral, we have 12 *magga* in this context. These are the 12 constituents of the path, or the way. The good constituents will lead to the blissful state and up to *nibbāna*. If the constituents of the path are unwholesome, they will lead you to the woeful state.

Let's start by talking about the meaning of the 12 constituents of the path:

1) *Sammādiṭṭhi* (right understanding)
2) *Sammāsaṅkappa* (right thinking, or right intention)
3) *Sammāvācā* (right speech)
4) *Sammākammanta* (right action)
5) *Sammājīva* (right livelihood)
6) *Sammāvāyāma* (right effort)
7) *Sammāsati* (right mindfulness)
8) *Sammāsamādhi* (right concentration)

These are the good constituents of the path. These realities lead to the blissful state, or *nibbāna*.

9) *Micchādiṭṭhi* (wrong view)
10) *Micchāsaṅkappa* (wrong thoughts)
11) *Micchāvāyāma* (wrong effort)
12) *Micchāsamādhi* (wrong one-pointedness)

Let's look at their realities now:

1) *Sammādiṭṭhi*: *paññā cetasika*

We have 52 kinds of mental factors. This is the last one. It is wisdom.

2) *Sammāsaṅkappa*: *vitakka cetasika*
3) *Sammāvācā: sammāvācā cetasika*
4) *Sammākammanta*: *sammākammanta cetasika*
5) *Sammājīva*: *sammājīva cetasika*

These last three factors are called abstinences, right? They are called *virati*.

6) *Sammāvāyāma*: *viriya cetasika*
7) *Sammāsati*: *sati cetasika*, or mindfulness
8) *Sammāsamādhi*: *ekaggatā cetasika*, or concentration
9) *Micchādiṭṭhi*: *diṭṭhi cetasika*

10) *Micchāsaṅkappa*: *vitakka cetasika*

Vitakka can associate with 55 types of consciousness, including unwholesome consciousness.

11) *Micchāvāyāma*: *viriya cetasika*

Effort is not necessarily connected to morality, right? Here, it's immoral.

12) *Micchāsamādhi*: *ekaggatā cetasika*

Okay, let's stop here for today. Thank you. *Sādhu, sādhu, sādhu.*

...

Today is February 7, 1999. Last week, we started talking about the 12 *maggaṅga*, or constituents of the path. Today, I would like to continue by explaining to you in detail about these constituents. We may already know their names but we should also know their realities and their natures in detail.

Sammādiṭṭhi

We may be familiar with this. It is right understanding. The reality here is *paññā (amoha)*. Among the 52 mental states, it is the last one. *Amoha* associates with 47 types of consciousness.

Right understanding has to do with understanding the law of *kamma*. Even a non-meditator can understand this point. It is understanding that doing good things gives good results. It is also understanding that doing evil things yields bad results. This is the law of *kamma*, or the law of cause and effect.

If we have right understanding, it is right view. This is *sammādiṭṭhi*. That's why we need to study. Otherwise, we won't understand the law of *kamma*. It is because of our belief in the law of *kamma* that we try to refrain from evil deeds and we try to develop virtue perfections. It is because of this belief that we try to do good things. This is why we try to be good.

Q: Diṭṭhi refers to wrong view, right?

Diṭṭhi is wrong view. In detail, we have 62 types of wrong view. Mostly, though, we just talk about three types:

1) Self-delusion

When we see something, we think "I see that." Actually, it's not you, a man or a woman. Who sees? Seeing-consciousness. But someone with wrong view thinks "I see that." They think that they see with their eyes. The Buddha explained that there is really just the five aggregates arising and disappearing together.

Thinking there is a person, an individual, a soul—that's one kind of *diṭṭhi*.

2) Eternalism

Some people think that they have a soul or an ego that persists after we die. They think it comes out of our body after death and then enters another body. They think the soul lasts forever. But this is wrong view. The Buddha said there is just mind and matter arising and disappearing. It's not the same mind, nor is it the same matter. To think otherwise is the wrong view called eternalism.

3) Annihilation

Some people think that there's nothing more than this life. They think that there is no future life after we die. This is wrong view.

There are also those who say that there's nothing—no this world, no previous life, no future life, no heaven, no hell, no mother, no father. This is wrong view too.

According to the law of *kamma*, everything has a cause. For something to occur, there must be a cause. But some people don't believe that. They don't believe in causes. And some people reject the notion of effects. Some reject causes and results—whether good or bad. They believe that even if you do something bad, there's no *kamma* connected to it. These people don't believe in anything. This is wrong view.

Now, though, I'll explain right understanding:

Belief in the law of *kamma* is *sammādiṭṭhi*.

Understanding and realizing phenomena of mind and body is right understanding. Without practicing meditation, this kind of knowledge cannot occur. To understand phenomena of mind and matter, we have to practice meditation. We need to know our mind and body, and their nature, which is arising and disappearing: impermanent. And because mind and body are oppressed by arising and disappearing, we call it suffering, or *dukkha*. It's dissolution. Also, there is nothing that we can control and force to remain the same, last long or follow our desires. Everything is beyond our control. That's what we call *anattā*, or no-soul.

We need to understand these three characteristics of our mind and body. This understanding is *sammādiṭṭhi* too. To gain this wisdom and understanding, we need to practice meditation. Then, we will know the nature of mind and body for what they really are.

Also, when we gain enlightenment, we come to understand the Four Noble Truths. As students of *Abhidhammā*, we know about the Four Noble Truths. We know suffering, we know the cause of suffering, we know the cessation of suffering, and we know the way leading to the cessation of suffering. We know these things, but it's not really wisdom. When we gain enlightenment, that's when we really know and understand the Four Noble Truths.

What knows the Four Noble Truths? *Sammādiṭṭhi*.

Please remember that *sammādiṭṭhi* (right understanding) understands the law of *kamma*, understands the nature of mind and body, and understands the Four Noble Truths. This is called *sammādiṭṭhi*.

The reality of *sammādiṭṭhi* is *paññā (amoha) cetasika*. What is *amoha*? It is wisdom.

Sammāsaṅkappa

This is right thinking, right intention or right thought. Its reality is *vitakka* (initial application).

Vitakka associates with 55 types of consciousness, but in this context we're just talking about *vitakka* associating with the 24 types of beautiful sense-sphere consciousness and 11 types of first *jhāna* consciousness. Altogether, that's 35 types of consciousness.

What is the meaning of right thinking, right intention or right thought?

1) Thought of renunciation
2) Thought of non-killing
3) Thought of non-cruelty

Sammāsaṅkappa is these three thoughts.

As an example of thought of renunciation, when we practice tranquility meditation we focus our mind on observing our object until we gain the first *jhāna*. What are the factors of the first *jhāna*? *Vitakka* (initial application), *vicāra* (sustained application), *pīti* (joy, or rapture), *sukha* (happiness) and *ekaggatā* (one-pointedness).

If your mind only observes your *jhāna*, in that moment no hindrances come to disturb it. You are only thinking about your *jhāna*. Doing so is called renunciation because there are no mental hindrances in that moment. Your thoughts are focused on renunciation.

As another example of thought of renunciation, sometimes we think about becoming a monk or a nun. This is right thinking. Or perhaps we think about going on a weeklong meditation retreat. This type of thinking is also called right thinking. These are thoughts of renunciation. Perhaps you consider spending an entire day off from work practicing meditation, or even just plan to sit in meditation for an hour. These are thoughts of renunciation, right?

So, thoughts of ordaining, practicing meditation, or thoughts of renunciation. This is *sammāsaṅkappa*.

Also, when we practice insight (*vipassanā*) meditation, we contemplate our mind on our primary object—or any object of mind and matter. In other words, we observe mind and matter. As we do, as we observe the object, this is 'thought' of renunciation. When we fix our mind on mind and matter—the object of our insight (*vipassanā*) meditation—we are just thinking, observing, contemplating (they mean the same thing in this context). We observe that the object is arising in this moment, disappearing in this moment, now there is heat, now there is cold. We're just observing, right? This heat has come, and now it goes. Another experience comes and then goes. We are just thinking about what is happening in mind and body. We are just observing experiences.

This is considered thought of renunciation.

There may be times when you think about the peace of *nibbāna*. Whether this is by direct knowledge or inference, it is also considered thought of renunciation.

Whatever we think about that is wholesome can be called thought of renunciation. Maybe you want to be generous—"I want to donate"—or perhaps you want to observe additional precepts, do chanting or sit in meditation. "I want to gain *jhāna*" or "I want to practice meditation to gain enlightenment." Even in worldly affairs, it is thought of renunciation if it is a matter of good and wholesome consciousness.

Q: There are a lot of bad things happening in the world. What if we watch the news and feel sorrow about what is happening? What if we want things to be better?

It depends on your thinking. If you feel sad after listening to the news, it's unwholesome consciousness. For the most part, watching the news is useless for spiritual practice. However, if wholesome consciousness arises after you watch the news, this is good thinking. See how it depends on your thinking? It depends on whether we have wise or proper attention. If we get angry while watching the news, it is not *sammāsaṅkappa*. But if we see images of people killing each other and have thoughts of goodwill and a desire for them to be released from suffering, this is right thinking.

It depends on our thinking. If we see something and feel unhappy, it's not good.

Good or bad, we should keep this in mind:

> *An action, act of speech or thought which does not harm any person and brings good effect to oneself and to others is certainly good and moral.*

Think about this. After watching or listening to the news, is there any harm to yourself or others? If the answer is no, then it's good. After watching television or a movie, how do you feel? If you have loving-kindness or wisdom, you're thinking the right way. This is right thought.

We've been talking about thought of renunciation.

Now, let's talk about thought of non-killing.

If your thinking is such that you don't want to kill anyone and you don't want anyone to be killed, this is right thinking. If you feel the same way about animals—even small insects—and reflect that all beings are afraid to die, this too is right thinking. This kind of thinking is called *sammāsaṅkappa*. It is wholesome consciousness when we think like this.

This is thought of non-killing.

How about thought of non-cruelty? Non-killing is regarding *mettā*, or loving-kindness. Non-cruelty, on the other hand, is regarding compassion. It is the wish to not harm or hurt anyone. It is the desire for no one to suffer. Thinking like this is also *sammāsaṅkappa*.

If you don't want anyone to be hurt, harmed or suffer because of your thoughts, speech or deeds, this is right intention, or right thinking.

The next three *maggaṅga*—that is, *sammāvācā*, *sammākammanta* and *sammājiva*—are called *virati*. Among the 52 kinds of mental factors, these are called *virati*, or abstinences. They are the three abstinences.

The reality of *sammāvācā* is *sammāvācā cetasika*, right? This, *sammākammanta* and *sammājiva* associate with 16 kinds of consciousness: the eight kinds of sense-sphere wholesome consciousness and the eight kinds of supramundane consciousness. They are found collectively in supramundane consciousness. That is, when we gain enlightenment, all three associate with this consciousness together. When the three abstinences associate with the eight types of sense-sphere wholesome consciousness, they associate separately because their objects are different.

Sammāvācā

This is right speech. What is right speech?

1) No lying to anyone
2) No slandering
3) No speaking harshly
4) No speaking vainly

It is refraining from these four kinds of evil verbal action. This is *sammāvācā*. "I will not lie. I will not gossip or speak in a way that leads to disharmony between others. I will not speak harshly. I will not speak frivolously."

Sammākammanta

This is right action. It is refraining from killing, stealing and committing sexual misconduct.

Sammājiva

This is right livelihood. It regards our way of earning a living.

When we have right livelihood, we don't kill, we don't steal, and we don't commit sexual misconduct as a part of our making money. There's also no lying, no slandering, no harsh speech and no vain talk.

Some people earn a living by killing or stealing, right? *Sammājiva* refrains from doing the three evil physical actions:

1) Killing
2) Stealing
3) Committing sexual misconduct

It also refrains from doing the four evil verbal actions:

1) Lying
2) Slandering
3) Harsh speech
4) Vain talk

Additionally, right livelihood refrains from five kinds of trading:

1) Selling arms (weapons)
2) Selling human beings (slaves)

Even nowadays, people may kidnap and sell someone, right? Human trafficking. Others sell human beings as pimps do with prostitutes. *Sammājiva* doesn't do this.

3) Selling intoxicants (alcohol or drugs)
4) Selling poison
5) Selling flesh (animals for slaughter or meat)

These five kinds of things should not be sold. Real Buddhists are not supposed to sell them.

This is *sammājiva*, or right livelihood.

So, do we have good livelihood or not? Think about these things.

Q: What about people who gamble for a living?

People mostly gamble for pleasure. But for a living? This isn't a matter of wrong livelihood, as the Buddha did not specifically say it was such. However, he taught that gambling is a way of ruin. As such, we should not do it.

In particular, meditators who want to attain enlightenment in this life should stay far away from gambling. In my opinion, it's best if we don't gamble. Before gambling, while gambling, and after you gamble, what do you feel? I think that 99% of people suffer when they gamble.

Some people will steal or sell their prized possessions to cover their gambling addictions. A better use of time would be doing chanting and practicing meditation to gain peace of mind, to gain enlightenment, and to realize the supreme bliss. Instead, they go to the casino and gamble. It's a waste of time, and as such, a waste of their life. They waste opportunities to do good things. They waste everything.

Sammāvāyāma

This is right effort. The reality is *viriya cetasika*.

Viriya cetasika can associate with 73 types of consciousness. With *sammāvāyāma* (right effort), though, *viriya cetasika* associates with the 59 types of beautiful wholesome consciousness.

This right effort is very important for everyone. It means endeavoring to discard evil that has already arisen; preventing the arising of unarisen evil; developing unarisen good; and promoting good which has already arisen.

So we have four, right? I will explain these to you one-by-one.

Viriya (good effort) is one kind of predominance. In order to achieve our goal, right effort is very important. We must have it.

1) Discard evil that has already arisen

What does this mean? How do we discard evil that has already arisen?

The meaning is not clear, so we have to use an example:

Maybe you used to kill animals. Now, whenever you think about what you have done, how do you feel? Sad, right? Why do you feel sad? There is remorse about having done something bad. When you think about your past bad deeds, unwholesome consciousness arises in your mind.

The Buddha said that we have to discard evil that we've already done. This means: Don't think about it. Forget it. If you cannot stop your thinking, you will suffer as long as it persists. This thinking is like a fire, right? It's burning your mind. Do you remember when we talked about *dosa* burning us? We can't sleep. We can't eat. We suffer.

This is why we need to stop thinking about our past bad deeds.

This is very easy for meditators. Whenever the mind thinks about the bad things we've done in the past, we feel sorrow. As we do, just note it—"sorrow, sorrow." Just make a mental note and the thinking will stop right away. Then, try to focus your mind on your primary object. You can focus on your breath or the movement of your abdomen. You can focus it anywhere. Just change the object—don't think about your past misdeeds.

Rather than indulge in thinking about your past evil deeds, try to focus your mind on your primary object. If thinking arises in your mind, just make a mental note. The thinking will stop.

Also, if you used to kill animals, don't do it again. You can reflect: "I used to kill animals but I will never do that again." This means that we are discarding evil that has already arisen.

Understand that, right? Do you understand these techniques to discard evil that has already arisen? Don't think. If thinking arises, make a mental note and then try to put your mind on your primary object. Don't allow the same thoughts to arise again.

2) Prevent the arising of unarisen evil

This means that if you've never before killed an animal, you will not kill any animals for the rest of your life. It's very easy for us, right? If you never drank alcohol, it's having the resolve to never drink alcohol.

This is right effort. It is preventing the arising of unarisen evil. It is saying to oneself: "I won't do this. I've never killed an animal and I will never kill an animal. I've never stolen and I will never steal."

This is resolving not to do what one has never before done.

Especially before we go to bed each evening, it's good for us to reflect on the day and consider our deficiencies. What do we need to quit or improve upon? We know ourselves best. Here, we're endeavoring to prevent the arising of unarisen evil.

3) Develop unarisen good.

The third one is the endeavor to develop unarisen good. This means that there's more to do than simply discard past evil and prevent new evil.

Let's look at some examples:

If you never used to do any charity or practice generosity, try to do it. If you do generous things but do not fulfill your morality, try to observe your precepts. If you practice generosity and keep your precepts, you have to develop and elevate your mind—higher and higher.

If you're someone who is generous and observes your precepts but never does chanting or sitting meditation, perhaps you should start to do some chanting. There are also those who chant but don't sit in meditation.

We need to elevate these things. We need to sit in meditation too. This is what it means to develop unarisen good.

If you already practice generosity and have good morality, work more on your concentration and sit in meditation. If you haven't gained enlightenment yet, you should keep developing these things until you gain enlightenment. This is how we develop unarisen good, step-by-step. Whatever you never did before, you start to do it.

4) Promote the good that has already arisen.

The fourth one is to promote the good which has already arisen. This means that you already do meritorious things—that's generosity, morality, concentration and meditation–but you now try to promote them and make them bigger and bigger. Whereas the third one is to develop what you've never done before, this one is to take what you already do and make it higher and bigger.

Let's say you normally donate $10 a year, but (according to your financial situation) you now try to donate $15 a year. You increase it, right? Maybe you typically observe the five precepts but now you endeavor to observe the eight precepts. Eight is higher than five, right? Perhaps you chant once a day but decide that you will start to chant twice a day. Or maybe you used to sit in meditation for one hour each day but will increase it to two hours each day.

Here, we are increasing our good actions. We are promoting the good that has already arisen. As we do, in time we will fulfill our spiritual practice—*dāna*, *sīla* and *bhāvanā*. *Dāna* is generosity, *sīla* is morality and *bhāvanā* is mental culture, or meditation. After you fulfill these three things, you will accomplish your goal—you will gain enlightenment.

Even if you have to be reborn again, you don't have to worry because you've already prepared everything for your next life. If you've been generous, you won't have to worry about property. If you've had good morality, you won't have to worry about your health. You'll have good health. If you've practiced meditation a lot, even if you don't gain enlightenment in this life you'll be smart in the next life. You will be a smart person, and then you might gain enlightenment in that life.

This is why we have to do these three things—so we don't have to worry about future lives. We need to practice generosity, morality and meditation every day. This is *sammāvāyāma*, or right effort.

Sammāsati

This is right mindfulness. The reality here is *sati cetasika*, which associates with beautiful wholesome consciousness.

We practice mindfulness meditation, right? We'll talk about this in more detail in the next chapter, but I'll talk about it briefly now:

Right mindfulness means that we observe our body. We are aware of what's happening in our body. We are aware of our physical activities. We also try to observe our sensations and feelings—maybe pleasant, unpleasant, or perhaps neutral. We try to be aware of whether there's pain or happiness. We observe these feelings. When we practice meditation, we know what's happening and what we are experiencing. We make a mental note and just observe these sensations or feelings.

We're also aware of our mind. We know whether it's wholesome or unwholesome. Whatever occurs in the mind, we try to be aware of it. This is *sammāsati*, or right mindfulness.

Whatever you see or hear, just make a mental note—"seeing" or "hearing"—and be aware of it. If there's smelling, just make a mental note—"smelling"—and be aware of it. Otherwise, if you're not aware that there's simply "seeing," then perhaps greed or hatred will arise, depending on whether the object is desirable or undesirable.

If you see, just be aware and know that there is just "seeing." If you hear, just be aware and know that there is just "hearing." Just observe these objects. Then, there will be no attachment, even if the object is good or desirable. No attachment will occur. In the same way, if the object is undesirable, no hatred will occur. You will just know that there is seeing or hearing, and so on. You have awareness.

This is called right mindfulness. Be mindful of all physical activities and mental thoughts. This is *sammāsati*.

Q: Is that the same as sacca?

No, *sacca* is truth. This is *sati*. Mindfulness is awareness. Different.

Sammāsamādhi

This is right concentration. The reality is *ekaggatā*, or one-pointedness. *Ekaggatā* can associate with all kinds of *citta* because it's a universal mental factor. But since we're talking about *maggaṅga* (the constituents of the path) here, this is *ekaggatā* that associates with beautiful consciousness.

What is right concentration?

You concentrate your mind on the right thoughts, the right points, in the right way. Especially when we sit in meditation, we try to observe our mind with one-pointedness. This is *sammāsamādhi*.

Where will these eight constituents of the path lead us? They will lead us toward the blissful state of *nibbāna*. This means that you can gain enlightenment if you fulfill right understanding, right thinking, right speech, right action, right livelihood, right effort, right mindfulness and right concentration.

Even if you don't gain enlightenment in this life, in the next life you will be reborn in a blissful position as a human being, a celestial being, or perhaps in the *Brahma* realms. If you fulfill these eight constituents, it will lead you to enlightenment and *nibbāna*.

What are the remaining four *maggaṅga*? They are *micchaādiṭṭhi* (wrong view), *micchāsaṅkappa* (wrong thinking), *micchāvāyāma* (wrong effort) and *micchāsamādhi* (wrong one-pointedness).

These four kinds of constituents lead to the woeful states. If these are present, you will suffer about it. As we have wrong view, wrong thoughts, wrong effort and wrong one-pointedness, we might go to the woeful states in the next life.

This is why *magga* means "the way." We have two ways: one way goes to the blissful state up to *nibbāna*, and the other way leads you to the woeful states.

Micchādiṭṭhi

Wrong view. We've studied this already, right? I don't need to explain this again.

The reality here is *diṭṭhi cetasika*. It associates with four types of consciousness, right? Among unwholesome consciousness, we're talking about the types that associate with wrong view. So *micchādiṭṭhi* is really *diṭṭhi cetasika*.

Micchāsaṅkappa

Wrong thought refers to thoughts of sensual desire. This is greed and craving. What are the sensual desires? We think about forms, colors, sounds, smells, tastes and touches. This is sensual desire. If you think about these things, it's wrong thinking, or *micchāsaṅkappa*.

"I want to watch a movie." This is wrong thinking. It's a thought based on sensual desire.

"I want to listen to music." Same. "I want to wear perfume" or "I want to try Italian food." Same again. "What outfit should I wear tomorrow?" Thinking about sensual desire is wrong thinking.

Wrong thought also refers to thoughts of killing. Maybe you get angry and want to kill someone. Or maybe you want them to die. Thinking like this is wrong thought. These thoughts are full of hatred.

Wrong thought also has to do with thoughts of cruelty. Perhaps you want someone you dislike to get hurt. You want them to suffer. It's not that you want them to die; rather, you want them to suffer or get hurt.

All of these things are called wrong thoughts. They are of three kinds, right?

1) Thoughts of sensual desire
2) Thoughts of killing
3) Thoughts of cruelty

Without practicing meditation, our thinking is comprised of these three kinds of thoughts.

What's the reality of *micchāsaṅkappa*? *Vitakka* (initial application). *Vitakka* can associate with wholesome or unwholesome consciousness, right? But in this context where we're talking about wrong thought, *vitakka* associates with the 12 types of unwholesome consciousness.

Micchāvāyāma

This is wrong effort. The reality here is *viriya cetasika*. It associates with the 12 types of unwholesome consciousness. *Viriya*, of course, can associate with moral or immoral consciousness. When we studied *cetasika*, we learned that it can associate with 73 types of consciousness, both wholesome and unwholesome. But this is wrong effort, so it associates only with immoral consciousness.

As an example, maybe you go fishing or hunting. This requires effort or energy, right? But this is wrong effort. You're trying to kill, right? Whatever you're doing, if it's unwholesome, it's wrong effort. If you hit someone, beat someone, kill someone, it's wrong effort. It's not wholesome.

Micchāsamādhi

This is wrong one-pointedness. The reality is *ekaggatā cetasika*, which in this context associates with 11 types of unwholesome consciousness. It does not associate with *uddhacca sahagata citta*, which is the last of the various types of unwholesome consciousness.

Sometimes, we might sit somewhere and think about something that's not good. Our mind might be deeply focused on one object, but it's not a good object. This is wrong one-pointedness.

When you try to shoot something—such as when you're hunting—what do you need? One-pointedness. Without one-pointedness, you can't shoot the animal, right? You need one-pointedness.

But, here, this one-pointedness is wrong one-pointedness. It is wrong because *ekaggatā* is associated with unwholesome consciousness. You want to kill the animal, so you concentrate your mind. You need concentration, right? *Ekaggatā* is concentration.

It's not right concentration, though.

Sometimes, you may think about killing someone. As you think about this, it's concentration too. But there is right one-pointedness and wrong one-pointedness. They differ.

Can we see why *micchādiṭṭhi* (wrong view), *micchāsaṅkappa* (wrong thinking), *micchāvāyāma* (wrong effort) and *micchāsamādhi* (wrong one-pointedness) can lead us to woeful states? It's because they associate with unwholesome consciousness.

But the first eight, which we've discussed many times, are the Noble Eightfold Path.

Indriya

Now we go to *indriya*. This is faculties. Usually, we talk about *indriya* as being of five types. Here, though, we're talking about 22 kinds. These 22 faculties are possessed of controlling power in their respective domains. This doesn't mean that they control everything. They have controlling power in their respective domains.

We'll study these one-by-one, including how and what they control.

1) *Cakkhundriya*

When we do *Paṭṭhāna* chanting, we chant about *cakkhu indriya*, right? What is the reality here? What is the *paramattha dhamma*? It is *cakkhu-pasāda*, which is eye-sensitivity. It's the sensitive part of the eye.

This means that eye-sensitivity is one kind of *indriya*, or faculty.

What is the controlling power here? What does eye-sensitivity control? It controls the quality of seeing, right?

That's why we say they possess the controlling power in their respective domains. Can ear-sensitivity come and disturb or interfere with what eye-sensitivity perceives? No, because eyes are for seeing. But eyes cannot hear, right? Eye-sensitivity cannot control hearing, only seeing.

Understand that, right? Eye-sensitivity controls the quality of seeing. That's why we call it *indriya*, or faculty.

2) *Sotindriya*

The reality here is *sota-pasāda*. This is ear-sensitivity. It controls the quality of hearing.

3) *Ghāṇindriya*

The reality is *ghāṇa-pasāda*, which is nose-sensitivity. This nose-sensitivity controls the quality of smelling.

4) *Jivhindriya*

The reality is *jivhā-pasāda*, which is tongue-sensitivity. Tongue-sensitivity controls the quality of tasting.

5) *Kāyindriya*

This is *kāya-pasāda*, or body-sensitivity. It controls the quality of touching.

6) *Itthindriya*

This is femininity. It controls the character of sex, as a female.

7) *Purisindriya*

Masculinity controls the character of sex, as a male.

Can you see how these *indriya* control their respective spheres?

From 1-7, these *indriya* are *rūpa*, or matter. That is, eye-sensitivity, ear-sensitivity, nose-sensitivity, tongue-sensitivity, body-sensitivity, femininity and masculinity are *rūpa*, or materiality.

8) *Jivitindriya*

This is vitality. Here, the reality is *jivita-nāma* and *jivita-rūpa*. This means mental vitality and physical vitality, respectively.

We have two here, right? Physical and mental vitality. When we studied the 28 kinds of material properties, we learned about physical vitality, or *rūpa-jivitindriya*. This physical vitality controls the life term of its associates.

We also studied mental vitality when we went through the chapter on mental factors. This was *jivitindriya cetasika*. It's one of the mental factors. Being a universal mental factor, *jivitindriya* always arises no matter what kind of consciousness it is.

So, for this eighth *indriya*, the realities are twofold: *jivita-nāma* (mental) and *jivita-rūpa* (matter). Each of them controls the life terms of its associates. This means that when *jivitindriya cetasika* (mental vitality) arises, it controls the concomitants that it associates with. In the same way, *jivita-rūpa* controls the eight inseparable *rūpa* that it associates with. Do you remember vital-nonad?

This is why we call these *indriya*, or faculty. They have controlling power. What do they control? These *indriya* control the life terms of their associates.

9) *Manindriya*

This is mind (*citta*, or consciousness). What does *manindriya* control? It controls its concomitants and knowing the object. Without mind, the 52 mental states cannot arise, right? They depend on the mind to arise. That's why we say that mind controls its concomitants, which means the 52 mental factors. *Manindriya* also has the controlling power to know the object. Although there are 52 kinds of mental factors, *cetasika* cannot know the object. They just support the mind. It is the mind that knows the object exactly.

So, *manindriya* controls its concomitants and knowing the object.

We have two, right? What's the controlling power of this *indriya*? Controlling concomitants and knowing the object.

We studied the five aggregates, right? When you see something, the seeing happens because of eye-sensitivity, which is *rūpa*. *Rūpa* is one of the aggregates. When you see, you have a feeling about it—good, bad or neutral. *Vedanā*—another aggregate—will arise. As you see, there is perception—"Ah, this is John." Perception is an aggregate. The fourth aggregate is mental formations, which is the remaining 50 kinds of mental factors. They don't know the object, but support the mind to know. And the fifth aggregate is consciousness. It is consciousness that knows the object.

This is why we say that the controlling power of *manindriya* is knowing the object.

So, the first seven *indriya* are only matter. The eighth *indriya* is *nāma* and *rūpa*, and the ninth is mind only.

We'll study the remaining *indriya* next week. Thank you. *Sādhu, sādhu, sādhu.*

Let's take a couple of minutes for a quick review of what we've talked about previously:

How many *āsavā* are there? Four. There is *kāmāsava, bhavāsava, diṭṭhāsava* and *avijjāsava*. What is the reality of *kāmāsava*? Lobha. *Bhavāsava*? Also *lobha*. *Diṭṭhāsava*? *Diṭṭhi*. And *avijjāsava*? *Moha*. What's the nature of *lobha*? Attachment. *Diṭṭhi*? Wrong view. *Moha*? Delusion.

If you know this much, it's good. *Oghā* and *yogā* are the same.

What about *ganthā, upādānā, nīvaraṇā, saṃyojana* and *kilesa*? I want you to remember these.

...

Today is February 14, 1999. Last week, we started to study the 22 kinds of *indriya*, or faculties. We studied *cakkhuindriya* (eye-faculty), *sotindriya* (ear-faculty), *ghāṇindriya* (nose-faculty) and *jivhindriya* (tongue-faculty), as well as *kāyindriya* (body-faculty), *itthindriya* (femininity), *purisindriya* (masculinity), *jivitindriya* (vitality) and *manindriya* (mind-faculty).

Today, we will continue with the next one:

10) *Sukhindriya*

Sukha is happiness, and *indriya* is faculty. This is a pleasant bodily feeling.

The reality of *sukhindriya* is *vedanā*, though *sukhindriya* is specifically a pleasant bodily feeling. When we studied *sukha sahagata kāyaviññāṇa* as we talked about rootless consciousness, we learned that this *vedanā* will associate with it. This is regarding the body, right?

What does *sukhindriya* control? It controls its concomitants. When *kāyaviññāṇa* (body-consciousness) arises, it associates with the seven universal mental states. Among these seven, *vedanā* has the power to control the other six universal mental states.

Again, this feeling is regarding the body.

11) *Dukkhindriya*

This is pain. It is bodily pain. It's the pain-faculty.

The reality of *dukkhindriya* is *vedanā*. This *vedanā* associates with *dukkha sahagata kāyaviññāṇa,* which is one of the types of rootless consciousness. This is a painful feeling in the body.

12) *Somanassindriya*

Somanassa is pleasure, and *indriya* is faculty. This is the pleasure-faculty.

The reality is *vedanā*. This *vedanā* associates with 62 types of consciousness. These types of consciousness are accompanied by pleasure—*somanassa sahagata citta*.

13) *Domanassindriya*

This is displeasure. *Somanassa* is a mental feeling. It regards the mind. In the same way, *domanassa* is mental displeasure.

We should know the difference between *dukkha* and *domanassa*. Pain and displeasure are different. Pain is in reference to the body, while *domanassa* is a mental feeling. It is displeasure.

The reality of *domanassindriya* is *vedanā*. This *vedanā* associates with *domanassa sahagata paṭigha sampayutta*. We have two kinds of *dosa citta* in unwholesome consciousness, right? This *vedanā* will associate with these two *dosa citta*.

14) *Upekkhindriya*

This is *upekkhā indriya*, or equanimity. The reality is *vedanā*. This *vedanā* associates with 55 types of consciousness.

Do you remember when we classified consciousness in terms of *vedanā*? We have one type that is *sukha vedanā*, one type that is *dukkha vedanā*, 62 types that are *somanassa vedanā*, two types that are *domanassa vedanā*, and 55 types that are *upekkhā vedanā*. Altogether, that's 121 types of consciousness.

This is just a review. When we know the 121 types of consciousness and how they associate with the various kinds of *vedanā*, it makes it very easy, right? We're talking about realities. Even though we have five *vedanā*—again, *sukha vedanā*, *dukkha vedanā*, *somanassa vedanā*, *domanassa vedanā* and *upekkhā vedanā*—their realities are just one, which is *vedanā* (feeling).

These five kinds of feelings can be grouped into one as *vedanā*.

Whenever someone asks you what the reality of *sukha*, *dukkha*, *somanassa*, *domanassa* or *upekkhā* is, you can just say *vedanā*. It's feeling, right? But there are different kinds of feeling. We have feelings regarding the body, right? How many? Two. They are *sukha vedanā* and *dukkha vedanā*. And we have feelings regarding the mind, which include *somanassa*, *domanassa* and *upekkhā*.

So we have five *vedanā*.

15) *Saddhindriya*

This is *saddhā indriya*. *Saddhā* is confidence. This confidence (faith) will associate with the 59 types of beautiful consciousness. Confidence has the controlling power to control the concomitants with which it associates.

16) *Viriyindriya*

This is effort-faculty. *Viriya* is effort. The reality of effort-faculty is *viriya*. This *viriya* associates with 73 types of consciousness.

17) *Satindriya*

Satindriya is mindfulness-faculty. The reality is *sati*. This *sati* will associate with the 59 types of beautiful consciousness.

In the first chapter, we talked about the 59 types of beautiful consciousness. There are 12 types of unwholesome consciousness and 18 types of rootless consciousness. That's a total of 30 types of consciousness. So, excluding these 30 types of consciousness, that leaves 59 types of consciousness that are *sobhaṇa* (beautiful) *citta* (consciousness).

So, here, *sati* is the reality that associates with these 59 types of consciousness.

It's good for us to know exactly what these realities are; otherwise, we might doubt whether something is wholesome or unwholesome. But when we know their realities—like *sati*, for example—we can know exactly. We will know that *sati* is never unwholesome. It only associates with wholesome (beautiful) consciousness.

This is why we need to know these realities.

Satindriya (mindfulness-faculty) is *sati cetasika*. This mental factor will associate with the 59 types of beautiful consciousness.

18) *Samadhindriya*

This is concentration-faculty. The reality of this faculty is *ekaggatā cetasika*, which is one of the universal mental factors. Usually, *ekaggatā* associates with all types of consciousness. But here, it takes just 72 types of consciousness.

What are these 72 types of consciousness?

We start by excluding the one type of doubt (*vicikicchā*) consciousness. Then we exclude the 16 types of rootless consciousness that are not associated with *viriya* (effort). We call these the 16 types of *aviriya citta. Viriya* means effort, and *'a'* means not associated with. Of the 18 types of rootless consciousness, the first 16 types are *aviriya*. To make it easy, we call the first 16 types of rootless consciousness by the term *aviriya citta*. They are not associated with *viriya*.

Add the one type of doubt consciousness to the 16 types of *aviriya citta* and that's 17 types of consciousness. The remaining 72 types of consciousness can associate with *samadhindriya*.

19) *Paññindriya*

This is wisdom-faculty. This reality is *amoha*. Generally-speaking, *amoha* associates with 47 types of *citta*. Mostly, this is the case. But strictly-speaking, it takes 39 types of consciousness. So, *amoha* (wisdom) associates with 39 types of consciousness, but generally-speaking, it associates with 47 types.

Why 39 types of consciousness?

Because it can't take supramundane consciousness. When we subtract the eight types of supramundane consciousness from the 47 types, that leaves 39 types of consciousness. When we practice meditation, we know "this is mind" and "this is matter." We know "this is cause" and "this is effect." We also know "this is impermanent," "this is suffering" and "this is non-self."

Who knows that? Wisdom. *Paññindriya* is *amoha*, which associates with 39 types of consciousness because it is not supramundane yet. It is *vipassanā-ñāṇa*. This wisdom is *vipassanā* knowledge; hence, 39 types of consciousness, rather than 47 types.

20) *Anaññātassāmitindriya*

Aññā means knowing, and *anaññā* means the unknown. This term refers to knowing that which was previously unknown.

What is our desire or purpose in practicing meditation? To gain enlightenment, to realize the Four Noble Truths. It is to experience these ourselves through direct knowledge. So we practice meditation because we want to realize that which was unknown to us before. We want to know that which was previously unknown to us—the Four Noble Truths, reality, *nibbāna*.

Now, as you have the desire, you practice meditation. After you practice meditation, you eventually gain the first stage of enlightenment and become a stream-enterer. When you do, this knowledge (wisdom, or *amoha*) is called the "faculty of one who practices with the thought that he will know what was previously unknown to him." In other words, upon realizing the Four Noble Truths for the first time (this is the knowledge of the path of the stream-enterer), he has now realized wisdom previously unknown to him.

What did he realize? The Four Noble Truths. These were unknown to him before. That was *anaññā*. *Anaññā* means unknown. But now he knows. This is the wisdom that knows what was unknown to him before.

There are eight types of supramundane knowledge, right? What's the first one? *Sotāpatti magga citta*. When you practice *vipassanā* meditation and gain the first stage of enlightenment, in that moment there is *parikamma*, *upacāra*, *anuloma*, *gotrabū*, and then, *magga citta* arises.

Sotāpatti magga citta is *amoha*. This *amoha* (wisdom) associating with *sotāpatti magga citta* is called *anaññātassāmitindriya*. Normally, wisdom associates with 47 types of consciousness, but here, this wisdom associates only with *sotāpatti magga citta*.

Understand? This is only for *sotāpatti magga citta*. Remember the eight types of supramundane consciousness, the first of which is *sotāpatti magga citta*. This wisdom associates only with *sotāpatti magga citta*.

Q: What about phala?

Phala is a different one. This is for *sotāpatti magga citta* only. *Anaññātassāmitindriya* is specific to *sotāpatti magga citta*.

21) *Aññindriya*

This is *aññā indriya*. It refers to what is already known. The reality is *amoha*, right? This means wisdom.

This is wisdom that is within the limit of realization. It is wisdom associated with the three upper *magga*. We have four *magga* and four *phala*, right? What are the three upper *magga*? *Sakadāgāmī magga*, *anāgāmī magga* and *arahatta magga*. And with the three lower *phala*. What are they? *Sotāpatti phala citta*, *sakadāgāmī phala citta* and *anāgāmī phala citta*.

How many types of consciousness is that? Six. So, this is wisdom which associates with the three upper *magga* and three lower *phala*. It is called *aññindriya*.

What does this mean? When you gain enlightenment, *sotāpatti magga citta* is *anaññātassāmitindriya*. Then, *phala* will come. This is called *aññindriya*. This wisdom is different. But it's not special.

What is *sotāpatti magga*? It is already known. We're talking about the Four Noble Truths. *Sotāpatti magga citta* knows it. Now, these six types of consciousness already know that which *sotāpatti magga citta* knew. That's why we say it's not special. This is why we say that *aññindriya* is within the limit of realization.

22) *Aññātāvindriya*

The reality is *amoha*, or wisdom. This wisdom, this faculty, is associated with *arahatta phala citta*. *Arahatta phala citta* is the last of the eight types of supramundane consciousness. Becoming an *arahant* and knowing the fruit of *arahantship* is called *aññātāvindriya*.

Aññātā refers to fully realizing the Four Noble Truths. The first seven types of supramundane consciousness haven't fully realized them, right? But *arahatta phala citta* has fully realized the Four Noble Truths.

So this is wisdom associated with *arahatta phala citta.*

So, the 20th, 21st and 22nd types of *indriya* pertain only to supramundane consciousness. This is when you gain enlightenment, right?

We have 22 types of *indriya* by name. How many realities are there among these 22 types? Only sixteen. There are just 16 controlling factors.

What are they?

The reality of *cakkhundriya* is eye-sensitivity; the reality of *sotindriya* is ear-sensitivity; the reality of *ghāṇindriya* is nose-sensitivity; the reality of *jivhindriya* is tongue-sensitivity; the reality of *kāyindriya* is body-sensitivity; the reality of *itthinidrya* is femininity; and the reality of *purisindriya* is masculinity. These seven are just matter, or *rūpa.*

What about *jivitinidrya*, or vitality? Among vitality, we have two realities: physical vitality and mental vitality. In *Pāli*, they are called *rūpa-jivitindriya* and *jivitindriya cetasika.* When we studied the 52 mental factors, one of them was *jivitindriya cetasika.* It is a universal mental factor. And when we studied matter, we learned about *rūpa-jivitindriya.* That's why the reality here is twofold: physical and mental vitality.

How about *manindriya*, or mind (consciousness)? All 89 or 121 types of consciousness are called *manindriya.*

As for the next group of five feelings—*sukhindriya, dukkhindriya, somanassindriya, domanassindriya* and *upekkhindriya*—what's their reality? Only *vedanā.*

Saddhinidrya is *saddhā cetasika, viriyindriya* is *viriya cetasika, satindriya* is *sati cetasika*, and *samadhindriya* is *ekaggatā cetasika.*

The remaining four have *amoha* (wisdom) as their reality.

Altogether, there are just these 16 realities among the 22 *indriya.*

See that, right? The 10th through the 14th becomes just one—only *vedanā.* The 19th through the 22nd are only wisdom. And the 8th becomes two. Altogether, there are sixteen.

Among the 22 faculties, how many are just physical faculties? The 1st through the 7th are *rūpa*-only. The 9th is the only faculty that is mind-only. The 8th is the only faculty that is both physical and mental. And how many are only mental states? The 10th through the 22nd.

Q: So even though sukhindriya and dukkhindriya are bodily feelings, they're only mental states?

Yes, they regard the body but their reality is *vedanā*. *Vedanā* is not found in *rūpa*; only in the 52 kinds of mental states.

Why do we need to study the 22 *indriya*? Because these are the objects of our *vipassanā* meditation. When we practice meditation, these are all objects of *vipassanā*.

So, how many are mental faculties only? From the 10th through the 22nd, right? That's 13 types. Matter only? Seven. Mind only? One. Physical and mental? One. Altogether, that's 22 types.

Now that we've classified them in terms of mind, mental states and matter, let's look at the 31 planes of existence.

How about in our world? How many faculties can we get in the human world?

All 22 faculties can occur in the *kāmāvacara* (sensual) realm.

Q: But they can't all happen in other realms, right?

Well, how about the *rūpa* realm? What about the mindless realm? If there is no mind, there can be no mental states. They have vital-nonad, right? Just nine. That's it for beings in that realm. They can have only those eight inseparables, plus there's physical vitality, right? So, just one *indriya* for mindless beings.

Q: So they have only physical vitality as an indriya?

Yes, mindless beings just have physical vitality. That's the only one.

Q: So, they don't have cakkhundriya because that's eye-consciousness? Does that mean they don't have eyes too?

They have physical eyes and so on, but no sensitivity. They look like statues.

How about the remaining 15 *Brahma* realms? How many *indriya* can they get?

Brahmā don't have nose-sensitivity, tongue-sensitivity, body-sensitivity, femininity or masculinity. So we can remove those five *indriya*. How about mind? They can get that. And how about *sukhindriya* and *dukkhindriya*? Can *brahmā* experience bodily happiness and pain? No, because they don't have body-sensitivity. Remove those two. So that's seven that have been removed. What else? *Domanassindriya*? No, there is no *dosa* consciousness because *domanassa vedanā* cannot arise.

The remaining 15 realms of form-sphere consciousness cannot get these eight *indriya*. As such, they can only have 14 kinds of *indriya*.

What about for the *arūpa* (formless) sphere? How many *indriya* can they get? They can't get the 1st through the 7th because those are *rūpa*. They also don't get physical vitality, though they have mental vitality. They also can't get *sukhindriya, dukkhindriya, somanassindriya* or *domanassindriya*. They get *upekkhindriya*. They also get *saddhindriya, viriyindriya, satindriya, samadhindriya* and *paññindriya*.

But what about the 20th faculty? Can *sotāpatti magga citta* arise in the formless-sphere? No, there is no *sotāpatti magga*. Worldlings living in the formless-sphere cannot gain the first stage of enlightenment because they don't have eyes or ears to learn the *Dhamma* from someone.

Q: So there's no vedanā in that realm?

Only *upekkhā*. *Arūpa citta* is accompanied by two *jhāna* factors: *upekkhā* (equanimity) and *ekaggatā* (one-pointedness of mind).

How many faculties do they have in the *arūpa* realm? The formless-sphere can get the following 10 kinds of faculties: mental vitality, *manindriya, upekkhindriya, saddhindriya, viriyindriya, satindriya, samadhindriya, paññindriya, aññindriya* and *aññātāvindriya*.

Q: They can get the 21st indriya?

Yes, sure. It's possible. But they can't get the 20th *indriya*.

Okay, now we know about the 22 facilities, as well as how they can occur amongst the 31 planes of existence.

<u>*Bala*</u>

Now we go to the nine kinds of *bala*. This means power. We have nine powers.

Why do we call them powers?

Because they are strong and firm. Your *saddhā* is confidence, right? Everyone has confidence but the confidence of some people is not strong. If it's not strong, we can't call it a power. When a human being becomes strong and firm, he can't be shaken by opposing forces, right? In the same way, these *bala* are strong and firm and can't be shaken by opposing forces.

They also strengthen their concomitants. They make the concomitants that associate with them energetic and powerful.

This is why we call these *bala*.

A person in the Army who becomes a major or a general does so because they are strong and firm, right? They can't be shaken, but they also strengthen their soldiers. If they are not strong, the name might be the same (take *saddhā* as an example) but we can't call it a power.

What are these *bala*?

1) *Saddhābala*

This is confidence. The reality is *saddhā cetasika*, which associates with the 59 types of beautiful consciousness.

What is the opposing force of *saddhā*? Faithlessness. Someone might say: "I don't believe that."

But when we have *saddhābala*, its power is opposed to faithlessness. Even if someone says something to try to change your mind, your mind won't change. It's not shaken by opposing forces. No matter what they say, you won't believe it.

2) *Viriyabala*

This is energy or effort. The reality is *viriya cetasika*, which associates with 73 types of consciousness.

This *viriya* is opposed to laziness. When we have energy and effort, it opposes laziness; otherwise, we might say, "I don't want to do that; I'm lazy." When energy and effort become powers, there is no laziness.

3) *Satibala*

This is *sati*. The reality is *sati cetasika*, which associates with the 59 types of beautiful consciousness.

This *sati* is opposed to forgetfulness. When you practice meditation, you might think: "I forgot to make a mental note. I forgot to be aware." But when your *sati* becomes *bala*, you will remember and be aware of everything.

This is why *satibala* is opposed to forgetfulness.

4) *Samadhibala*

The reality is *ekaggatā*, which associates with 72 types of consciousness. Why only 72 types? Because we must exclude the 16 types of *aviriya citta*, as well as doubt-consciousness.

We have 18 types of rootless consciousness, right? The first 16 are not associated with *virya*. Whenever we talk about *aviriya citta*, we are referring to the first 16 types of rootless consciousness.

When we exclude the aforementioned 17 types of consciousness, that leaves 72 types of consciousness. These 72 types are associated with *ekaggatā*.

Ekaggatā is opposed to restlessness. When your *ekaggatā* becomes *bala*, there is no restlessness. That's why we need to develop our *saddhā*, *viriya*, *sati*, *samādhi* and *paññā* higher and higher.

5) *Paññābala*

Amoha, or wisdom. *Amoha cetasika* associates with 47 types of *citta*.

This *amoha* is opposed to ignorance. You don't see the characteristics of mind and body and you don't see the Four Noble Truths because of ignorance. It's because you don't have wisdom. But *amoha* is opposed to ignorance.

6) *Hiribala*

What is *hiri*? Moral shame. Its reality is *hiri cetasika*, which associates with the 59 types of beautiful consciousness.

This *hiri* is opposed to moral shamelessness.

7) *Ottappabala*

Ottappa is moral dread, or moral fear. Its reality is *ottappa cetasika*, which associates with the 59 types of beautiful consciousness.

Ottappa is opposed to fearlessness.

This *hiri* and *ottappa* strongly support moral action. Some of the discourses call these two the "guardians of the world." They are very important. These two guardian principles rule the world. Without them, no civilized society can exist.

If we lacked moral shame or moral dread, we might consider our sister or mother as no different from any other woman and engage in inappropriate behavior, right? If we did, this world might become like the animal kingdom, right? This would be because of a lack of *hiri* and *ottappa*.

These first seven *bala* are strong and firm and cannot be shaken by opposing forces.

8) *Ahirikabala*

This is moral shamelessness. Its reality is *ahirika cetasika*, which associates with the 12 types of unwholesome consciousness.

9) *Anottappabala*

This is moral fearlessness. Its reality is *anottappa cetasika*, which also associates with the 12 types of unwholesome consciousness.

Why do we call *ahirikabala* and *anottappabala* powers?

It doesn't mean that they can't be shaken by opposing forces. As I said before, one meaning of *bala* is that it's strong and firm and can't be shaken by opposing forces. But a second meaning is that it strengthens its concomitants. The first seven *bala* have both meanings.

But *ahirikabala* and *anottappabala* only have the meaning of strengthening their concomitants. They associate with unwholesome consciousness, right? When they do, they strengthen their concomitants and lead the way to immoral action. We do immoral things because of moral shamelessness and moral fearlessness. If we have moral shame and moral dread, we don't do bad things.

Q: So these are the opposites of the previous two?

Yes.

Adhipati

Let's go to *adhipati*. This means predominance.

We have four kinds of *adhipati*, or dominating factors. They include *chandādhipati* and so on. When we do *Paṭṭhana* chanting, you may recognize that we say "*adhipati paccayo*."

Adhipati is compared to a king. As the sole heir of the estate, no one is higher than the king. This is like *adhipati*.

When we studied *indriya* (faculty), we talked about it having controlling power. As such, *indriya* is compared to a king's minister. It's lower than the king. When someone becomes a minister, he has control over his ministry, right?

Nowadays in the U.S., the president looks like *adhipati*. And the ministers look like *indriya*. In those days, they compared *adhipati* to a king but we can't do that these days. Why? Nowadays, some kings have no powers, right? A king might be a king but he can't rule anything.

In America, the president is the top, right? He's the sole heir of the estate. But in some countries, the president has no power. Instead, the prime minister might have the power. Or perhaps neither the president nor the prime minister have power, and some other person controls everything. Maybe a general is in charge.

See how it depends on the policy of the nation? But in those days, they compared *adhipati* and *indriya* to a king and his ministers, respectively. This is very clear, right? The king is the top (like *adhipati*) and the king's ministers are like *indriya*. They can only control their respective ministries without interference from others.

Like, eye-sensitivty is called *indriya*, right? What does it control? Eye-sensitivity controls its coexisting *rūpa*. We have the eye-decad, right? Eye-sensitivity just controls the coexisting nine kinds of *rūpa*. It also has controlling power over seeing. Ear-sensitivity cannot come and interfere with seeing, right?

Nowadays, in politics we have figures like foreign ministers. They have power over their respective departments. Other ministers cannot come and interfere.

So, this is how we make the distinction between *adhipati* and *indriya*.

We have four kinds of *adhipati*, or dominating factors:

1) *Chandādhipati*

This is intention, or wish to do. The reality is *chanda* (cognition, or desire). It's one kind of mental factor. This *chanda* is a dominating factor.

Two *adhipati* cannot exercise supreme authority simultaneously. Only one can. When one of these four is *adhipati*, the others just follow.

This is the first of the four *adhipati*. Two cannot be *adhipati* at the same time. One country is not supposed to have two presidents with equal power, right? We can't have two kings.

Anyhow, the reality is *chanda*. *Chanda* is a little harder to memorize.

Chanda associates with how many types of consciousness? Normally, it associates with 69 types of consciousness. But here, it just associates with 52 types of *javana*. In other words, we're talking about *chanda* which associates with 52 *javana*.

How many *javana* do we have? We have 55 types. What are the three that we're excluding? We exclude the two types of *dosa mūla citta* and the one type of smile-producing consciousness. The *chanda* that associates with the remaining 52 *javana* is called *chandādhipati*.

2) *Viriyādhipati*

This is energy, or effort. Its reality is *viriya cetasika*, which normally associates with 73 types of consciousness. Here, though, it just associates with the same 52 types of *javana* as *chandādhipati*.

3) *Cittādhipati*

This is mind, or thought. The reality is *citta*, but not all *citta*. *Cittādhipati* associates with 52 *javana*. We exclude the two types of *moha mūla citta* and the one type of smile-producing consciousness.

4) *Vimaṃsādhipati*

This is reason, or intellect. This is wisdom, right? The reality is *amoha*. *Amoha* mostly associates with 47 types, but here, it only associates with the 34 types of *tihetuka javana*.

What are they? We have eight types of beautiful wholesome consciousness, though only four of them are *ñāṇa sampayutta*. Among *kāmāvacara citta*, we also have eight types of great functional consciousness, with four types that are *ñāṇa sampayutta*. That's a total of eight types of consciousness that are *ñāṇa sampayutta*. We also have 26 types of *appaṇā javana*.

In total, that's 34 types, which we call *tihetuka javana*.

These four types of *adhipati* are very important. Whatever you do—even worldly affairs—will not succeed if you don't have strong desire, strong effort, strong mind and wisdom. See that? If one of these is lacking, you can't succeed. We have to fulfill *adhipati*.

Especially when you practice meditation, you must have *chandādhipati*, or 'wish to do'. You should have the wish: "I want to gain enlightenment." You need to have strong desire, right?

You also need to have strong energy. You can't care what happens to your life or body. You try hard.

You need a strong mind. Even if something disturbs you, you can't care.

And you need wisdom. You study, you practice, and then you can succeed in attaining your goal.

When we set a fire with straw, it burns temporarily then is gone. But when someone sets a fire with branches, it burns for a long time. We can compare what we're talking about here with a straw fire and a branch fire.

Usually, when someone does something they start out with strong intention, strong energy and a strong mind. But they quit later. This is like a temporary straw fire. It burns very high at first but is temporary.

But branch fires burn for a long time—burning, burning, burning. We should be like this.

Whatever you do, if you don't have strong intention, so many things will come to disturb you until you quit. You get discouraged, right? So we need to have strong desire, strong effort, strong mind and strong wisdom. If you have *adhipati*, you will succeed in whatever you do, whatever you think, whatever your goal.

Think about your own situation. Whether it's in your business or in your meditation, what kinds of *adhipati* do you lack if you haven't succeeded yet? Maybe desire, maybe energy, maybe a strong mind, or maybe wisdom. So what do you need? Maybe all four. Or perhaps two or three of them.

We need to have these *adhipati*.

Āhāra

Now, we go to *āhāra*. *Āhāra* means nutriment. We have two kinds of nutriment, though the number is four. So, four kinds of nutriment, which we can also call food, cause or sustenance:

1) Kabalīkāra āhāra

This is edible food. These are the things we eat every day. Precisely, this is bodily food.

2) *Phassa* (contact)
3) *Manosañcetanā* (volitional activities)
4) *Viññāṇa* (rebirth consciousness, or relinking consciousness)

These last three are called mental food.

So, we have these two kinds of food, briefly.

Kabalīkāra āhāra

Why do we call this first one nutriment, cause or sustenance? Because we cannot survive without edible food. Edible food sustains the material body. If we don't eat for a month or two, we will die.

What do we need to have a long life? *Kabalīkāra āhāra*. That's why we need to eat every day, and work every day to get it. This edible food sustains or produces the material body. Otherwise, we cannot survive.

Phassāhāra

This is contact.

Let's look at the realities first. The reality of *kabalīkāra āhāra* is *āhāra*. Among the 28 types of material properties, one of them is *āhāra* (nutriment). The reality of *phassa* is *phassa cetasika*, which is a mental state. *Phassa* associates with all types of *citta*.

Contact sustains the five kinds of feelings. We will study this in detail in the upcoming chapter when we talk about Dependent Origination. When we say "*phassa paccaya vedanā,*" we mean that feeling arises because of contact. This is very important. And this is why we say that contact sustains the five kinds of feelings.

What are they? *Sukha vedanā, dukkha vedanā, somanassa vedanā, domanassa vedanā* and *upekkhā vedanā*. We would not have these five kinds of feelings without contact. But because of contact, feelings arise.

Where does contact come from? From the eyes, ears, nose, tongue, body and mind. It comes when objects come into contact with your eyes, your ears, your nose, your tongue, your body and your mind. And because of this contact, you have five feelings.

We have to work every day for good feelings, right? Why do we have to work? Because we want good feelings. We want to see certain colors, hear certain sounds and enjoy good smells, tastes, and mental objects. We want these good feelings, so we pursue them every day.

But they are constantly changing from one feeling to another. That's why the Buddha said that changing is suffering and there is suffering in change. Even a good feeling won't last long before it changes.

To be able to get this good feeling, we have to do something. We have suffering due to formation. Some people want to be beautiful, so they have to take care of their faces and bodies all the time. They get up each morning and spend one or two hours before they leave the house taking care of the body and trying to make it beautiful. Why? Because they want this good feeling. So they have to take care of this body and beautify it.

We call this *saṅkhāra-dukkha*.

This *dukkha* is suffering, though those who lack wisdom don't see it as *dukkha*. They just think: "I'm very beautiful." They don't see the *dukkha*. We call this *saṅkhāra-dukkha*. Your face may be very beautiful because you spent an hour or two beautifying it that morning. But how's it look by the time you get home in the evening? The beauty is gone, right? Your face looks normal again, so you start again the next day. This is *saṅkhāra-dukkha*.

This is suffering due to formation. It's called *saṅkhāra-dukkha* in *Pāli*.

We have contact when we eat, right? We want to eat tasty food, so we have to go to the market to buy the food, then we have to prepare and cook it. For what? For the good feeling of taste. It's for this desire that we spend a lot of time preparing to eat.

This is also suffering.

Then, after all that time spent preparing the meal, you're done eating the meal within 30 minutes. Most people don't reflect on how long it took us to prepare for that quick meal. Instead, they think only about how much they want to enjoy the meal. They just want that good taste.

We are slaves to our bodies. In order to study, work and practice meditation, we have to take care of ourselves.

Q: What about if you don't like the taste?

We can also experience *vedanā* when there's a bad taste. It's a kind of feeling.

Dukkha regards the body, right? If the food is so hot that it burns your tongue, that's *dukkha*. But if you find the flavor unpleasant, it regards the mind instead of the body. Then, it's *domanassa*.

Q: Is that also saṅkhāra-dukkha?

No, this is called *dukkha-dukkha*.

We have three kinds of *dukkha*, right? Painfulness as suffering is *dukkha-dukkha*. Everyone knows this kind of suffering, even without learning about it or practicing meditation. When we think "Oh, this is too hot!" it is *dukkha-dukkha*. It is painfulness as suffering.

Happiness changes to unhappiness (displeasure), right? This kind of *dukkha* is called *vipariṇāma-dukkha*. When you sit in a chair, you feel comfortable for about the first 15 minutes. What kind of feeling is that? It regards the body, so it's *sukha vedanā*. But what happens after you sit for about 30 minutes? Comfortable becomes uncomfortable. This is *dukkha* regarding the body, which is *dukkha vedanā*.

See? It changes. This is *vipariṇāma-dukkha*. Even good feelings change to something else and eventually become suffering. We call this *vipariṇāma-dukkha*.

So, we have these three kinds of dukkha: *dukkha-dukkha*, *vipariṇāma-dukkha* and *saṅkhāra-dukkha*.

Q: Can you give a different example of saṅkhāra-dukkha?

You want to be handsome, right? If you plan to go to a party this evening, you have to get ready by beautifying your hair and your face. If you're a woman, perhaps you have to add lipstick too. It takes a long time to maintain this face and this body to make it presentable for the party, right?

This is *saṅkhāra-dukkha*.

As soon as you finish beautifying your face and hair, what happens? Maybe the wind blows and you have to beautify your hair all over again. By the time you finish that, it's hot and you're sweating, so you have to fix your face again. In the meantime, you're worried about how you'll look for the party and whether you'll arrive on time.

I hope this example clarifies it for you.

Now, time is up. Thank you.

...

Today is February 21, 1999. Last week, we were studying *āhāra*. We have four kinds of *āhāra*, or food: *kabalīkāra āhāra, phassa, manosañcetanā* and *viññāṇa*. The last three are mental food.

Let's continue talking about *phassa* (contact, or sense-impact):

We need this because contact sustains and produces the five kinds of feeling. To be able to get good feelings, we go about in the world, right? Why? In search of eye-contact, ear-contact, nose-contact, tongue-contact, body-contact, and sometimes, mind-contact. Then, you get a good feeling, right?

Eye-contact, for example, sustains and produces the five kinds of feelings, including the good feeling that we're constantly looking for. This is pleasant feeling, right? So we do things like go to a show or watch television. Why? For the pleasure, for a pleasant feeling. This is *phassa*. When a good visible object contacts your eye, a good or pleasant feeling is produced. Getting this good feeling requires finding a good visible object.

It's the same way for sound. When a good sound contacts your ear-sensitivity—"Wow, what a beautiful song!"—you have a pleasant feeling. It's the same for the nose, the tongue or the body. We rely upon contact.

When we study dependent origination soon, we will learn that because of contact, feeling arises; because of feeling, clinging arises; because of clinging, *kamma* formation arises; because of *kamma* formation, rebirth arises; because of rebirth, aging, death, sorrow, lamentation, pain, grief, despair and so on—all kinds of suffering—occur.

This is how *phassa*—and these five kinds of feeling—make the process of our aggregates last so long in the cycle of rebirth, or *saṃsāra*. And this is why *phassa* is one kind of *āhāra*. It's because it is the cause of feeling.

Here, *āhāra* has different meanings, right? It might mean nutriment, cause or sustenance. As *phassa*, it is the cause of feeling. It produces feeling. When we practice meditation, we need to contemplate on this feeling. Feeling is just feeling; otherwise, it becomes craving. If it becomes craving, we cannot stop it. There will be clinging and so on.

We'll study all of this more later.

Manosañcetanāhāra

This is volitional activities.

We know that *phassa* is a universal mental factor, right? It can associate with all types of consciousness. The reality of *manosañcetanāhāra* is *cetanā*. Normally, *cetanā* can also associate with all types of consciousness. But here, *cetanā* is present only in the 29 types of moral and immoral mundane consciousness. This includes the 12 types of immoral consciousness. The remaining 17 types of consciousness include the eight types of sense-sphere moral consciousness and nine types of sublime moral consciousness.

Cetanā associating with these 29 types of consciousness are called *manosañcetanāhāra*.

Manosañcetanāhāra (volitional activities) sustain and produce rebirth in the sense-sphere, the form-sphere and the formless-sphere. This is why this *cetanā* just associates with 29 types of consciousness, not all types of consciousness.

What type of *cetanā* is it when we do demeritorious things? Is it moral or immoral? Immoral, right? If this *cetanā* associates with immoral consciousness, it will sustain and produce what kind of rebirth? In the lower realms, or the four woeful states—perhaps hell, the animal kingdom, or the realms of hungry ghosts or demons.

What is the rebirth consciousness for those reborn in the lower states? *Santīraṇa* (investigating consciousness). This *santīraṇa* is accompanied by indifferent feeling. It is *upekkhā sahagata santīraṇa citta*. This immoral volitional activity produces rebirth in the lower realms.

If volitional activity is associated with sense-sphere moral consciousness, what kind of rebirth will it produce? We have eight of these, right? We also have one type of wholesome rootless consciousness. We have two types of *santīraṇa* in this context, right? One is called immoral resultant consciousness, and the other is called moral resultant consciousness. Plus, there are the eight types of sense-sphere resultant consciousness. These nine types of consciousness produce rebirth.

If a being's rebirth consciousness is wholesome *santīraṇa* (investigating) consciousness, he will be blind, deaf or mute since conception in the mother's womb. Or he will be a lower *deva*, not one who lives in heaven. As for the eight types of *kāmāvacara* resultant consciousness, they will be reborn "normal," as we were. As such, this volitional activity in sense-sphere moral consciousness produces rebirth in the human world and the six celestial worlds. Between the human world and the six celestial planes, that's the seven planes of the blissful, sensual world.

Between these seven planes and the four woeful states we already talked about, that's 11 of the 31 planes of existence.

Cetanā which associates with the five types of form-sphere wholesome consciousness will produce rebirth in the form-sphere plane. How many form-sphere planes are there? Sixteen. And volitional activity that associates with the four types of formless-sphere wholesome consciousness will produce rebirth in the four formless-sphere planes, right?

According to this *kamma*, we will be reborn in one kind of existence within the 31 planes of existence. If people wonder where we have to be reborn after we die, it depends on this *cetanā*. If it associates with immoral consciousness, it will be in the woeful states. If it associates with sense-sphere wholesome consciousness, we will be reborn in the human or celestial worlds. This is when we do meritorious things like practice generosity, morality or meditation.

Where will you be reborn if you gain *jhāna*? This means that your *cetanā* is associated with the five kinds of form-sphere wholesome consciousness. If you gain the first *jhāna*, you will be reborn in the first *jhāna* plane. If you gain the second or third *jhāna*, you will be reborn in the second *jhāna* plane. If you gain the fourth *jhāna*, you will be reborn in the third *jhāna* plane. And if you gain the fifth *jhāna*, you will be reborn in the fourth *jhāna* plane.

So it depends on this *cetanā*. That's why we say that *manosañcetanā* sustains or produces rebirth in the three spheres. When you gain *arūpajhāna*, you'll be reborn in the formless-sphere.

None of this mentions *magga*, right? This is because *magga* eradicates rebirth; it doesn't produce rebirth. This is why we're just talking about these 29 types of moral and immoral consciousness.

Q: What's the difference between saṅkhāra and cetanā?

It depends on the context. *Cetanā* is sometimes the same as *saṅkhāra*, and sometimes different. For example, in teaching Dependent Origination, the Buddha said, "*avijjā paccaya saṅkhāra*." This means 'dependent upon ignorance, *saṅkhāra* arises'. In that context, it's referring to volitional activities. As such, this use of *saṅkhāra* means the same thing as *cetanā*. So, in the context of '*avijjā paccaya saṅkhāra*', *saṅkhāra* and *cetanā* are the same.

Sometimes the Buddha said, "*sabbe saṅkhāra anicca*." This means that all conditioned things are impermanent. *Saṅkhāra* in that context refers to all conditioned things, not just *cetanā*. *Saṅkhāra* means all mind and matter. All consciousness, all mental states and all material properties are called *saṅkhāra*.

So it depends on the context. In some contexts, the term *kāyasaṅkhāra* refers to the breath. This is why we need to study this.

But, here, *cetanā* and *saṅkhāra* are the same. This is why it's helpful for us to know their realities. Otherwise, we won't know how they differ. The reality of *manosañcetanāhāra* is *cetanā*. When we study *avijjā paccaya saṅkhāra*, we learn that the reality is also *cetanā*. They are the same. But sometimes, *saṅkhāra* is not only *cetanā*; sometimes it is all consciousness, all mental states and all *rūpa*.

Viññāṇāhāra

This is rebirth consciousness. *Viññāṇa* is mind, or consciousness. We have 121 types of consciousness, right? But here, rebirth consciousness consists of just 19 types.

How many types of rebirth consciousness do we have for the sense-sphere? We have two types of *santīraṇa* (investigating) consciousness and eight types of *kāmāvacara vipāka* (resultant) consciousness. That's a total of 10 types.

There are five types of *rūpavacara* resultant consciousness and four types of *arūpavacara* (formless-sphere) resultant consciousness too.

That's a total of 19 types of rebirth consciousness. So, in this context, *viññāṇa* is referring only to these 19 types of rebirth consciousness.

The reality here is *citta*. But this *citta* is only taking 19 kinds of rebirth consciousness. *Viññāṇa* rebirth consciousness sustains the mental states and material phenomena which arise simultaneously. Briefly, you can say that this *viññāṇa* sustains the *nāma* and *rūpa*. *Nāma* here does not mean consciousness.

Let's look at the rebirth consciousness of an animal:

An animal's rebirth consciousness is *santīraṇa*. It is unwholesome resultant investigating consciousness. When this *upekkhā santīraṇa citta* arises, how many mental states associate with it? Ten. We have seven universal mental factors, and six occasional mental factors. That's a total of 13 miscellaneous mental factors. Among those 13 mental factors, we exclude *chanda* (desire), *pīti* (joy) and *viriya* (effort). The remaining 10 mental states associate with this *santīraṇa* rebirth consciousness.

In the case of *arūpa*, do those reborn in the formless-sphere have *rūpa*? No. This is the formless-sphere, where there is no material phenomena. There is just *nāma*. *Nāma* here is only *cetasika* (mental states). So, how many mental states associate with the four types of *arūpa* (formless) resultant consciousness? When they arise, how many mental states associate with that consciousness? Thirty. We talked about this previously, so there's no need to go into it further right now. But what this means is that in the case of *arūpa* rebirth consciousness, it sustains only mental states, not *rūpa*.

In the case of the sense-sphere blissful world (human world and celestial worlds) and the 15 *rūpa* (form-sphere) worlds, there is both *nāma* and *rūpa*. When this rebirth consciousness takes place, mental states and material phenomena arise together, simultaneously. Mind only cannot arise. When consciousness arises, it has its concomitants. They arise together. When rebirth consciousness arises, there aren't just mental states. There are also material properties that arise.

But not all 28 types of material properties arise.

We already studied decads, right? We talked about *kāya-dasaka* (body-decad), *bhava-dasaka* (sex-decad) and *hadaya-dasaka* (heart-decad). These three decads arise together with rebirth consciousness.

Do you remember that when we studied the third chapter of the second book?

In our mother's womb, we take *paṭisandhi* (rebirth consciousness) and the three decads and mental states arise at the same time. This is why we say that *viññāṇa* rebirth consciousness—in the case of *kāmāvacara* (sense-sphere) resultant consciousness or *rūpavacara* (form-sphere) resultant consciousness—sustains mental states and material phenomena.

So, briefly, just remember that *āhāra* is nutriment, food or cause. *Kabalīkāra āhāra* (edible food) sustains and produces the material body. It makes your body survive and have a long life. *Phassa* (contact) sustains the five kinds of feelings. This means that it produces feelings. *Manosañcetanāhāra* (volitional activities) sustains and produces rebirth in the 31 planes of existence. And *viññāṇa* (rebirth consciousness) sustains mental states and material phenomena which arise simultaneously.

...

Last week, we studied *jhānaṅga, maggaṅga, bala, indriya* and *adhipati.* When we talked about their realities, it was a bit different from what we studied in the second chapter of the first book. Why do we talk about their realities differently? We'll talk about that now.

There is *ekaggatā* (one-pointedness of mind) and *upekkhā vedanā* (indifferent feeling). You already know about these, right? These are part of *jhānaṅga. Jhānaṅga* is *jhāna* factors, right? But these *jhānaṅga* are not present in *dvipañcaviññāṇa* (five-sense impression). We have two types of eye-consciousness, two types of ear-consciousness, two types of nose-consciousness, two types of tongue-consciousness and two types of body-consciousness. We call this *dvipañcaviññāṇa*.

Ekaggatā is a *cetasika* (mental state) that normally associates with all kinds of consciousness. It's a universal mental state, right? But when we studied the seven types of *jhānaṅga*, we learned that *ekaggatā jhānaṅga* only associates with 79 types of consciousness.

Why is this? Because no *jhāna* factors are present in the 10 types of sense-impression. This is why we subtract the 10 *dvipañcaviññāṇa*, but keep the remaining 79 types of consciousness.

We have seven *jhānaṅga*, right? Among these seven *jhānaṅga*, *ekaggatā* is a reality. There is *vitakka, vicāra, pīti*, and then, *ekaggatā*. The reality is *ekaggatā* but it only takes 79 types of consciousness. The 10 types of *dvipañcaviññāṇa* are not taken.

Why don't they take them? Because sense-impression is so weak and close perception of the object is absent. What is the meaning of *jhānaṅga*? It is *jhāna*, which closely and intently observes the object. *Dvipañcaviññāṇa* has no *vitakka* (initial application) associating with it, so how can the object be closely observed?

What's the characteristic or nature of *vitakka*? Lifting the concomitants to the object. If there's no *vitakka, ekaggatā* cannot be there as a *jhānaṅga*, closely and intently observing the object. The object is very weak, right?

This is the reason why *ekaggatā jhānaṅga* is not in *dvipañcaviññāṇa*.

Let's also look at *upekkhā vedanā*. How many types of *upekkhā* consciousness are there? Fifty-five. But in this context, *upekkhā vedanā* associates only with 47 types of *upekkhā* consciousness.

Why only 47 types of consciousness?

We subtract the two types of eye-consciousness, the two types of ear-consciousness, the two types of nose-consciousness and the two types of tongue-consciousness from the original 55 types of *upekkhā* consciousness. That leaves 47 types. *Upekkhā vedanā* as a *jhānaṅga* associates only with these 47 types of consciousness. Again, this is because they are so weak.

Also, *ekaggatā* is not *bala* in *dvipañcaviññāṇa, sampaṭicchana* (receiving consciousness), *santīraṇa* (investigating consciousness), *pañcadvārāvajjana* (five-sense adverting consciousness) and *vicikicchā* (doubt-consciousness). These first 16 types of consciousness have no *viriya* because *viriya* does not associate with effortless kinds of consciousness. Without *viriya*, it's not so strong, right? And if it's not strong, we can't call it *bala*, right? *Bala* is so strong and powerful.

Ekaggatā normally associates with 89 types of consciousness, but we're talking about *bala* now, right? How many *bala* are there? Nine. And what is *ekaggatā*? *Samādhibala*, right? When we studied *samādhibala*, the reality was *ekaggatā*. This *ekaggatā* will associate with only 72 types of consciousness because there is no *bala* in effortless consciousness. This is because they are not strong because there is no *viriya* associating with these types of consciousness.

Looking at *vitakka*, we see that it is not *maggaṅga* in *sampaṭicchana, santīraṇa, pañcadvārāvajjana, manodvārāvajjana* and *hasituppāda*.

How many *maggaṅga* are there? Twelve. Among these 12 *maggaṅga*, what is *vitakka*? It is *sammāsaṅkappa*, or right thinking. This is *vitakka*. It can normally associate with 55 types of consciousness, but here, it takes only 35 types. Why? *Vitakka* is not *maggaṅga* in *sampaṭicchana* and so on because these are types of rootless consciousness. As such, *vitakka* here takes only the 24 types of beautiful sense-sphere consciousness and the 11 types of first *jhāna* consciousness.

So *vitakka* is not *maggaṅga* in *sampaṭicchana, santīraṇa, pañcadvārāvajjana, manodvārāvajjana* and *hasituppāda* because they are rootless. What's rootless? No root. If there is no *lobha, dosa, moha, alobha, adosa* or *amoha*, the object cannot be taken firmly. It cannot be *maggaṅga* if the object cannot be taken firmly.

This is why when we take *sammāsaṅkappa*, the reality is *vitakka* but it only takes 35 types of consciousness.

How about *viriya*? *Viriya* is not *maggaṅga* in *manodvārāvajjana* and smiling-producing consciousness. What's *viriya* in *maggaṅga*? It's *sammāvāyāma*, or right effort. The reality is *viriya*. *Viriya* normally associates with 73 types of consciousness, but here, just 35 types. It associates with the 24 types of beautiful sense-sphere consciousness and the 11 types of first *jhāna* consciousness.

See? It's the same 35 types as *vitakka*. It's not *maggaṅga* in mind-door adverting consciousness and smile-producing consciousness.

Why? Because these two kinds of consciousness are rootless. There's no root. For that reason, the object cannot be taken firmly.

Also, *ekaggatā* is not *maggaṅga* in the 18 types of *ahetuka citta* (rootless consciousness) or doubt-consciousness. That's a total of 19 types of consciousness.

What is *ekaggatā* in the context of *maggaṅga*? It is *sammāsamādhi*. *Ekaggatā* is a universal mental factor, but in *maggaṅga* we actually have two types: *sammāsamādhi* and *micchāsamādhi*. See that, right? Among the 12 *maggaṅga*, there is *sammāsamādhi* (right concentration) and *micchāsamādhi* (wrong concentration).

When we take the reality of right concentration, it takes just 59 types of consciousness. What are they? It takes the 59 types of beautiful consciousness. It does not take unwholesome or rootless consciousness.

And when we take *micchāsamādhi* (wrong concentration), the reality is just taking 11 types of consciousness. There is no doubt, or *vicikicchā*. Doubt can't make a decision about the object, right? Because it's *maggaṅga* here, it's the same—doubt can't make a decision on the object.

So, *ekaggatā* is not *maggaṅga* in rootless consciousness and doubt-consciousness.

Also, when we studied the 22 faculties, we saw that *ekaggatā* is not *indriya* in *vicikicchā citta*. What is *ekaggatā* called in the context of *indriya*? *Samādhindriya*. The reality is *ekaggatā*. It's a universal mental state, but here, it only takes 72 types of consciousness. There is not this *indriya* among *ahetuka citta* or *vicikicchā*. That's why it takes just 72 types of consciousness.

As for *adhipati*, there are not the two types of *moha mūla citta* or the one type of smile-producing consciousness. When we studied *adhipati* (predominant), we talked about it taking *javana*. How many total *javana* are there? Fifty-five, right? But here, when we take the reality of *adhipati*, it mostly just takes 52 types of *javana citta*. It takes 52 types when it's *chandādhipati*. It takes 52 types when it is *viriyādhipati*. It takes 52 types when it's *cittādhipati*, and it takes just 34 types when it's *vimaṃsādhipati*.

We studied this last week, right?

The two types of *moha mūla citta* and smile-producing consciousness are *javana*, but we don't take these as the reality of *adhipati*. Why? Because the two types of *moha mūla citta* have just one root. Only *moha cetasika* associates with *moha*. And smile-producing consciousness has no root.

This is why we subtract these three types of *javana*, thus leaving 52 types.

Okay, the last one is *viriya*. It is not *adhipati* in the two types of *moha mūla citta* or the one type of smile-producing consciousness.

Consider the four *adhipati*. *Viriyādhipati* is energy or effort. The reality is *viriya*. How many *javana* does this *viriya* take? It takes 52 types of *javana*. It doesn't take all types of *javana* because the two types of *moha mūla citta* and the one type of smile-producing consciousness have only one root and no root, respectively. For that reason, they can't be *adhipati* (predominant).

As we study, it's good for us to understand these various realities, whether they do or do not take various types of consciousness, and why. We should understand these things.

...

So, now we've studied mixed categories.

How many mixed categories are there? Among *missakasaṅgaha*, we have *hetu, jhānaṅga, maggaṅga, indriya, bala, adhipati* and *āhāra*. That's seven departments, names or categories.

If we want to know their realities, we can explore them one-by-one:

Paññā is *amoha*, or wisdom. Wisdom has how many names here? It has five names, departments or categories. When we studied *hetu*, we saw *paññā* among the six roots, right? What's it called? *Amoha*. In *maggaṅga*, *sammādiṭṭhi* (right understanding) is *paññā*. This is *amoha* too. What's *paññā* called in *indriya*? It's *paññindriya* and so on. It is the last four *indriya* we spoke of. These are all *amoha*. What about *bala*? It's *paññābala*. And with *adhipati*, it's *vimaṃsādhipati*.

So, how many names for *paññā*? Five.

How many names are there for *viriya*? Four. With *maggaṅga*, we have *sammāvāyāma* and *micchāvāyāma*. There are two, right? For *indriya*, there is *viriyindriya*. For *bala*, there is *viriyabala*. And for *adhipati*, there is *viriyādhipati*. Four names.

How many names for *ekaggatā*, or *samādhi*? Four names. They include *ekaggatā* (*jhānaṅga*), *sammāsamādhi* and *micchāsamādhi* (*maggaṅga*), *samādhindriya* (*indriya*) and *samādhibala* (*bala*).

There are three names for *sati*. What are they? *Sammāsati* (*maggaṅga*), *satindriya* (*indriya*) and *satibala* (*bala*). There are also three names for *citta*: *manindriya* (*indriya*), *cittādhipati* (*adhipati*) and *viññāṇāhāra* (*āhāra*).

How many names are there for *vedanā*? Only two. With *jhānaṅga*, what kind of *vedanā* do we find? *Somanassa vedanā*, *domanassa vedanā* and *upekkhā vedanā*. And how about for *indriya*? *Sukhindriya*, *dukkhindriya*, *somanassindriya*, *domanassindriya* and *upekkhindriya*. Just two names for *vedanā*.

There are only two names for *saddhā*. What are they? *Saddhindriya* and *saddhabala*. Likewise, there are two names for *vitakka*: *vitakka* (*jhānaṅga*) and *sammāsaṅkappa* (*maggaṅga*).

The remaining realities have just one name: *Lobha hetu* (*hetu*), *dosa hetu* (*hetu*), *moha hetu* (*hetu*), *alobha hetu* (*hetu*), *adosa hetu* (*hetu*), *vicāra* (*jhanaṅga*), *pīti* (*jhānaṅga*), *sammāvācā* (*maggaṅga*), *sammākammanta* (*maggaṅga*), *sammājīva* (*maggaṅga*), *sammādiṭṭhi* (*maggaṅga*), *micchādiṭṭhi* (*maggaṅga*), *hiribala* (*bala*), *ottappabala* (*bala*), *ahirikabala* (*bala*), *anottappabala* (*bala*), *chandādhipati* (*adhipati*), *phassāhāra* (*āhāra*), *manosañcetanāhāra* (*āhāra*), *jīvitindriya* (*indriya*, for mental vitality), *cakkhundriya* (*indriya*, for eye-sensitivity), *sotindriya* (*indriya*, for ear-sensitivity), *ghāṇindriya* (*indriya*, for nose-sensitivity), *jīvhindriya* (*indriya*, for tongue-sensitivity), *kāyindriya* (*indriya*, for body-sensitivity), *itthindriya* (*indriya*, for femininity), *purisindriya* (*indriya*, for masculinity), *jīvitindriya* (*indriya*, for physical vitality) and *kabalīkāra āhāra* (*āhāra*).

If you want to know the various realities here and how many names they have within mixed categories, you can look right here. If you do, you'll know right away.

Bodhipakkhiyasaṅgaha

Now we'll study *bodhipakkhiyasaṅgaha*. This is very, very important. Very important. When we practice meditation, we experience all of this *bodhipakkhiyasaṅgaha*. If we develop these to perfection, we gain enlightenment.

Bodhipakkhiyasaṅgaha concerns itself with the four *satipaṭṭhāna*, the four *sammappadhānā*, the four *iddhipādā*, the five *indriya*, the five *bala*, the seven *bojjhaṅgā* and the eight *maggaṅga*. How many sections is that? Seven. We'll study these in detail because they're very important. Meditators in particular should understand these one-by-one. Maybe some of you will experience all of these *bodhipakkhiya*.

First, we should be sure that we understand the meaning of *bodhipakkhiyasaṅgaha*. *Bodhi* means enlightenment. *Pakkhiya* means 'on the side of'. So *bodhipakkhiya* means 'on the side of enlightenment', factors of enlightenment or requisites of enlightenment. To gain enlightenment, we need all of these factors. So, *bodhipakkhiyasaṅgaha* is the compendium of categories pertaining to enlightenment, or briefly, the factors of enlightenment.

The Four Satipaṭṭhāna

Let's start by looking at *satipaṭṭhāna*. You already know this, right?

How many *satipaṭṭhāna* do we have? Four. We will talk about the four *satipaṭṭhāna*.

What does *sati* mean? Mindfulness, or awareness. *Paṭṭhāna* means foundation. *Satipaṭṭhāna* is the foundation of mindfulness.

When you study the *Satipaṭṭhāna Sutta*, you will see how the Buddha talked about there being just one way for the purification of being, the overcoming of sorrow and lamentation, the cessation of pain and grief, the attainment of the supramundane path, and for the realization of *nibbāna*. He said there's only one way. If we go another way, we cannot gain enlightenment and experience these things.

The Buddha said there is only one way. What is the way? He explained that the only way is the foundation of mindfulness. This means that if we really want to achieve purification of being, we need to follow this way. Without doing so, our mind cannot be purified.

So I'd like to explain why they call this purification of being. What does this mean?

We studied *kilesas* (impurities), right? We have 10 kinds of impurities. If any one of these 10 impurities arise in a person's mind, that person's mind is not pure. To accomplish purity of being, we need to eradicate all of these mental impurities.

So what do we need to do? We need to practice meditation. When we follow the foundations of mindfulness meditation, we can eradicate all of these various kinds of mental defilements or impurities.

When beings have *lobha* (greed), hatred, delusion and so on, their minds are not pure. As their minds are not pure, their verbal and physical actions are bad. That is, they say and do bad things. They will have to take responsibility for what they've done in this present life, and in the next life they might have to be reborn in a woeful state. Even if they've done enough meritorious things to support them to be reborn as a human being again, they might be born with bad teeth, poor health, or perhaps a short life. This is because of these impurities.

So to get rid of these impurities, we need to practice meditation. The Buddha explained that this is the one way that leads to the purification of being.

What about overcoming sorrow and lamentation?

If you do something wrong and then think about it afterward—"Oh, I did something terrible"—sorrow occurs, right? Or perhaps you lose a member of your family or someone near and dear to you—perhaps your husband or wife, a parent, a child, or maybe a friend. You feel sorrow, right? You lament, cry and cry all the time. Some people even cry when they lose their cat, right?

What do we need to do? Practice meditation. Be aware of your mind. If your mind has any kind of thought, just make a mental note. Try to stay with your mindfulness. Then, you don't need to cry.

So the Buddha said that we need to practice *satipaṭṭhāna* (mindfulness meditation) to overcome sorrow and lamentation.

What about the cessation of pain and grief? Pain regards the body, right? And grief regards the mind.

What do we need to do? Just practice meditation. Just follow the foundations of mindfulness meditation. You can get rid of pain and grief.

What about those who would like to attain the supramundane path, or enlightenment? You can't do it by simply praying. We need to practice mindfulness meditation to gain enlightenment.

How about the realization of *nibbāna*? What is the ultimate goal of Buddhism? *Nibbāna*. It is liberation. What do we need to do to realize *nibbāna*? We just need to practice meditation. There is only this one way.

So *sati* is very important. It prevents the mind from wandering around the sense objects. It's like a security guard. You have six doors, right? You have the eye-door, ear-door, nose-door, tongue-door, body-door and mind-door. We need to be mindful all the time. If there is no security guard at these six doors, who will come? A thief. He will get in your house and take valuable things. You will lose.

If you lack mindfulness at your eye and see something attractive, what happens? "I like that. I want it." What is that? Craving, or attachment. It's greed. This is because the object is attractive and desirable.

If the object is undesirable, what do you feel? "I don't like that. I hate it." Hatred, anger. Or maybe jealousy. Why? No mindfulness.

With *satipaṭṭhāna*, if we see something, what do we have to do? Just know: "seeing." If you see something, note it—"seeing, seeing"—then come back to your primary object. If we have *satipaṭṭhāna*, it's like a security guard. No mental defilements can get in. Then, these mental impurities can't steal anything from you.

When you practice meditation and are aware all the time—in every moment—you develop your morality, your concentration, and your wisdom. You will understand the nature of mind and matter in every moment. This means that with every moment you are developing your virtue perfections—your *sīla*, *samādhi* and *paññā*—to make it higher and higher.

When you lack mindfulness, *lobha* and *hatred* come instead of wholesome consciousness. When unwholesome consciousness arises in your mind, you lost your opportunity, right?

Sati is very important. And it's not just for the eyes. When you hear, smell, taste, touch or think about something, you should be mindful. *All the time*. Whatever your practice is—maybe you practice tranquility meditation, or perhaps insight (*vipassanā*) meditation too—you need *satipaṭṭhāna*. The foundations of mindfulness meditation is the one way to gain enlightenment.

So, *satipaṭṭhāna* consists of how many realities? There are four kinds of mindfulness, right?

1) *Kāyānupassanā-satipaṭṭhāna*
2) *Vedanānupassanā-satipaṭṭhāna*
3) *Cittānupassanā-satipaṭṭhāna*
4) *Dhammānupassanā-satipaṭṭhāna*

There is just one reality. What is it? The *paramattha dhamma*, the essential property, is just *sati*.

Sati is a beautiful mental factor. Whichever of the 59 types of beautiful consciousness arises, *sati* is always associated with it, right? But, here, it associates with only 42 types of consciousness, including the eight types of sense-sphere beautiful consciousness, the eight types of sense-sphere functional consciousness, and the 26 types of *appaṇā javana*. Altogether, that's 42 types of consciousness.

Q: Can you please remind me what the appaṇā javana are?

They are sublime *javana*. Sublime refers to *rūpavacara* and *arūpavacara*. These 26 *appaṇā javana* include the nine types of sublime wholesome consciousness, the nine types of functional consciousness, and the eight types of supramundane consciousness.

Let's look at the meaning of *kāyānupassanā-satipaṭṭhāna*.

Kāya here does not only refer to the body. Sometimes *kāya* means the body, right? But here it refers to the body breathing in and breathing out. In this context, *kāya* means *āṇāpāṇa*. And the word *anupassanā* means 'repeated contemplation on'.

Q: It's not about movement; it's more about breath here?

It's specifically about breathing in and breathing out, but also includes movement. We'll discuss it in more detail later. It's contemplation of the body.

Vedanānupassanā-satipaṭṭhāna is contemplation of feelings, and *cittānupassanā-satipaṭṭhāna* is contemplation of thoughts. Lastly, *dhammānupassanā-satipaṭṭhāna* is contemplation of *dhamma*, which means mental objects in this context.

Kāyānupassanā-satipaṭṭhāna

When it comes to contemplation of breathing in and breathing out, we have many techniques we can use. Some people count the breath, for example: breathing in ("one"), breathing out ("one"), breathing in ("two"), breathing out ("two"). In other words, they count each breath cycle from one to ten. This is for tranquility meditation.

Other people do it a little differently: breathing in ("one"), breathing out ("two"), breathing in ("three"), breathing out ("four"). They count each breath segment from one to ten. There are also people who just concentrate on the touching sensation at their nostrils as they breathe in and breathe out: "breathing in" and "breathing out." Either way is okay for *kāyānupassanā-satipaṭṭhāna*. *Kāya* here means breathing in and breathing out.

But also, we can contemplate on our posture, whether we're standing, sitting, walking or lying down. When you sit, you know you're sitting: "sitting, touching, sitting, touching." You know you're sitting. When you're walking, you know you're walking: "walking, walking, walking." You know the movement of your legs and body. When you're standing, you know you're standing. And when you're lying down, you know you're lying down.

When you contemplate on these four postures, it's called *kāyānupassanā-satipaṭṭhāna*.

There's also something called contemplation on comprehension. Comprehension here means that you contemplate in this way: when you are going forward, you know you're going forward; when you are going backward, you know you're going backward; if you turn back, you know you're turning back; if you look forward, you know you're looking forward; if you look backward, you know you're looking backward; if you're bending, you know you're bending; and if you're stretching, you know you're stretching.

Comprehension is all about awareness of whatever it is that the body is doing. If you are reaching, you know you're reaching; if you're taking something, you know you're taking; if you are leaning down, you know you're leaning down. This is comprehension of whatever you're doing. In the same way, if you're talking, you know you're talking; if you're listening, you know you're listening. As you prepare your property or your clothes, you know this too. We call this comprehension.

This is all regarding the body, right? We call it *kāyānupassanā-satipaṭṭhāna*.

Also, when you eat, know that you're eating, chewing, swallowing, taking food. All of these are comprehension. See? It's not merely *sati* (mindfulness); we should have comprehension, which is knowing what we are doing.

Sometimes, we may contemplate the 32 parts of the body, including hair of the head, hair of the body, nails, teeth, skin, and so on. If you contemplate the 32 parts of the body, it's also *kāyānupassanā-satipaṭṭhāna*. Most of these 32 parts are internal.

We can also analyze the four elements in terms of their characteristics. The characteristics of the earth-element are hardness and softness, the characteristics of the fire-element are cold and heat/warmth, the characteristics of the air-element are supporting or moving, and the characteristics of the water-element are cohesion and fluidity. These are their characteristics. If you contemplate the four kinds of elements in terms of their characteristics, it is also considered *kāyānupassanā-satipaṭṭhāna*.

Kāya concerns the body, right? So, breathing in and out, posture, movement, the 32 parts of the body, and the four elements are considered *kāyānupassanā-satipaṭṭhāna*.

We can also compare our body with a dead body. In the old days, meditators would go to a cemetery. They didn't cremate dead bodies like we do today. And even if they did, they would put the dead body in a cemetery for a few days or a week. Meditators would go there to look at the dead bodies and compare them to their body in terms of loathsomeness. They did this to get rid of craving. This technique is also considered a part of *kāyānupassanā-satipaṭṭhāna*.

Satipaṭṭhāna has just one reality, right? It's *sati*. Then why did the Buddha teach four kinds of *satipaṭṭhāna*? Because their objects differ.

What's the object of *kāyānupassanā-satipaṭṭhāna*? The body, right? What's the object of *vedanānupassanā-satipaṭṭhāna*? Sensation or feeling. The object of *cittānupassanā-satipaṭṭhāna*? Thought. And the object of *dhammānupassanā-satipaṭṭhāna*? Mental objects.

So the objects differ. Also, the seeing is different, as well as the abandoning. This is why there are four kinds of *satipaṭṭhāna* –the object, the seeing, and the abandoning or eradication are different.

We'll talk about this more next time. Time's up for today. Thank you.

Any questions?

Q: Are kāyānupassanā-satipaṭṭhāna and vedanānupassanā-satipaṭṭhāna mostly about the body, and in contrast, cittānupassanā-satipaṭṭhāna and dhammānupassanā-satipaṭṭhāna mostly about mind?

Kāyānupassanā-satipaṭṭhāna contemplates the body. *Vedanānupassanā-satipaṭṭhāna* contemplates only feeling. But this includes bodily and mental feeling, right? If we have a painful feeling, it regards *kāya*, right? Remember that we have five kinds of feeling. Two kinds regard the body, and three kinds regard the mind. But, here, we don't say that one feeling is body and another is mind—it's just feeling.

Q: Do these satipaṭṭhāna go in the order you described them? I mean, do they get more and more subtle? Kāya is very gross and dense, so you just pay attention to the body. But do these satipaṭṭhāna get more subtle? In other words, is dhammānupassanā-satipaṭṭhāna the most subtle of the four?

It depends on your concentration. No matter which *satipaṭṭhāna* is your object, everything is subtle if you have good concentration. Even with *kāyānupassanā-satipaṭṭhāna*, you might experience your breath disappearing. So it depends on your concentration.

Q: I just wanted to get clarification on your answer to a question I had earlier. I think you said that saṅkhāra can be the same as cetanā, but saṅkhāra can also be other things. Can cetanā be other things?

No, *cetanā* can only be volition.

...

Today is March 7, 1999. We will continue talking about *satipaṭṭhāna*, or the four foundations of mindfulness. Mindfulness is very important for meditators because it prevents the mind from wandering to other sense-objects and also keeps the mind fixed attentively and firmly on a single object of meditation. Therefore, the four foundations of mindfulness are indispensable for the development of tranquility meditation and insight (*vipassanā*) meditation.

The reality of these four foundations of mindfulness is only *sati cetasika*. But even though there is just that one reality, the Buddha explained mindfulness in a fourfold way, right? This is because they have different objects. The object of *kayānupassanā-satipaṭṭhāna* is body, the object of *vedanānupassanā-satipaṭṭhāna* is feelings, the object of *cittānupassanā-satipaṭṭhāna* is mind, consciousness or thoughts, and the object of *dhammānupassanā-satipaṭṭhāna* is *dhamma* objects or mental objects.

Two weeks ago, we talked about the first *satipaṭṭhāna*, which is *kayānupassanā-satipaṭṭhāna*. We learned what *kāya* means, and what we need to contemplate on.

One of the things we can contemplate on with regard to the body is its 32 impure parts, including hair of the head, hair of the body, nails, teeth, skin, flesh, bones, sweat, blood, saliva, urine, feces, and so on. We'll study these 32 parts in detail later. But what do we see when we contemplate on these 32 parts one-by-one? We see the body as disgusting.

See how the object is different, and the seeing is different? You will see the body as disgusting. The Buddha taught us to contemplate our body to see its disgusting aspects. When you see these disgusting aspects, you will eradicate the wrong view that the body is beautiful.

Some people say, "My body is so beautiful." But when we see how disgusting it actually is, we can eradicate and abandon the wrong view that the body is beautiful. So can you see how abandoning is also different?

When we contemplate on the body, the object is the body, the seeing is disgust, and abandoned is the wrong view that the body is beautiful.

Vedanānupassanā-satipaṭṭhāna

This is contemplation of feelings. We have five kinds of feelings, right? Two of them regard the body, and three of them regard the mind. Briefly, there are three types of feeling: pleasurable, displeasurable, and neutral.

What will you see if you focus your mind on feeling? First, you may see a pleasurable feeling. Then, that pleasurable feeling will turn into a displeasurable feeling. The feeling changes. It changes all the time. And when you see these feelings changing all the time, you will see that these feelings are oppressed by arising and disappearing, arising and disappearing. What do you see then? *Dukkha*, or suffering. Mostly, you'll see suffering.

You might notice: "Just then, I felt comfortable but now I'm uncomfortable." You will see the changing of feeling. We call this *dukkha*. See how it's not just pain that is *dukkha*? Suffering here also refers to whatever is being oppressed by arising and disappearing. This suffering will be clear to your view.

So when you contemplate on feelings, you will see suffering. When you see suffering, you can eradicate the wrong view that this feeling—and this mind and body—are sources of pleasure. It is because you see suffering that you will know that *sukha* just leads to *dukkha*. By seeing this, you will eradicate the wrong view that this body and mind are pleasurable. They are just *dukkha*.

This *vedanānupassanā-satipaṭṭhāna* is very important. It's very obvious to everyone. When we practice meditation, *vedanā* occurs to the eyes, ears, nose, tongue, body and mind.

Let's look at some examples:

When an external object comes in contact with your eye, what happens? If it's a desirable object, what kind of feeling arises? Pleasurable. If the object is undesirable, a displeasurable feeling arises. And if the object is neither good nor bad, an indifferent feeling arises.

If you don't contemplate on *vedanā*, when you see a desirable object, a pleasurable feeling will arise and that will lead to craving (*lobha*). If it's an undesirable object, a displeasurable feeling will arise and lead to *dosa* (anger). If there's a neutral feeling, *moha* arises. You either won't know the nature of the object, or you'll ignore it, right? Ignorance is *moha*.

So, if we don't contemplate *vedanā*, there will be *lobha*, *dosa* and *moha*.

Q: Ultimately, do we want to experience all of our sensations as upekkhā? Instead of feeling pleasure or pain, should we see them all in a neutral way?

Just see them as they really are. Usually, pleasurable feelings or displeasurable feelings are very obvious and clear. But neutral feelings are usually not so clear. If we don't watch our eyes, ears, nose, tongue, body and mind, we won't understand the feelings and we may end up ignoring them.

If we see something as just 'seeing', there is just seeing-consciousness arising and disappearing. Seeing-consciousness is *cakkhuviññāṇa*. It is *upekkhā sahagata cakkhuviññāṇa*, right? It is eye-consciousness accompanied by indifferent feeling. If we have just "seeing, seeing," we are contemplating with *upekkhā*.

Without mindfulness, the three kinds of feelings can produce *lobha*, *dosa* and *moha*. As you know, pleasurable feelings can become craving, displeasurable feelings can become anger, and neutral feelings can become *moha*. You ignore neutral feelings, right? This is why we have to be aware of feelings all the time with whatever occurs at our six sense-doors, otherwise *lobha*, *dosa* and *moha* will arise.

We should practice in accordance with these foundations of mindfulness. We should contemplate on feelings. Whatever kind of feeling arises in the body or mind, it must be realized and stopped right there. If you're happy, just know "happy, happy, happy" and it will stop right there and go no further. If you don't stop it right there and it goes further, it will lead to grasping and you may think, speak or act with the intention to get or prolong that feeling.

We call this *paṭiccasamuppāda*, or the law of dependent origination. It just keeps on going. That's why we need to stop *vedanā*. When we see, it's just "seeing." When we hear, it's just "hearing." When we smell, it's just "smelling." When we taste, it's just "tasting." When we touch, it's just "touching." And when we think, it's just "thinking, thinking." When we practice like this, it will stop right there.

So what do we need? We need *sati*, or mindfulness.

Q: So we should keep upekkhā with all experiences? We're trying to keep upekkhā, right?

Yes, you can say that too.

But when you see suffering, you can abandon the wrong view of pleasure.

Cittānupassanā-satipaṭṭhāna

Sometimes our mind is passionate, sometimes it is dispassionate, sometimes it is angry, and sometimes it is lazy. Whatever occurs in the mind, we should make a mental note, realize it and identify it right away. We should know: "I'm angry" or "I'm lazy." Realize it and know.

Briefly, we should know what kind of consciousness we are experiencing. We studied 121 types of consciousness, of course, but meditators can't contemplate all of these. We can only contemplate mundane consciousness. We cannot make supramundane consciousness the object of our meditation.

When you want something, we call this having a passionate mind. If it arises, just realize it. And when that mind goes away, know that too. Or if you don't want something or you get angry, know that. If you feel lazy, know it as well.

Contemplating our mind like this is called *cittānupassanā-satipaṭṭhāna*.

The arising and disappearing of the mind is more obvious than that of matter. Do you remember when we talked about how mind arises and disappears 17 times faster than matter? On the occasion of matter arising and disappearing a single time, mind has arisen and disappeared 17 times.

So, mind is 17 times faster than matter. When you contemplate on this mind, you will see your mind just wandering around. You'll want something—this or that—and then you'll get angry about something else. Then you'll feel happy as a new pleasurable stimulant presents itself. All of this will occur in just a few minutes. The mind can change many, many times.

You will see this changing more clearly than when you contemplate on the body. You see that the mind moves very quickly—arising and disappearing. You can try to sit in meditation for five minutes, but your mind can travel all over the world in that time, right? You can see this impermanence.

When you contemplate the mind, you see impermanence very clearly. There is just arising and disappearing over and over. This impermanence is mostly what you see. When you see this impermanence, you can abandon the wrong view that the mind is permanent.

Some people hold the view that their mind doesn't really change. They may think that they've had essentially the same mind since they were born. The fact of the matter is that it's not the same mind. As we study and practice meditation, we know that the mind arises and disappears all the time. It is so clear to us that the mind is impermanent.

So, when you see impermanence, you will abandon the wrong view of the mind being permanent. It's the opposite, right? If you see impermanence, you know that there is not permanence.

We have to know the object, the seeing, and the abandoning.

Dhammānupassanā-satipaṭṭhāna

This is contemplation on *dhamma*, or mental objects. In this context, there are five *dhamma* (mental objects):

1) *Nīvaraṇa* (hindrances)

We already studied these.

2) *Khaṇḍa* (the five aggregates)
3) *Āyatana* (bases)

This is the eye-base, and so on.

4) *Sacca* (the truth)

The Four Noble Truths, right?

5) *Bojjhaṅga* (the factors of enlightenment)

We call these the five *dhamma* objects. We already study hindrances, but we will study the others today or the next time we meet. Although we haven't already studied all of them, all of you already know what the five aggregates are, right? You've already been introduced to the six sense-bases and the Four Noble Truths too. We'll study the seven factors of enlightenment later.

If we contemplate on one of these *dhamma* objects, we can't see them with the eyes, ears, nose, tongue or body. But we can see them with the mind. That's why we call them mental objects.

What is *nīvąraṇa*? Hindrances. They include sense desire, ill will, sloth and torpor, restlessness, and remorse or doubt.

When you contemplate on these *dhamma* objects, you may see that you want something—"I want this" or "I want that." This is sense desire. Your duty is to recognize that a hindrance is present in your mind. When sense desire disappears, you need to know that too. This means that you know when a hindrance arises and when it disappears. This is an example of *dhammānupassanā-satipaṭṭhāna*.

Sometimes, there will be ill will. You might get angry with someone. Or perhaps you feel unsatisfied about something. This ill will arises in the mind. You should know it: "Oh, I got angry." But you should also know when the anger disappears.

There is sometimes sloth and torpor also. This is when you don't want to do anything. You don't want to sit in meditation or do anything else that is skillful. There is drowsiness in that moment. This is sloth and torpor. You should know when this hindrance is present. And when it goes away, you should recognize: "Oh, now I don't feel sleepy. It went away." You know this. In other words, you should know when hindrances arise and disappear.

Sometimes the mind just wanders. Despite your best efforts to control the mind, it continues to wander. The mind is distracted. You should know that. And when you try to focus your mind on your primary object and your awareness is steady, you should know that your wandering mind has disappeared and been replaced with concentration. Know this.

You also sometimes feel remorse over things you've not done well. You may think about the past and feel sorrow. Try to know when this occurs, and when this state of mind has disappeared. You should know these things.

There are also times when you feel doubt. You have doubt about something and can't make a decision. "What should I do?" There's doubt, right? This is *vicikicchā*. When it arises in your mind, realize it. When it disappears, know that too.

I'm talking about *dhammānupassanā*, or mental objects. Everyone has experience with these. Perhaps we didn't know their names previously, but now we've studied their names and their natures. So, if someone says, "I have this emotion," you can know that it's a *dhamma* object. Whatever arises in the mind, just observe it. This is *dhammānupassanā*. It is an object of meditation.

Sometimes we try very hard to focus our mind on our primary object but it just wanders. We get angry with ourselves when this happens, right? If you know the proper technique, you know that this is an inappropriate way to react to the mind's behavior. If there is anger, just acknowledge that you're angry. Know that anger has occurred. Then, it will go away. It's impermanent, right?

Just try to observe whatever occurs in the mind.

What about *khaṇḍa*? We have five aggregates. What are they? They are body, feelings and sensations, perceptions, mental formations, and consciousness. Whichever one of these five occurs, just know "this body" or "this feeling" or "this perception" or "this mental formation" or "this consciousness" has arisen. Know when it has disappeared as well. These are also *dhamma* objects that we should know and contemplate on.

As for *āyatana*, we have these six bases: eye-base, ear-base, nose-base, tongue-base, body-base and mind-base. We've already studied these. When you see something, concentrate your mind on your eye and make a mental note: "seeing, seeing." When you see, what do you see? You see the object. In order to see the object, there is eye-sensitivity. When we have an eye-base, a visible object, and eye-sensitivity, eye-consciousness arises.

You should know that in every moment, objects present themselves to their respective doors and consciousness arises. It then disappears. It just arises and disappears. This is why we need to contemplate on and observe the eyes, ears, nose, tongue, body and mind. As we do, we are contemplating mental objects. Mentally note these experiences: "seeing...hearing...smelling...tasting...touching...thinking" and so on, as appropriate to the experience.

Sacca is the Noble Truths. We should know: "This is suffering." Why is there suffering? We should also know the cause. In other words, you know suffering and the cause. When you contemplate on suffering and its cause, you are contemplating on *dhamma* objects.

The last one is *bojjhaṅga*, of which there are seven. We'll study these later. They include mindfulness, investigation, effort, rapture, joy, concentration and equanimity. If you contemplate on these seven, you are contemplating on *dhamma* objects.

The scope of this contemplation is very wide, right? We can contemplate on these five areas, but in brief, whatever we contemplate on—maybe our body, *vedanā*, consciousness, or the hindrances, aggregates, bases, truths or factors of enlightenment—it's called *dhammānupassanā-satipaṭṭhāna* if we see the impermanent and suffering nature of those objects.

If we contemplate on the body—*kāyānupassanā-satipaṭṭhāna*—and see the arising and disappearing of the body, it is *dhammānupassanā-satipaṭṭhāna*. *Dhammānupassanā-satipaṭṭhāna* sees the nature of mind and body.

Q: How can we tell the difference between cittānupassanā-satipaṭṭhāna and dhammānupassanā-satipaṭṭhāna?

Citta is mind. If your mind wants something, we call it a passionate mind. If you want something, this mind arises. If you don't want something, that mind arises. If it wants something, contemplate on that. Know that your mind wants something. Know that a passionate mind has arisen. Then, it disappears. Know that there is no longer a passionate mind.

Sometimes, there is an angry mind. You're angry. Know that an angry mind has occurred. Later on, your angry mind goes away. Know that there is no longer an angry mind.

As *dhamma* objects, the mind contemplates hindrances, aggregates, bases, truths, and the factors of enlightenment. But briefly, if you see the nature of mind and body as arising and disappearing—in other words, you don't see body, feelings or *citta*, but only arising and disappearing—then we call this *dhammānupassanā-satipaṭṭhāna*.

Q: So citta is about mental states coming and going?

It's just mind. It's thought. It's consciousness.

But, to make it easy, *dhammānupassanā-satipaṭṭhāna* means that you see the nature of mind and matter as arising and disappearing. When you see *dhammānupassanā-satipaṭṭhāna*, you contemplate this mental object and see only arising and disappearing. You see this nature. There's no person here. You don't see anything as an entity, right? There's no individual. Instead, you just see arising and disappearing, which we call *anattā*. This means no-self. You see no-self, or *anattā*.

Whether it's *kāya* (body), *vedanā* (feeling) or *citta* (mind), you have no control over their arising. This is because it's their nature to arise and disappear all the time. When you know this *anattā* nature of arising and disappearing, you see no body, no man, no woman. You see *anattā*. When you see *anattā*, you can abandon the wrong view that there is self, soul or body, man or woman. You eradicate this wrong view. This is nature.

So, the objects are fourfold, right?

With *kāyānupassanā-satipaṭṭhāna*, what do we see? Disgust or impurity in the body. Which wrong view can we then eradicate? The beauty of the body. When we contemplate *vedanānupassanā-satipaṭṭhāna*, we see suffering. In seeing this suffering, we abandon the belief that this body and mind are pleasurable. With *cittānupassanā-satipaṭṭhāna*, we see impermanence. When we see impermanence, we eradicate the wrong view of permanence. And when we contemplate *dhammānupassanā-satipaṭṭhāna*, we see no self and uncontrollability. When we do, we eradicate the wrong view of self or soul. We see that there is no immortal soul.

So now we know the objects of these four foundations of mindfulness, as well as their seeing and abandoning. They're different, right? That's why the Buddha taught us *satipaṭṭhāna* as being fourfold.

These four foundations of mindfulness are especially necessary for those of us who practice insight (*vipassanā*) meditation. Without *satipaṭṭhāna*, we cannot experience *bojjhaṅgā*. This is strong mindfulness, investigation, effort, rapture, tranquility of the mind, concentration and equanimity (or neutrality) of mind. When we practice meditation and see the arising and disappearing of mind and matter, these seven factors of enlightenment will eventually occur. We can then realize the Noble Truths and gain enlightenment.

So, whatever technique you make your primary object of meditation, it's not insight (*vipassanā*) meditation if it doesn't consist of the four foundations of mindfulness. While some contemplate on external objects, we especially contemplate internally—our body, our feelings and our consciousness. As we see the nature of this body, feelings and consciousness, this is *dhammānupassanā-satipaṭṭhāna*.

The Four Sammappadhānā

Now we go to the four *sammappadhānā*. These are the four supreme efforts. I already explained to you about *sammāvāyāma*, or right effort. Right effort and supreme effort mean the same thing. So, *sammappadhānā* refers to the four kinds of right effort.

1) *Uppannānaṃ pāpakānaṃ pahānāya vāyāmo*

The name is long. Remember *vāyāmo*? What is this? Effort. *Uppannānaṃ pāpakānaṃ pahānāya vāyāmo* means the effort to discard evil that has arisen. *Uppannānaṃ* means arisen. *Pāpakānaṃ* means evil. *Pahānāya* means discard, or remove. And *vāyāmo* means effort. That's why this term means the effort to discard evil that has arisen.

When we practice meditation, anger, hatred, envy and so on can arise in our mind. As they arise, we have to realize it and label it. We have to identify it. Make a mental note. How we manage it depends on our specific technique, you know. As we make a mental note, we let greed, hatred, envy, jealousy go—right away. This is what is meant by effort to discard evil that has arisen.

I already explained to all of you about *sammāvāyāma* when we talked about the 12 *maggaṅga*. This is discarding evil that has arisen. If we have done something that is demeritorious, don't allow it to occur again. Don't think about it; try to forget it. If we don't repeat the bad things we've done in the past, then we can call that discarding old evil that we've done.

2) *Anuppannānaṃ pāpakānaṃ anuppādāya vāyāmo*

Anuppannānaṃ means unarisen, *pāpakānaṃ* is evil, and *anuppādāya* means not arising. So the full meaning of *anuppannānaṃ pāpakānaṃ anuppādāya vāyāmo* is the effort to prevent the arising of unarisen evil. This means not allowing new evil to occur in the mind.

This has to do with something you've never done before, right? Don't let it happen in your mind. Don't let new evil happen. For example, if you never before drank alcohol, put forth the effort to never start drinking alcohol.

3) *Anuppannānaṃ kusalānaṃ uppādāya vāyāmo*

Anuppannānaṃ means unarisen. *Kusalānaṃ* means good, or moral. *Uppādāya* means to develop, or to grow. *Vāyāmo* means effort. So *anuppannānaṃ kusalānaṃ uppādāya vāyāmo* means the effort to develop unarisen good. What you have never done before, try to do it. This has to do with moral actions, or good and meritorious things. For example, if you never practiced meditation before, start to do it.

4) *Uppannānaṃ kusalānaṃ bhiyyobhāvāya vāyāmo*

Uppannānaṃ means arisen, *kusalānaṃ* means good, and *bhiyyobhāvāya* means to promote. This is the effort to promote the arisen good. This refers to promoting and increasing meritorious things that we have already done but have not yet brought to perfection.

For example, if you normally sit in meditation twice a day, you now try to sit in meditation three times a day. Or if you usually practice meditation for one hour per day, you start to meditate for two hours each day.

See? You're increasing good things that you already do. This is the effort to promote arisen good.

We already discussed these four *sammappadhānā*, or supreme efforts, when we learned about *sammāvāyāma*, so I don't need to explain this in detail again.

What is their essential element? *Vāyāma* means *viriya*. *Viriya*, of course, is one kind of mental state. Usually, *viriya* associates with 73 types of consciousness. In this context, it only associates with 21 types. The *viriya* that associates with 21 types of wholesome consciousness is called *sammappadhānā*. This section talks about *bodhipakkhiya*, right? As factors of enlightenment, these *viriya* only take 21 types of wholesome consciousness. That's the reality of *sammappadhānā*.

See that, right? The reality of the four *satipaṭṭhāna* is just *sati cetasika*, and the reality of the four *sammappadhānā* is just *viriya*.

The Four Iddhipādā

Now we go to *iddhipādā*. *Iddhi* means accomplishment, and *pādā* means foundation, so the four *iddhipādā* means the four foundations of accomplishment. To be successful in our goals or aims, we need the four *iddhipādā*.

The four *iddhipādā* look like the four *adhipati*, or predominance:

1) *chandiddhipādā* (which is *chanda iddhipādā*)
2) *viriyiddhipādā* (which is *viriya iddhipādā*)
3) *cittiddhipādā* (which is *citta iddhipādā*)
4) *vīmaṃsiddhipādā* (which is *vīmaṃsā iddhipādā*)

Recently, we studied the four *adhipati*: 1) *chandādhipati*, 2) *viriyādhipati*, 3) *cittādhipati*, and 4) *vimaṃsādhipati*. They're the same as *iddhipādā*, right? But their names differ. *Chandiddhipādā* is will, the wish to do, or desire. *Viriyiddhipādā* is effort, *cittiddhipādā* is thought, and *vīmaṃsiddhipādā* means wisdom or reason.

Chandiddhipādā

Whatever you do, you need to have strong desire and strong will, otherwise, you cannot reach your goal. This is *chanda*. The reality is *chanda*. It's one kind of mental factor. This *chanda* is found in 21 types of wholesome consciousness, where it's called *chandiddhipādā*.

In our practice, we need to have the desire to be generous, practice morality (observe precepts), and do meditation. If we want to gain enlightenment, we have to have a strong desire to do these things. If we lack strong desire, what happens when we face obstacles in our practice? We want to quit, right? So we need strong desire. "I will try until I attain my goal." This is not normal *chanda*, or desire.

Viriyiddhipādā

This is strong effort. The reality—*viriya*—is another kind of mental factor. This *viriya* is found in 21 kind of wholesome consciousness.

Even if we have strong desire, we won't reach our goal if we are lazy and don't have strong effort too. We must have strong effort. One day has 24 hours, right? But how often do we sleep for 10 hours? We can't succeed in anything—even worldly affairs—if we behave like this.

It's sufficient to sleep 5-6 hours a night. By that, I don't mean you should sleep five or six hours but then spend the rest of your time watching television and movies. Spend your waking hours doing skillful things like practicing meditation. Please don't think: "Las Vegas Sayādaw said I should only sleep five or six hours, so I'll sleep six hours then get up and listen to music all day." That's not right. Instead, try your best to be mindful all the time. Practice meditation and use strong effort to fulfill your spiritual goals.

Cittiddhipādā

This is thought, consciousness—the mind. This mind is *citta*, right? How many types of *citta* do we have? We have 89 types, right? Here, we're talking about the eight types of supramundane consciousness. This is *magga* and *phala*.

We do not let the mind quit. We don't let someone or something stand between us and our goal. We try until we succeed. Especially when we are practicing meditation, we should make the decision: "As I practice meditation, I will let my body be reduced to skin and bones. I will let my flesh and blood dry up. I will try the best I can. Even if my life comes to an end, I will not quit until I reach my goal." Make this strong decision.

This is *iddhipādā*. It's not at a normal level, right? This is a foundation of accomplishment.

Again: "Let my body be reduced to skin and bones, let my blood and flesh dry up, let my life come to an end; I will not stop until I succeed." You should keep this in your mind.

Vīmaṃsiddhipādā

This is reason, or wisdom. Its reality is *amoha*. When we studied *cetasika* in the second chapter of the first book, we learned that wisdom associates with 47 types of consciousness. But here, it takes only 17 types of wholesome consciousness.

What are the 17 types? Wisdom associates with the four types of *mahākusala ñāṇa sampayutta*, right? It also associates with the nine types of sublime (*rūpa* and *arūpa*) wholesome consciousness. That's 13 types of consciousness. Plus, there are the four types of *magga citta*. We call these 17 types of consciousness by the term wholesome *ñāṇa sampayutta*. They are accompanied by wisdom. Their reality is *amoha*. When this is present in supramundane consciousness, it is called *iddhipādā*, or accomplishment. When we develop our mind—our desire, our effort, our thoughts, and our wisdom—to the highest level, which is supramundane consciousness, we call it *iddhipādā*.

When we practice meditation, we develop *bodhipakkhiyasaṅgaha*, or the factors of enlightenment. We experience the four *satipaṭṭhāna*, right? We experience body, feelings, thoughts and mental objects. We also experience *sammappadhānā*. We try so hard to gain enlightenment. We put forth *viriya*. And there's also *iddhipādā*. We have desire, effort, thought and wisdom. But, as I said, there must be a strong decision to develop this *iddhipādā*. If you're still attached to your body—"If I practice too hard, maybe I will injure my body and I could die"—you cannot gain enlightenment. You can't be concerned about things like this. Whatever happens—even if you have to die—that's fine; have the resolve: "I will not quit. I will try the best I can until I reach my goal."

The Five Indriya

Now we go to *indriya*. These are faculties. How many *indriya* did we study previously? Twenty-two. But those 22 *indriya* concerned mind and matter, mental states, and mind and mental states. Here, though, we're just talking about the five spiritual faculties. Why just five? Because they are factors of enlightenment.

Maybe all of you know these:

1) *Saddhindriya* (confidence or faith)
2) *Viriyindriya* (effort or energy)

3) *Satindriya* (mindfulness or awareness)
4) *Samādhindriya* (concentration)
5) *Paññindriya* (wisdom)

We must possess these five faculties strongly and powerfully, sharply and balanced, in order to gain enlightenment.

How about *saddhindriya*, or confidence? What is the reality? *Saddha cetasika*. This *saddha* is found in the eight types of *mahākusala*, the eight types of *mahākiriyā*, and the 26 types of *appaṇā javana*. That's a total of 42 types of consciousness with which this *saddha cetasika* associates. When we studied the second chapter of the first book, we learned that *saddha* associates with the 59 types of beautiful consciousness, right? But here, it associates with just 42 types because this *saddha* is a factor of enlightenment.

Viriyindriya (effort) is *viriya cetasika*. It associates with 42 types of consciousness. They are the same as *saddha*. For *satindriya* (mindfulness), the reality is *sati*. It associates with the same 42 types of consciousness as *saddha* and *viriya* here. The reality of *samādhindriya* (concentration) is *ekaggatā cetasika*. With how many types of consciousness can it associate? Normally, 89 types but here just 42 types of consciousness. Once again, this is because we're talking about factors of enlightenment. We are not concerned with something like *akusala* (unwholesome) consciousness here.

What about *paññindriya*, or wisdom? This *amoha* takes just 34 types of consciousness. What are they? They are the four types of *kusala* sense-sphere consciousness (*mahākusala*) accompanied by wisdom, the four types of *mahākiriyā ñāṇa sampayutta*, and the 26 types of *appaṇā javana*. That's a total of 34 types of consciousness. *Appaṇā javana* refers to the nine types of sublime wholesome consciousness, the nine types of sublime functional consciousness—that's 18 types—and the eight types of supramundane consciousness. That's 26 types in total. So, wisdom can normally associate with 47 types of consciousness, but only 34 types here.

Please remember that *saddha, viriya, sati, samādhi* and *paññā* here are not normal *saddha, viriya, sati, samādhi* and *paññā*. *Saddha* should be firm and strong confidence. It's not blind faith; instead, it should be based on right understanding. To gain enlightenment, we need strong and firm *saddha* that is based on right understanding. *Viriya* should be strong and strenuous effort or energy. *Sati* should be sustained and uninterrupted mindfulness. Be aware of every moment—just *sati, sati, sati, sati, sati, sati, sati, sati*—sustained and uninterrupted. This is the kind of mindfulness required here. As for *samādhi*, it should be deep concentration. And wisdom should be penetrative.

Wherever you go to practice meditation—whatever meditation center it may be—the teachers all talk about these *indriya* (faculties). They do this because these *indriya* are very important for meditators. If they are not balanced—that is, if one *indriya* is in excess—you cannot gain enlightenment.

What do I mean?

The Buddha taught us that our *saddha* (confidence) and our wisdom must be balanced if we are to gain enlightenment. If we have excessive confidence but deficient wisdom, then it leads to blind faith. Blind faith is an unreasonable belief. Therefore, we have to balance confidence with wisdom.

On the other hand, if we have excessive wisdom and deficient confidence, it leads to a lack of concentration. In other words, we'll practice meditation but have no concentration. Instead, due to our excessive wisdom, we'll be investigating everything—thinking about this and that—but without concentration. This is why the Buddha said that excessive wisdom with deficient confidence leads to no concentration.

In worldly affairs, good wisdom that lacks faith or confidence leads to dishonesty or cunningness. A person with good wisdom who knows everything but doesn't have confidence or faith can become a dishonest or cunning person that can't be trusted.

But, again, meditators with excessive wisdom and deficient confidence find themselves lacking concentration. They get lost in thinking about this or that. That's why we should balance *saddha* and *paññā*.

Our *samādhi* and *viriya* must be balanced too. *Viriya* means energy, right? It's effort. Great effort with weak concentration leads to restlessness. We might try so hard that we can't sleep. Perhaps we practice walking meditation too much, such that our energy overpowers our concentration. We then end up restless, distressed and distracted. This is why we should balance *viriya* and *samādhi*.

What about if we have strong and deep concentration with deficient energy? It leads to sluggishness or drowsiness. Some people sit in meditation a lot but barely practice walking meditation. They might walk for 10 minutes then sit in meditation for six hours. They might have good concentration, but they lack energy. What happens? They become sleepy and sluggish.

So, remember that *saddha* and *paññā* should be balanced. *Viriya* and *samādhi* should also be balanced.

But what about *sati*?

Strong *sati* is always necessary. There is no such thing as excessive *sati*. As such, it need not be balanced with any factors. So much, so strong—so good!

So, five faculties, right? Among the five, strong *sati* is always necessary.

It is very important for meditators to remember and follow this guidance. When we reflect on our meditation practice, we should bear this in mind. Consider our *saddha* and *paññā*. How are they? If we spend our time in meditation thinking about "the five aggregates," "the six sense-bases," or "*indriya*"—in other words, thinking instead of meditating—we may have a lot of wisdom but probably no concentration. On the other hand, if we have excessively strong faith, we may try to practice but don't have any understanding of how to practice properly. That's not good. For this reason, *saddha* and *paññā* should be balanced.

And don't forget that *viriya* and *samādhi* should be balanced as well. If we only practice walking meditation, that's not good. Practicing only sitting meditation isn't good either. Our postures should be balanced. After sitting in meditation, we should walk in meditation. And after doing walking meditation, we should do sitting meditation. Balance *viriya* and concentration.

And, once again, we should always have *sati*. It is necessary to be aware of any object—whether it occurs in our body or in our mind.

The Five Bala

This means power. These are the five powers:

1) *Saddhābala*
2) *Viriyabala*
3) *Satibala*
4) *Samādhibala*
5) *Paññābala*

So what's different from *indriya*? They are the same thing. Faculties and powers are the same. Their realities are the same. They are identical.

But *indriya* and *bala* have distinct properties. *Indriya* (faculties) have the ability to control the mind. *Bala* (powers) have the ability to be firm and cannot be overcome by opposing force.

In order to gain enlightenment, we need to sharpen our five faculties (*indriya*). If they are weak, it means that they are not sharp enough. As such, we can't gain enlightenment. So to gain enlightenment, we need to sharpen them. We have nine ways to sharpen the five mental faculties, which some of you may already know.

1) Realize the impermanence of mental and physical processes.

This is very important.

When you practice meditation, you might contemplate on your body, your feelings, your mind, or perhaps *dhamma* objects such as the hindrances or the five aggregates. But your aim should be to realize impermanence. You should see impermanence in every moment.

For example, you might contemplate on feelings or sensation and see pain. If you just see pain (*vedanā*), it's not enough. What do we have to see? The impermanence of *vedanā*. Feeling just arises and disappears, arises and disappears. It does this all the time, in every moment. You have to see this in your feelings. Feeling is just arising and disappearing all the time.

As another example, you might practice walking meditation and know that as you step you are lifting, pushing and dropping the foot. But just seeing the movement is not enough for a meditator who practices insight (*vipassanā*) meditation. We have to know the arising and disappearing of physical and mental processes in every moment. This is what is meant by realizing the impermanence of mental-physical process. This is very important. You should see this, and if you do, we call it *vipassanā* meditation. Otherwise, it's tranquility meditation.

I try to guide people to concentrate on the rising and falling of their abdomen. If they just see rising and falling, it's not enough. What do they have to see? They have to realize the impermanence. There is rising, then it goes away. There's nothing left, right? Then there's falling, which then goes away. Again, nothing left. In every moment, see impermanence.

If you see something pass in front of you—"seeing"—it's not enough if you only know the seeing. That's tranquility meditation. What passes in front of you appears and then disappears. See the impermanence. Whatever you see, hear, smell, taste, touch or think, see the impermanence (*anicca*).

Realizing the impermanence of mental-physical process is one way to sharpen our faculties. We have nine ways, but we'll just talk about this one today. We'll discuss the remaining eight ways next week.

Time's up. Thank you.

Any questions?

Q: When we contemplate the disgustingness of the body to overcome the feeling that it's beautiful, isn't that going to the other extreme?

No, it's not extreme. This practice encourages us to consider the hair on the head, the hair on the body, the skin, the nails, the teeth, the lungs, the kidneys—the body inside and out—to see impurities. When we see impurities, we see that which is disgusting. We will see that the body is not beautiful.

If we think that the body is beautiful, we call that *subha*. But when we see *asubha* (impurity), we discard the wrong view that the body is pretty and beautiful inside and out. When we see the impurity of our body, we eradicate this wrong view.

Q: The body is just energy, right? Isn't it the mind that labels the body as being beautiful? The body isn't different from anything else—it's just a neutral thing made of cells.

Yes, but some people have the wrong view about their body. For example, they might look at their hair and think it's so pretty. Then they become attached to their hair. Craving follows. But to get rid of craving, the Buddha taught us to contemplate on the 32 impure parts of the body. This is the main purpose of this technique.

...

Today is March 14, 1999. Last week, we started talking about the nine ways to sharpen the five mental faculties. Remember? We were talking about the first one. What was it? Aim to realize the impermanence of mental-physical process.

Before starting to practice meditation, we learned that mind and matter are impermanent. We know this in an intellectual sense, but not through practical knowledge. So when we start to practice meditation, we need an aim. The aim should be to see the impermanence of mind and body.

We practice the four kinds of mindfulness meditation, right? When we contemplate the body, it's not enough if we just see the movement of the body. If we just see feeling and don't see the impermanence (arising and disappearing), it's not enough. We have to see the arising and disappearing of mind and body.

When we practice meditation, we have to aim to realize the impermanence. Whatever our primary object is—maybe a sensation, the nostrils, breathing in and out, the movement of the abdomen—we need to see the impermanence. If we contemplate on the rising and falling of the abdomen but don't see impermanence, then it's not *vipassanā*. When we see impermanence, we call it insight (*vipassanā*) meditation.

Sometimes people practice meditation and experience a painful feeling. They might reflect: "Five minutes after starting the meditation, there was pain. And it stayed there for the whole hour!" People usually think that they experienced one long, prolonged feeling of pain. But it's not like that. Pain, too, just arises and disappears. Old water flows out and new water flows in. It's the same. It continues, right?

To see the arising and disappearing of experiences step by step, we need to aim to see impermanence while practicing meditation. This is one way to sharpen our mental faculties.

2) Practice seriously and with respect.

This means practicing with respect to our meditation technique. We have learned how to practice sitting meditation, how to transition from standing to sitting, from sitting to standing, and how to practice walking meditation, right? With walking meditation, we know there are different steps, different sections. We know how to practice this technique. So when we know the technique, we have to seriously practice and with respect to the technique.

As an example, we observe our abdomen as our meditation technique. This is our primary object. Our mind should be fixed on the right place and the right time. When there is rising, our mind should be on the movement of our abdomen rising. As for the 'right time', it should be the present moment. We shouldn't note "rising" after the abdomen has risen. Doing so is not respecting the technique. We should observe the primary object at the right place and the right time.

When we go from sitting to standing up, our movements should be slow. Slow down movements whenever practicing meditation. Movements should be slow and gentle. As we slowly stand up—step by step—we can see our movements one by one. This is what it means to seriously practice with respect to the technique of meditation.

When we walk, there is a lifting of the legs. From the beginning of the lifting, the mind should focus on the movement of the lifting of the leg. The mind follows the movement. When pushing forward, the mind should observe the pushing forward of the foot. This knowing of 'pushing' or 'moving' should be in the present moment. Next, dropping of the foot follows. Again, we're talking about practicing with respect to the technique. It should be at the right place and the right time.

Whatever our daily activity, we should slow down and closely and attentively observe our object. As we do, we can gain concentration. Otherwise, we can't control the mind. We have to focus our mind on our object—perhaps the eyes, the ears, the nose, the tongue, the body, the mind, or sensations. Practice seriously and with respect.

3) Maintain continuity of awareness.

Your awareness should be uninterrupted. From moment to moment, just be aware of whatever occurs in your body or mind. Just try to observe and contemplate whatever object is present. Be mindful all the time. No resting. Just continue your awareness from moment to moment.

We might sit in meditation and contemplate the four foundations of mindfulness for one hour. Afterward, we might feel tired and think we should lie down and take a nap. "Maybe I'll stop for a while." You cannot do that. Awareness should be uninterrupted. This is necessary to sharpen our mental faculties.

4) Suitability must be observed.

We have seven kinds of suitabilities. Perhaps some of you already know about these.

Suitable Place

The place where you practice meditation should be quiet. It should also be clean. If it's too old, it will need to be repaired again and again. This could lead to a loss of concentration. This is why your place should be suitable.

Suitable Resort

Many monks have to go out each day with their alms bowls and walk to collect food for survival. The place, the resort should not be too far or too close to the place where meditation is practiced. It should be suitably easy to get food to survive.

In the context of lay meditators, this means that food should be very easy to get. It shouldn't be difficult. If you are staying somewhere for meditation and it's very difficult to acquire available food, then it's not suitable resort. When you practice meditation, food should be easy to get.

Again, for monks, going on alms round to get food should be neither too far nor too close to where we practice meditation.

Suitable Speech

This means that when we're practicing meditation, it's best for us if we don't talk. Perhaps we get confused about something or have a doubt about our meditation technique. It then becomes necessary to discuss the matter with our meditation teacher. Otherwise, quiet is best.

Suitable speech is to talk only when really necessary.

Suitable Person

This is especially referring to a teacher. When you practice meditation, you should have a suitable meditation teacher. When a teacher gives you instruction, you can gain concentration easily. As you do, you can realize the nature of mind and matter.

Also, though, suitable fellow meditators are important. When we practice meditation with others, how do we feel if we don't get along with one of the people? This isn't good for meditation. But, especially important is a suitable meditation teacher.

Suitable Food

The food that we eat every day should be suitable for our health. If we can't get suitable food, we can't gain concentration. Of course, we sometimes need to adjust our attitude to accept whatever food is available to us. But Asian people, for example, cannot always eat all types of American food. They might not be able to eat bread or hot dogs. If they have to eat these foods and then go practice meditation, they may feel hungry later. Their hunger may be unsatisfied, thus leading to difficulty gaining concentration.

Suitable food is necessary.

Suitable Climate

If the place where we practice meditation is too hot or too cold, we can't easily gain concentration. People practicing meditation in America don't usually have to worry about this because we have air conditioning and heaters. But people in some countries don't have a chance to adjust their climate. They just have to accept whatever nature brings to them. As such, sometimes it's very hot or very cold.

Suitable Posture

We have four postures, right? We have sitting, standing, walking and lying down. A beginner meditator should not practice lying down meditation because they might fall asleep very quickly. This is not a suitable posture for beginners. On the other hand, if we practice only standing meditation then we will experience pain very easily. This pain may make it difficult to gain deep concentration. What's best, then, is to practice a combination of sitting and walking meditation.

If we just sit in meditation all day, even our good concentration eventually turns to drowsiness. As such, we should not sit in meditation the entire day. But if all we do is practice walking meditation all day, we will find our mind getting distracted. So, we should adjust as needed to a suitable posture. This means doing sitting meditation and then walking meditation. These two postures of meditation are suitable postures.

Additionally, we should pay attention to which postures are suitable to our health and body. Folks lacking strong legs can't easily do walking meditation, right? They need to sit in meditation. So it depends on our health and body too.

So we have seven kinds of suitabilities. These suitabilities must be observed in order to develop and sharpen the five mental faculties.

5) Remember how to achieve the concentration that was attained previously.

After we have practiced meditation many, many times over many, many days and years—especially if we sometimes spend a few days or a week or two in a retreat—we may remember a time when we sat in meditation and gained deep concentration. When that happens, try to remember what type of position you were in. In other words, how were you working with the mind when you gained that good concentration? Then, whenever you get into a difficult situation in your meditation and you're having difficulty controlling your mind, you may be able to remember the causes of your previous good mindfulness and concentration and establish them again.

So try to notice what circumstances led to this good practice. While working with the mind and gaining good concentration, how did you experience a sensation such as pain? If there was pain, how did you overcome it to gain concentration? Remember your personal experience and try to use the same technique.

We're talking here about remembering how to achieve the concentration that was attained previously.

6) Develop the seven factors of enlightenment.

The seven favors of enlightenment are called *bojjhaṅga*. They include *sati, dhammavicaya, viriya, pīti, passadhi, samādhi* and *upekkhā*. *Sati* is mindfulness, right? *Dhammavicaya* means investigation of the truth, *viriya* is effort, *pīti* is rapture or joy, *passadhi* is tranquility of the mind, *samādhi* is concentration, and *upekkhā* is equanimity.

We have to develop these seven factors of enlightenment. It's not necessary to adjust *sati*, as we learned previously. But as for investigation, effort, rapture, we'll become agitated if we have too much of them. Therefore, we need to adjust and balance some of these factors of enlightenment. As for how to do that, we'll discuss that later.

7) Disregard body and life.

This means courageous effort. When we practice meditation, we don't have to worry about our body or our life. Some people might think: "I practiced meditation from 3 am to 11 pm. I'm tired. I hope I don't get sick from not resting enough." They worry about their body and health, right? There's no need to worry about that.

We have this good opportunity while we're still young and strong to practice meditation. If we get sick, or when we become too old, we won't have a chance to practice like this. So use this time, this life, this good opportunity, to practice meditation. We don't have to worry about our health, our body or our life.

If we're sitting in meditation and have a painful feeling, we might think: "Oh, I need to change my position or I might become paralyzed." Sometimes people worry like this. "I hope I don't fall down from doing so much walking meditation!" Don't worry about that. Nothing will happen. The more you have concentration, and especially deep concentration, the more easily you can overcome painful sensations.

So, courageous effort is necessary to develop in order to sharpen our mental faculties.

8) Have patience and perseverance in the face of pain.

Every meditator comes across painful sensations. But we have to be patient with these sensations. This is *vedanā*. It is not our enemy. Rather, it is our friend. If you are patient with unpleasant sensations and try to attentively observe their nature, you will see the arising and disappearing of sensation. You will know its nature as impermanent. As you do, a sensation like pain can lead you to attain enlightenment. So, a painful sensation is not your enemy. Try to stay with it. A painful sensation won't last long.

Mostly, when we sit in meditation, we fail to observe feelings. We usually ignore them. We might feel numb from sitting a long time but often don't know that we're numb until we get up from the meditation. This is because of a lack of concentration. When we practice meditation and try to develop concentration and eventually gain deep concentration, we will easily feel pain because of that very concentration. When we sit in meditation with good concentration, whatever happens to our head or face—maybe itching, or even the slightest small thing touches our body—we will know it because of our good concentration. But if we lack concentration, we will not know it. Be patient with sensations, especially painful ones.

Suppose you sit in meditation for five minutes and start to feel pain. If you can't be patient with the pain, you'll change your position. If the pain keeps coming back, you'll keep changing your position. If you're changing your position every five minutes, you can't gain concentration. Without concentration, you can't gain wisdom. We have to know the nature of experiences, right?

We should be patient and closely observe painful feelings. If we do, we will see their nature. We will see what they really are. They're like flames. When a fire burns, a flame arises. But it's not just one flame. The flame burns out then a new flame continues on. It has the appearance of being a continuing fire, so we say it's the same thing, but it's not just the same flame over and over.

In the same way, a painful feeling is not the same painful feeling from beginning to end. Every moment, there is just arising and disappearing, arising and disappearing. We will see vibration, arising and disappearing. We'll see our noting mind too. What will we see? We won't see the shape of our body. Instead, we will just see sensation and the noting mind. The sensation and the noting mind arise and go away, arise and go away, in every moment. This means we're seeing impermanence, right? Just arising and disappearing.

So we have to be patient with sensations of pain.

But not only painful feelings. We also need to be patient with other obstacles that disturb us. If someone makes a noise, be patient. If you lack patience, you won't gain concentration. Meditators in particular sometimes need to force themselves to be patient. As we settle into meditation, be patient for at least that hour of practice. If we change our position 10 or 20 times over the course of the hour, that's not right.

9) Do not stop halfway to your goal.

What is our goal? Enlightenment. Enlightenment here doesn't mean the first stage of enlightenment. The first stage to the fourth stage—until we gain *arahant* and eradicate all mental defilements—that is our goal. Do not stop halfway. Do not stop until you gain the fourth and final stage of enlightenment.

Make a strong determination: "Until I gain the first stage...the second stage...the third stage...the fourth stage of enlightenment, I will not stop my spiritual work. I will try to practice meditation." This should be a strong determination. Otherwise, as soon as your concentration starts to get a little better, you stop. Then, you can't gain anything else. See? It's not just enlightenment here. A lack of determination also stands in the way of deepening concentration.

In the time of the Buddha, they didn't have matches. If they needed to make a fire, what did they do? They would use two sticks or two stones and rub them together until they got warm, and then hot, and then later, fire. See? They'd get fire from rubbing two sticks or stones together until a fire was started. But what happens if you rub two stones together until they get warm, then hot, then hotter, and then you stop just before a fire starts? The stones get cold again. Then, if you start again, the stones get warm. But what if you stop again? Cold.

You can't make a fire that way, right?

Try the best you can for the rest of your life. Don't stop halfway. From the time you get up in the morning until the time you fall asleep at night, try to practice the best you can. This is our duty. We should do this until we reach our destination and succeed at our goal.

These are the nine ways to sharpen our mental faculties. When our mental faculties become powerful and strong, we gain enlightenment. What are the five mental faculties? Confidence/faith, effort, mindfulness, concentration and wisdom. We need to use these nine ways to sharpen them so that they can be powerful and strong.

If we haven't gained enlightenment yet, why is that? It is because our mental faculties aren't so strong or powerful. Why aren't they so strong or powerful? Because we lack one of these nine ways. So we should examine ourselves to know what way, thing or technique we still need to fulfill. Use these techniques, use these guidelines, and you can fulfill your spiritual goal.

The Seven Bojjhaṅga

Now we go to *bojjhaṅga*, or *bodhi-aṅga*. *Bojjhaṅga* means *bodhi-aṅga*. *Bodhi* means enlightenment, and *aṅga* means factor or constituent. So *bojjhaṅga* means the constituents of enlightenment.

If we practice meditation and reach the knowledge of rising and falling—that is, we see the arising and disappearing of mind and matter—at that time, we are experiencing the seven *bojjhaṅga*.

1) *Satisambojjhaṅga*

Sam here means good. *Sati* is mindfulness, right? This is mindfulness, which is one of the constituents of enlightenment. We're talking about mindfulness, or awareness.

The *paramattha dhamma* (reality) is *sati*. *Sati* can normally associate with how many types of consciousness? It can normally associate with the 59 types of *sobhaṇa* (beautiful) *citta*. But here, it associates with only 42 types of consciousness. What are they? They are the eight types of *mahākusala*, the eight types of *mahākiriyā*, and the 26 types of *appaṇā javana*.

So *sati* in these 42 types of consciousness is called *satisambojjhaṅga*.

2) *Dhammavicayasambojjhaṅga*

Dhamma means truth, right? *Vicaya* means investigation. So this is investigation of the truth. The truth means the nature of mind and body.

The reality of investigation of truth is *amoha*. What's *amoha*? It is wisdom. But it's not normal wisdom. It is *vipassanā* knowledge. This wisdom sees mind and matter as they truly are. This is *amoha*.

This *amoha* is one kind of mental factor. It normally associates with 47 types of consciousness, but here, it only associates with 34 types. What are they? They are the four types of sense-sphere wholesome consciousness accompanied by wisdom, the four types of sense-sphere functional consciousness accompanied by wisdom, and the 26 types of *appaṇā javana*. This is the reality of *dhammavicayasambojjhaṅga*.

The reality is very important. If we study *Suttanta* (discourses), we won't see mention of realities. They just call it wisdom. But now we know exactly what realities are.

3) *Viriyasambojjhaṅga*

This is effort or energy, right? We can also say that it's endeavor or diligence.

Viriya normally associates with 73 types of consciousness, but here, it just associates with 42 types. It is the same 42 types as *satisambojjhaṅga*. *Viriyasambojjhaṅga* refers to *viriya* in these 42 types of consciousness.

4) *Pītisambojjhaṅga*

Pīti is rapture or joy. *Pīti* normally associates with 51 types of consciousness, but here, just 38 types. What are they? To begin, they are the combined eight types of *mahākusala* and *mahākiriyā somanassa*. This is the four types of sense-sphere wholesome consciousness accompanied by pleasurable feeling and the four types of sense-sphere functional consciousness accompanied by pleasurable feeling. Do you remember this from the first chapter of the first book?

Okay, the 38 types also includes the combined three types of *rūpāvacara* (form-sphere) first *jhāna*, second *jhāna* and third *jhāna* wholesome consciousness. It doesn't include resultant consciousness—just wholesome and functional consciousness. Do you remember when we studied form-sphere consciousness? They have first *jhāna*, second *jhāna* and third *jhāna* wholesome consciousness, and first *jhāna*, second *jhāna* and third *jhāna* functional consciousness. There's no resultant consciousness taken here. We're talking here about the factors of enlightenment. *Vipāka citta* cannot function as part of a meditation practice. That's why we're only taking wholesome and functional consciousness.

What are the factors of the first *jhāna*? *Vitakka, vicāra, pīti,* and so on. What about the second *jhāna*? *Vicāra, pīti,* and so on. The third *jhāna* starts with *pīti*. Can you see how *pīti* associates only with the first, second and third form-sphere *jhānas*? The fourth *jhāna* starts from *sukha*, with no *pīti*. So, we can call the first, second and third *jhāna* by the term *javana*. *Javana* is not *vipāka*—not resultant. It is just wholesome and functional consciousness.

So if we take the three types of *rūpāvacara* wholesome consciousness and the three types of *rūpāvacara* functional consciousness, that's six types of consciousness. Plus, we had the four types of sense-sphere wholesome *somanassa citta* and the four types of sense-sphere functional *somanassa citta* we already talked about. That's a total of 14 types of consciousness.

Next, we add the eight types of supramundane first *jhāna* consciousness, the eight types of supramundane second *jhāna* consciousness, and the eight types of supramundane third *jhāna* consciousness. That's 24 types of consciousness.

These, plus the 14 types we just talked about, totals 38 types of consciousness. *Pīti* associating with these 38 types of consciousness is called *pītisambojjhaṅga*.

Can you see why you weren't supposed to forget when we studied consciousness in the first chapter of the first book?

5) *Passadhisambojjhaṅga*

This is quietude or tranquility of the mind. Its reality is *passadhi*: *kāyapassadhi* and *cittapassadhi*. When we studied the second chapter of the first book, we learned about these. *Kāyapassadhi* and *cittapassadhi* are mental states, or *cetasika*. They are calmness, serenity or tranquility.

This *passadhi* is in 42 types of consciousness, same as *sati*.

Do you remember *kāyapassadhi* and *cittapassadhi*?

6) *Samādhisambojjhaṅga*

This is concentration. Its reality is *ekaggatā cetasika*. It associates with 42 types of consciousness, same as *sati*.

7) *Upekkhāsambojjhaṅga*

This is equanimity or neutrality of mind. Its reality is *tatramajjhattatā cetasika*, which is one kind of mental factor. *Tatramajjhattatā* is in 42 types of consciousness.

Tatramajjhattatā is equanimity. In the second chapter of the first book, we studied the 52 types of mental states, right? This is one of them. When we talk about the four sublime *brahmā vihāra*, we talk about *mettā, karuṇā, muditā* and *upekkhā*. *Upekkhā* is *tatramajjhattatā*. It's not a feeling; it's equanimity.

So, these are the seven *bojjhaṅga*. We experience these when we practice meditation well.

The first one is *sati*, or awareness. You know if you have good mindfulness, right? Before you do something, know your mind first. Whatever you do, have good *sati*. In terms of *bojjhaṅga*, you will experience this good mindfulness.

The second one is investigation of truth. This is seeing mind and matter as they truly are. You'll know: "Oh, this arises and disappears, comes and goes away. It doesn't last long. It's impermanent." You will know this when you practice meditation well and gain *udayabbaya ñāṇa*—the knowledge that sees arising and disappearing.

The third one is *viriya*. Here, your energy is not like it was before. It's now so strong.

The fourth one is *pīti*. Some of you have experienced rapture before. We have five kinds of *pīti*. When there is *bojjhaṅga*, you will experience one of these five kinds of rapture.

The fifth one is *passadhi*, or tranquility of mind. The body will feel light and tranquil too. Your body and mind will experience this.

The sixth one is concentration. You will have good concentration. You will know that today's concentration was not like yesterday's concentration. You will notice an improvement in your concentration.

The last one is *upekkhā*, or equanimity. In the past, you would have gotten angry if you encountered an undesirable object. Or craving would occur if the object was desirable. Now, there's no love or hate. There is just equanimity.

You will experience all of these constituents of enlightenment when you practice meditation. Not in the beginning, of course. When you reach *udayabbaya ñāṇa*—step by step—you will gain concentration and see impermanence, suffering and non-self. Especially, you will see the arising and disappearing of mind and matter. Then, you will experience these seven kinds of *bojjhaṅga*.

These seven *bojjhaṅga* are like the five mental faculties, in that we sometimes need to adjust them. When we studied the mental faculties, we learned that our faith and wisdom should be balanced, right? Our concentration and effort should also be balanced. Well, it's the same thing with *bojjhaṅga*. Investigation, effort and rapture must sometimes be adjusted with tranquility, concentration and equanimity. As I've told you, if we have too much investigation, effort and rapture, we will become agitated. If there's too much tranquility, concentration and equanimity, we become sluggish and drowsy. These two groups should be balanced. Of course, *sati* doesn't need to be balanced with any factors.

Now, I'd like to briefly share about how to develop these *bojjhaṅga*, or constituents of enlightenment.

Sati

To gain mindfulness, what do we need?

1) Constant noting of one's motion. We should always be aware of our daily physical activities.
2) Associating with the mindful.

There are many, many things we can do, but I just told you two.

Dhammavicaya

What do we need to do to develop investigation of the truth? We need to balance between *saddhā* (faith), wisdom, effort, concentration, and so on.

Viriya

What do we need to develop our effort?

1) Contemplating the dangers of the woeful states of existence, keeping in mind the benefit of energy.

2) Contemplating the greatness of the path and fruition.

Contemplating the dangers of the woeful states of existence means that as we are now human beings, we have opportunities to do good things like practice meditation. If we are unfortunate enough to be reborn in a woeful state after death, we will have no opportunity to practice meditation because we will have to suffer all the time. As human beings, we sometimes come across painful feelings or sensations, but this is quite different from what we would experience in the woeful states.

Why do we practice meditation? To gain enlightenment. If you gain the first stage of enlightenment, you will never again be reborn in a woeful state.

If you think about this, energy and effort will arise. It's also good to bear in mind the benefit of having energy. If you use your energy when you practice meditation, you will get the result—no mental defilements will come to interfere with or disturb your mind.

As for contemplating the greatness of the path and fruition, it's helpful to reflect that we can gain *magga* (path) and *phala* (fruition) through our practice of meditation. If we gain even the first stage of enlightenment, we will have to be reborn no more than seven more times. And, of course, we could have gone to hell upon death if our wrong actions in the past gave their results. But when you gain enlightenment, the door to the woeful states is closed.

So, think about these things. If you do, you'll want to try the best you can. These are good ways to develop your *viriya*.

Pīti

To develop rapture, recollect the attributes of the Buddha, the Dhamma, and the Saṅgha. When we do our chanting, we reflect on the attributes of the Buddha, his teachings, and his disciples. Recollecting these things can lead to rapture. Sometimes we need to do this, such as when the mind becomes lazy and drowsy. We use *pīti* to overcome these states.

Passadhi

To develop tranquility of mind, we should have wholesome food, agreeable weather conditions, comfortable postures, and so on. In other words, we need suitable food, weather and posture to develop tranquility of mind.

Samādhi

To develop concentration, just balance between *saddhā* and *paññā*, effort and concentration, and so on.

Upekkhā

To develop equanimity, maintain the balance between loving and hating by contemplating the fact that *kamma* alone is one's possession.

The Eight Maggaṅga

Now we go to *maggaṅga*. This is very, very important for meditators.

Maggaṅga is *magga aṅga*. *Magga* means path, the way. *Aṅga* means constituents. So *maggaṅga* means path constituents, which we call the Noble Eightfold Path.

Magga is a *Pāli* word comprised of two words, two syllables. *Ma* means kill, and *gga* means goes. So, kill and go. What do we have to kill? Mental defilements. Where do we go? We go to *nibbāna*.

Please remember these two words: *ma* and *gga*. Very easy. *Ma* is killing—the killing of passion and mental defilements that allows us to go to *nibbāna*.

This is *magga*:

1) *Sammādiṭṭhi* (right understanding)

2) *Sammāsaṅkappa* (right thought, or right thinking)
3) *Sammāvācā* (right speech)
4) *Sammākammanta* (right action)
5) *Sammājīva* (right livelihood)
6) *Sammāvāyāma* (right effort)
7) *Sammāsati* (right mindfulness)
8) *Sammāsamādhi* (right concentration)

What are their *paramattha dhammas* (realities)?

Sammādiṭṭhi

The reality is *amoha* (wisdom), which associates with 34 types of consciousness. These are the same as *dhammavicayasambojjhaṅga*.

Sammāsaṅkappa

The reality of right thought is *vitakka*. This *vitakka* takes only 26 types of consciousness. What are they? Normally, *vitakka* takes 55 types of consciousness, but it takes just these 26 types because we're talking about the path of enlightenment. We're not concerned with unwholesome consciousness here. The 26 include the eight types of *mahākusala* (that's sense-sphere wholesome consciousness), the eight types of *mahākiriyā* (sense-sphere functional consciousness), and first *jhāna*.

How many first *jhāna* are there? Here, it's taking just 10 types of first *jhāna*. It does not take *rūpāvacara vipāka* first *jhāna* because *vipāka citta* in *rūpāvacara* does not function as part of the path of enlightenment. So it just takes 10 types of first *jhāna*.

What are the 10 types? They are the one type of *rūpa* (form-sphere) wholesome consciousness and the one type of *rūpa* functional consciousness. That's two. We don't take *vipāka*, right? Plus, we take the eight types of supramundane first *jhāna*. That's a total of 10 types.

So, that's the eight *mahākusala*, the eight *mahākiriyā*, and first *jhāna javana*. If we see the word *javana*, it means there's no *rūpa vipāka*. So we're subtracting one type from the 11 types. That one type being subtracted is *rūpa vipāka*. Excluding that one, we take just form-sphere wholesome first *jhāna*, form-sphere functional first *jhāna*, and supramundane first *jhāna*. Altogether, that's 26 types of consciousness.

This *vitakka* associates with these 26 types of consciousness. This is the essential element of *sammāsaṅkappa*.

Sammāvācā

The reality of right speech is *sammāvācā*, which arises in 16 types of consciousness. These include the eight types of *mahākusala* and the eight types of *lokuttara*.

Sammākammanta

This is right action. The reality—*sammākammanta*—arises in 16 types of consciousness.

Sammājīva

The reality of right livelihood is *sammājīva*, which associates with 16 types of consciousness.

Sammāvāyāma

This is right effort, whose reality is *viriya*. This *viriya* associates with 42 types of consciousness. But, here, *viriya* is not normal *viriya*. Right effort implies the four supreme efforts, which we've already discussed. You remember the four *sammappadhānā*, right?

Sammāsati

The reality of right mindfulness is *sati*, which associates with 42 types of consciousness.

Sammāsamādhi

This is right concentration. Its reality is *ekaggatā*, which associates with 42 types of consciousness.

We already talked about the natures of these when we studied the 12 types of *maggaṅga* when we discussed mixed categories, right?

Sammādiṭṭhi (right understanding) is right view, right belief or right knowledge. It is knowledge of the Four Noble Truths. All of our actions should be regulated by this wisdom.

When we practice meditation, we will come to see the Four Noble Truths. Later, we will discuss exactly what "noble truth" means. But in every moment, we experience Noble Truths, especially the truths of suffering and the cause of suffering. As for the cessation of suffering, we experience that just momentarily.

Let's look at an illustration of this:

When you practice sitting meditation, you may experience an intense painful sensation. This is suffering, right? If you're not aware of the nature of the sensation, you may feel a desire to get up and move away from the suffering. In other words, you'll want to change your position. What makes you want to change your position? Your desire.

But when we contemplate feeling and sensation, we see their nature. We will know the nature of *vedanā*. As we do, there is no craving and no desire that arises. We will see suffering and the cause of suffering. Why do we suffer? We will know this. As we see the nature of *vedanā*, we will momentarily see cessation, or *nirodha*. It's not really *nibbāna*, but in that moment our mental defilements (greed and craving) will not occur.

Why won't they occur? Because you observe the object. What's doing the observing? Right understanding, or right view. This is *magga*, right?

You will experience these Four Noble Truths.

The second factor is *vitakka*, or right thought. Right understanding leads to right thought. When you have right understanding, you have good thoughts. What are right (good) thoughts? You don't think about sensual desires, ill will or cruelty. Instead, you think about renunciation, loving-kindness, and non-cruelty. This is right thinking.

Right understanding and right thought—these two factors of the Path—lead to right speech, right action and right livelihood. So when you have right understanding, you have right speech, right action and right livelihood.

What do we need in order to have right understanding and right thought? We need right effort, right mindfulness and right concentration.

As all of you may know, right understanding and right thought are grouped as wisdom, which we can also call *paññā khandha*, or *paññā sikkhā*. *Sikkhā* means training. *Khandha* means group.

Right speech, right action and right livelihood constitute *sīla*, or moral training. We can also call this *sīla khandha*, or *sīla sikkhā*.

Right effort, right mindfulness and right concentration are included in *samādhi*, or concentration. We can call this *samādhi khandha*, or *samādhi sikkhā*.

These eight *maggaṅga*, which we call the Noble Eightfold Path, are very important for meditators. They are very, very important.

Right effort, right mindfulness, right concentration, right understanding and right thought—these five factors—are called the five workers. In every moment that you make a mental note and observe your primary object or your meditation object, these five factors are working together. That's why we call them the five workers.

So, what do we have to follow to extinguish all kinds of suffering and to gain enlightenment? We need to follow these eight *maggaṅga*. Another term for these is the Middle Way. The Middle Way is the Noble Eightfold Path.

...

If we look at the whole body of the Buddha's teachings—which consists of the three baskets, or three canons—when we take the essence of them, we see there is just these 37 *bodhipakkhiya*, or requisites (factors) of enlightenment. From the four types of mindfulness to the eight factors of the Path, that's 37 factors of enlightenment we've been talking about in this section. These 37 factors compose the Noble Eightfold Path.

But we can say that the Noble Eightfold Path is briefly comprised of just three factors. What are they? *Sīla*, *samādhi* and *paññā*. Right speech, right action and right livelihood are *sīla*, right effort, right mindfulness and right concentration are *samādhi*, and right understanding and right thought are *paññā*. So we can say that the whole of the Buddha's teachings comes down to these three components.

And looking further still, we can see that among the three baskets of the Buddha's teachings, *sīla* is Vinaya, or discipline. The essence of Vinaya is *sīla*. As for *Suttanta* (the discourses), this is *samādhi* in essence. Lastly, Abhidhammā has *paññā* as its essence.

So, just *sīla*, *samādhi* and *paññā*. We can say that the essence of the Buddha's teachings, or the heart of Buddhism, is morality, concentration and wisdom. This is the Noble Eightfold Path. When we practice meditation, we have to follow this Middle Way, which fulfills our *sīla*, *samādhi* and *paññā*.

Even though there are 37 factors of enlightenment, the essential elements amount to just 14 in number. These 37 factors of enlightenment are collectively found only in supramundane consciousness. That is, when we gain enlightenment we completely experience all of these.

On the other hand, according to the type of consciousness, with mundane consciousness we may experience some of them separately but not all of them completely. Do you see how this contrasts with enlightenment, when we experience all of them completely?

So, separately and within mundane consciousness, we talk about the seven categories of *bodhipakkhiya*. I'm talking about *satipaṭṭhāna*, *sammappadhānā*, *indriya*, and so on.

Now, let's take a look at *viriya*, which is effort. This occurs in nine of the 37 factors of enlightenment. What are they? They are the four types of supreme effort, the one type of foundation of accomplishment, and with *indriya*...

Actually, we'll talk about this more next week. For now, time's up. Thank you.

Q: Can I ask a question? Does consciousness arise with nirodha? I understand that there's no consciousness with nibbāna, but is there consciousness with nirodha?

Correct, there's no consciousness with *nibbāna*. But when we talk about *nirodha*, we're not always talking about true *nirodha*. When we practice meditation, our craving, desire and greed stop. This is like *nirodha*—but it's just momentary. This defilement stops just temporarily. But *nirodha* is extinction. When we practice meditation, we temporarily experience the extinction of desire and craving. When you practice meditation, there's no desire or craving, right?

Nirodha is *nibbāna*. But some discourses talk about momentary *nirodha*. If you see something beautiful and don't focus your mind and contemplate on this desirable object, craving may occur. But when you contemplate the object, craving does not occur. In this moment, your desire is extinct.

...

Today is March 21, 1999. We will finish *bodhipakkhiyasaṅgaha*. How many sections are included in *bodhipakkhiyasaṅgaha*? Well, there are the four *satipaṭṭhāna*, the four *sammappadhānā*, the four *iddhipādā*, the five *indriya*, the five *bala*, the seven *bojjhaṅga*, and the eight *maggaṅga*. We've already studied all of these.

Even though there are 37 of these factors of enlightenment, their essential elements are just 14 in number. What are they?

1) *viriya*
2) *sati*
3) *amoha*
4) *ekaggatā*
5) *saddhā*
6) *vitakka*
7) *passadhi*
8) *pīti*
9) *tatramajjhattatā*
10) *chanda*
11) *citta*
12) *sammāvāca*
13) *sammākammanta*
14) *sammājiva*

Viriya

This is effort. How many times does in occur in *bodhipakkhiyasaṅgaha*? It occurs nine times: the four *sammappadhānā* (their realities are effort, right?), *viriyiddhipādā*, *viriyindriya*, *viriyabala*, *viriyasambojjhaṅga*, and *sammāvāyāma*. These are just *viriya*, right? That's their reality.

So *viriya* occurs nine times in *bodhipakkhiyasaṅgaha*.

Sati

How many times does this occur? Eight times. It's found in the four *satipaṭṭhāna*, *satindriya*, *satibala*, *satisambojjhaṅga*, and *sammāsati*. Altogether, that's eight.

Amoha

This is wisdom. It occurs five times: *vīmaṃsiddhipādā*, *paññindriya*, *paññābala*, *dhammavicayasambojjhaṅga*, and *sammādiṭṭhi*.

Ekaggatā

Just four times. What are they? *Samādhindriya*. *Samādhi* and *ekaggatā* are the same, right? There's also *samādhibala*, *samādhisambojjhaṅga*, and *sammāsamādhi*.

Saddhā

Just two times: *saddhindriya* and *saddhābala*.

The remaining nine realities appear just one time each among *bodhipakkhiyasaṅgaha*: *vitakka* is *sammāsaṅkappa*, *passadhi* is *passadhisambojjhaṅga*, *pīti* is *pītisambojjhaṅga*, *tatramajjhattatā* is *upekkhāsambojjhaṅga*, *chanda* is *chandiddhipādā*, *citta* is *cittiddhipādā*, *sammāvāca* is *sammāvāca* in *maggaṅga*, *sammākammanta* is *sammākammanta* in *maggaṅga*, and *sammājiva* is *sammājiva* in *maggaṅga*.

So these are the 14 realities among the 37 *bodhipakkhiyasaṅgaha*.

Sabbasaṅgaha

Let's go to *sabbasaṅgaha*. *Sabba* means the whole. *Saṅgaha* means compendium, so we can call this section the compendium of the whole. In this compendium, we will see mind and matter. It covers all *paramattha dhamma*, or *nāma* and *rūpa*. For this reason, we can call *sabbasaṅgaha* the miscellaneous compendium.

This section is also very important. We'll be talking about *khandha* (the five aggregates), *āyatana* (bases), *dhātu* (elements), and *sacca* (truths). When we practice meditation, we have to contemplate these various things.

The Five Khandha

First, we need to know the meaning of the word *khandha*. It means group, aggregate, or mass. We can use any of these English words.

Here, we'll be talking about five *khandhas*, or five aggregates. What are they?

1) *rūpakkhandha* (matter, or corporeal realities)
2) *vedanākkhandha* (feeling)
3) *saññākkhandha* (perception)
4) *saṅkhārakkhandha* (mental states, or mental formations)
5) *viññāṇakkhandha* (consciousness)

Khandha means a group, right? But "group" doesn't mean that these are things that we put together. It doesn't mean that a group is formed. Instead, it means that we have to take 11 aspects into account.

What are these 11 aspects?

1) past
2) present
3) future
4) internal
5) external
6) inferior
7) superior
8) distant
9) near
10) gross

11) subtle

How many is that? Eleven, right? With each of these five *khandhas*, these 11 aspects much be taken into account. These 11 aspects are collectively called a *khandha*.

Now you know what group, or *khandha*, means, right? It means these 11 aspects.

Now, I'd like to explain what is meant by the past, the present, and the future.

Let's look at *rūpakkhandha*, or matter:

Rūpa is past *rūpa*, present *rūpa*, or future *rūpa*. In other words, it is *rūpa* in the past, *rūpa* in the present, and *rūpa* in the future. We can see any of these *rūpa*.

For internal and external, internal includes that which is inside our body, right? It's internal. External is something that we can see on the outside of our body, someone else's body, or on the exterior of something else. We have both, right? So we have internal *rūpa* and external *rūpa*.

For inferior *rūpa* and superior *rūpa*, we can consider the *rūpa* of ordinary worldlings to be inferior, but the body of a noble person (*arahant*) is superior *rūpa*. So we have inferior *rūpa* and superior *rūpa*.

As for distant and near, we can consider that anything far away from us—that is, 12 feet or farther away—is distant. In contrast, anything that is less than 12 feet from our body is near. Another way to consider this is that if something is very easy to see, we can call it near. Something that is hard to see or understand is distant.

Lastly, we have gross and subtle, which we've already studied. How many types of subtle matter did we discuss in the third chapter of the second book? There were 16 types of *sukhuma* (subtle) *rūpa*, right? There were also 10 types of gross *rūpa*. What are these 10 types? They are eye-sensitivity, ear-sensitivity, nose-sensitivity, tongue-sensitivity, body-sensitivity, visible object, sound, smell, taste, and tangible object. These are the 10 types of hard (or gross) matter. And we have 16 types of subtle matter.

These 11 aspects are not found *only* in *rūpa*. All *khandha* have these 11 aspects.

Look at *vedanā*:

We have past feelings, right? "I felt this way many years ago..." We also have present feelings: "I feel this way now." And we have future feelings as well. So we have past, present and future *vedanā*. These are groups, right? That's why we call them *khandhas*.

We also have internal and external feelings, as well as inferior and superior feelings. What's an inferior feeling? If we have a pleasurable or displeasurable feeling about a sensual object or something demeritorious, then it's called inferior. Sometimes, though, we have a pleasurable feeling after doing something meritorious, right? This is called a superior feeling. Can you see how feelings can be superior or inferior?

We can also have feelings that are distant or near, and gross or subtle. So think about these 11 aspects, which we group into *khandhas*.

What about *saññā*? It's the same. This is perception, right? We can have perceptions about the past, the present, or the future. We can also have perceptions that are internal, external, and so on.

It's the same for mental formations or *viññāṇa*. If you understand just *rūpa*, the remaining four will be understood as well. With *viññāṇa*, we have past, present and future consciousness, and so on. See that?

The Buddha taught this analysis of these five kinds of aggregates. Why? He wanted us to eliminate the wrong perception or the wrong view of ego, self, personality, and so on. The strategy is to analyze this so-called being into five groups. If we have the wrong view about this matter, our thoughts, our speech, and our actions will be directed wrongly. The Buddha wanted us to get rid of wrong view. If wrong view is rooted in our mind, our actions, words and thoughts will be wrong. This will cast us down to the lower states again and again.

What happens when we have wrong view? We take issue with one person, then another, then yet another. One country has problems with other countries, right? Why? Because of wrong view. If we have the wrong view of personality, we become selfish. And if we are selfish, problems will follow.

This is why the Buddha divided an individual into five aggregates. When we understand the nature of these five aggregates one-by-one, we will see that we experience all of them in every moment. We will come to see just five aggregates—no I, no you, no man, no woman—just performing their functions. They just arise and disappear. They are impermanent, suffering, and not-self.

When we really understand the nature and characteristics of the five aggregates, we won't have to worry or feel sorrow over the sufferings of this body, our position in life, or anything else. Otherwise, we will experience misery anytime things don't go as we wish they would.

So we need to study, and especially, practice meditation to understand these five aggregates. Normally, we think this is man, this is woman, this is I, or this is you. But, really, it's just five aggregates. They arise together and disappear together in every moment.

Right now, you're listening to what I'm talking about, but really, it's just five aggregates arising and disappearing. What's the first one? *Rūpakkhandha*. There is my voice, right? This is *saddha*, which is one kind of *rūpa*. There's also your ear-sensitivity, which is also *rūpa*. This *rūpa* is just arising, continuing, and disappearing. In *Pāli*, we call this *uppāda* (arising), *ṭhiti* (continuation), and *bhaṅga* (dissolution). So there's just *rūpa* in every moment.

When you hear what I'm talking about, you have a feeling. This is *vedanākkhandha*. The feeling may be pleasant, unpleasant, or perhaps neutral. It depends on your thought or reaction, right? Even if someone says something kind to us, sometimes we don't want to hear it and end up with an unpleasant feeling, right? Can you see how feelings arise?

There's also perception, or *saññākkhandha*. We speak using terms that we already know and understand. What's *khandha* mean? We've already learned what it means, so there's perception—"Oh, I know what this means." Because we have already talked about *khandha*, and you memorized the word, you know what I mean when I say it. This is perception.

What about *saṅkhārakkhandha*, or mental formations? It's hard to explain this one because there is no equivalent English term for it. We can get close by calling it mental states, or mental formations. It's not exact, though. *Saṅkhāra* here is referring to *cetanā* (volition). We have 50 *cetasika* here, right? *Cetanā* is predominant in the remaining 49 *cetasika*. If you have a good or bad heart, a good or bad feeling, a good or bad thought, this is because of *saṅkhāra*, which forms your mind to become good or bad. We call this mental formation. We can also call these mental states. So now you try to listen to what I'm saying. This is *saṅkhārakkhandha*. You're paying attention. What's paying attention? *Vitakka*, or initial application. *Vitakka* is one of the 50 *cetasika* included in *saṅkhārakkhandha*. See how *vitakka*, which we call *saṅkhāra*, arises?

And there's *viññāṇakkhandha*. This is consciousness. You know the meaning of what I'm talking about, right? *Rūpa* cannot know. *Vedanā* is just feeling, so it can't know about the object either. *Saññā* is just perception—just the memorization of a name or term. *Saṅkhāra* merely forms the mind to pay attention to what I'm talking about. But the knowing is consciousness. You know what I'm talking about, and so you take notes and record them. Right?

So in every moment there is just these five aggregates arising together and disappearing together. We can't find a person here, right? Is it man, or is it woman? Really, there are just these five aggregates. The Buddha taught this for the purpose of allowing us to eliminate the wrong perception and wrong view of ego, self, personality, and so on. That is why he analyzed the individual in terms of five groups or aggregates.

What about their realities?

What's the *paramattha dhamma* of *rūpakkhandha*? It is the 28 *rūpa* (material properties), which we studied in the third chapter of the second book. I don't mean that it's the entire group of 28 here. Even just one of these 28 material properties is *rūpakkhandha*. Even your eye-sensitivity, which is just one of the 28 *rūpa*, is *rūpakkhandha*.

The reality of *vedanākkhandha* is *vedanā*, or feeling. The reality of *saññākkhandha* (perception) is *saññā cetasika*. What about for *saṅkhārakkhandha*? The reality is the remaining 50 *cetasika*, which excludes *vedanā* and *saññā*. We have 52 mental states, right? When we exclude *vedanā* and *saññā*, it leaves 50 *cetasika* remaining. These remaining 50 *cetasika* are called *saṅkhārakkhandha*.

Most people are confused about *saṅkhārakkhandha*. They wonder: "What is *saṅkhārakkhandha*?" It's not just one thing. *Saṅkhāra* here is the name of *cetanā* (volition). Because these 50 kinds of mental states are headed by *cetanā*, we call it *saṅkhārakkhandha*.

I'll give you an example:

Sometimes, the president of the United States will come to Las Vegas. When he does, we say, "Today, the president is coming." But it's not just the president who's coming, right? After all, he's accompanied by an entourage of maybe 40 or 50 people. Yet we still just say that the president is coming.

In the same way, *saṅkhāra* is the name of *cetanā* (volition), yet *cetanā* is not the only *saṅkhāra*. The remaining 49 *cetasika* are called *saṅkhārakkhandha*. Understand that, right? *Cetanā* is predominant over the other 49 mental states.

And what about *viññāṇakkhandha* (consciousness)? The reality is all 89 types of *citta*. In other words, the 89 types of *citta* are called *viññāṇakkhandha*.

So among the five aggregates, the realities are *rūpa*, *cetasika* and *citta*. No *nibbāna*, right? We have four realities, or *paramattha dhamma*. They include *rūpa*, *cetasika*, *citta* and *nibbāna*. But there's no *nibbāna* here. Why can't *nibbāna* form an aggregate? *Nibbāna* lacks differentiation. That's why.

What's differentiation? We can't consider *nibbāna* in terms of past *nibbāna*, present *nibbāna*, or future *nibbāna*. This is because *nibbāna* is timeless. For this reason, we exclude it from the category of "aggregate."

Nibbāna is not only timeless. What about internal and external? Remember how we group the various aspects in terms of internal or external, inferior or superior, distant or near, and gross or subtle? *Nibbāna* is just one, so it can't form a group. For this reason, *nibbāna* is external. It is not internal. If someone says that "*nibbāna* is in our heart (or in our body)," it's not accurate. There is just suffering in our hearts and bodies, and *nibbāna* is not suffering. It is external and beyond our five aggregates.

How about inferior and superior? *Nibbāna* is superior. What about distant and near? It's distant. After all, if it was near then everyone could gain it. It's distant, so we have to try so hard. And how about gross and subtle? It's subtle.

So just one, right? This is what is meant by *nibbāna* lacking differentiation. There's no past, present or future, but as for internal or external (and so on), there's just one. Because it's just one, it can't form a *khandha*, or group. I can't form a group by myself, right? There must be you and I to form a group. In other words, we can call ourselves a group if we are together. An individual cannot form a group. *Nibbāna* is like this.

The Five Upādānakkhandhā

We have another kind of *khandha* here—that is, we also have five *upādānakkhandhā*. We're dividing *khandha* into two, right? The first *khandha*, which we just talked about, includes both mundane and supramundane. *Viññāṇakkhandha* includes the 89 types of consciousness, right? These 89 types include both the mundane and the supramundane. But as for the five *upādānakkhandhā*, only mundane is included.

What is *upādāna*? It's grasping, or clinging. We're talking now about aggregates of grasping or clinging. This means that these five aggregates are objects of clinging. What is clinging? We studied this before, right? What is it? Do you remember? It is *kāmupādānā*, *diṭṭhupādānā*, *sīlabbatupādānā* and *attavādupādāna*. Their realities are just *lobha* and *diṭṭhi*. *Kāmupādānā* (clinging to sensual pleasure) has *lobha* as its reality. The remaining three have wrong view (*diṭṭhi*) as their reality. So *upādāna* is just *lobha* and *diṭṭhi*.

So these five aggregates (*upādānakkhandhā*) are the objects of clinging. They are the objects of *lobha* and *diṭṭhi*, and the supramundane cannot be the object of either.

The Buddha explained *upādānakkhandhā* for the purpose of practicing *vipassanā* meditation. When he explained how to practice this type of meditation, he taught us which objects we need to observe. He tried to explain these five aggregates for that very purpose.

1) *rūpūpādānakkhandho*

The reality of *rūpakkhandha* is the 28 types of *rūpa*, right? But do you remember when we were studying material properties in the third chapter of the second book? We learned about *nipphanna rūpa* and *anipphanna rūpa*. We can take only the 18 *nipphanna rūpa* as meditation objects. The remaining 10 material properties that are not born of *kamma* are not treated as *ūpādānakkhandha*.

Why can we take the 18 *nipphanna rūpa* as meditation objects? Because they have the characteristics of impermanence, suffering, and non-self. What about the 10 *anipphanna rūpa*? This includes space, which is the space between *rūpa*. This cannot be our meditation object. We also can't use bodily and vocal intimation as meditation objects. And it's the same for the three mutable material properties and the four characteristics of matter. So, excluding these 10 *rūpa*, that leaves the remaining 18 *nipphanna rūpa* to be taken as meditation objects.

Please remember that, among *rūpa*, only these 18 *nipphanna rūpa* can be taken as objects of *vipassanā* meditation. In English, we call them concretely-produced matter. But, generally-speaking, these 28 kinds of material properties are mundane. Please remember the distinction between 28 *rūpa* and 18 *rūpa*. When we do morning chanting, you may recognize the part in which we chant "*rūpūpādānakkhandho, vedanūpādanakkhandho* (and so on)." This is what we're talking about.

2) *vedanūpādānakkhandho*

The reality here is just *vedanā*. But this *vedanā* is not the same *vedanā* as before. The *vedanā* of *vedanākkhandha* is found in all *citta*, but here we're just talking about *vedanā* in mundane *citta*. How many types of mundane *citta* are there? There are eighty-one. This is because we are excluding the four types of *magga citta* and the four types of *phala citta*.

Can you see how this differs from our previous discussion of *vedanākkhandha*?

3) *saññūpādānakkhandho*

This is just *saññā cetasika*. It is only in the 81 types of mundane *citta*. With *saññākkhandha,* we studied all *citta*, right? Here, it's just mundane.

4) *saṅkhārūpādānakkhandho*

The reality is the remaining 50 *cetasika*.

5) *viññāṇūpādānakkhandho*

This is *citta*. Here, it takes only the 81 types of mundane *citta*.

We're just talking about mundane *citta*, right? This is why it's just mundane *citta* that we can take as our meditation object. How can we take the four types of *magga citta* or the four types of *phala citta* as meditation objects if we haven't yet reached that level? We can't, which is why we can only take mundane *citta* until then.

So now we know about *khandhas*. These *khandhas* are especially suitable for meditators who are deluded by mentality, or *nāma*.

When we look at all *paramattha dhammas* (realities) here, what do we see? The first is *rūpa* (matter) and the second, third, fourth and fifth are *nāma*. How many *cetasika* (mental states) do we have? We have fifty-two. Among how many *khandhas* do we find these 52 *cetasika*? Three *khandhas*. What are they? They are *vedanūpādānakkhandho*, *saññūpādānakkhandho* and *saṅkhārūpādānakkhandho*. Where do these three *khandhas* come from? *Cetasika*. We call these *nāma*. And what about *viññāṇūpādānakkhandho*? This is *citta*, or consciousness.

So we have just one *rūpa khandha* and four *nāma khandhas*. For this reason, those who are deluded by *nāma* who study and practice with these *khandhas* as objects find that things become very clear—they will understand the nature of *nāma*, or mentality.

Those with keen mental faculties—that is, those with very sharp *indriya*—can study the *khandhas* and will understand right away. They can then practice meditation and gain enlightenment quickly. These are good objects for those with keen mental faculties.

The 12 *Āyatana*

We'll now talk about the 12 *āyatana*. We call these fields, or bases. What are they the bases of? They are the bases of *citta* and *cetasika*. They are the place of mind and mental states. In other words, mind and mental factors cannot arise without these *āyatana*.

I'll give an example:

If we don't have eye-sensitivity, then eye-consciousness cannot arise. But even if we have eye-sensitivity, if there is no visible object—this is *āyatana* too—then eye-consciousness cannot arise.

These are bases of consciousness and mental factors.

Āyatana cause the long cycle of misery. Why do we have to be reborn again and again in *saṃsāra*? Because of *āyatana*—because of eyes, ears, nose, tongue, body, mind, forms, sounds, smells, tastes, tangible objects, and cognizable objects. These are the 12 *āyatana*.

What are they?

1) *cakkhāyatanaṃ*

This is eye-base. When we do *Paṭṭhāna* chanting, we say "*cakkhāyatanaṃ, sotāyatanaṃ*..." This is what we're talking about.

Cakkhāyatanaṃ is eye-base. The reality is *cakkhu-pasāda*, or eye-sensitivity.

2) *sotāyatanaṃ*

This is ear-base. The reality is *sota-pasāda*, or ear-sensitivity.

3) *ghāṇāyatanaṃ*

This is nose-base. The reality is *ghāna-pasāda*, or nose-sensitivity.

4) *jivhāyatanaṃ*

This is tongue-base. The reality is *jivhā-pasāda*, or tongue-sensitivity.

5) *kāyāyatanaṃ*

This is body-base. The reality is *kaya-pasāda*, or body-sensitivity.

We call these first five *āyatana* the five sense-organs.

6) *manāyatanaṃ*

This is mind-base. The reality is *citta*. How many? The 89 *citta*.

7) *rūpāyatanaṃ*

This is visible object, or *rūpa*. Here, *rūpa* doesn't mean all 28 types of *rūpa*. In this context, it's referring to just one: form, or shape. You can see it, right? We call this *rūpa*.

8) *saddāyatanaṃ*

This is sound.

9) *gandhāyatanaṃ*

This is odor. *Gandha* is smell.

10) *rasāyatanaṃ*

This is taste. The word *rasa* means taste.

11) *phoṭṭhabbāyatanaṃ*

This is tangible object. What is this, though? It's *pathavī* (earth-element), *tejo* (fire-element) and *vāyo* (air-element). These are tangible objects. Notice how there's no water-element. This is because we can't touch water-element. We can only touch earth-element, fire-element and air-element.

What are the characteristics of *pathavī*? Hardness and softness. You can feel that, right? What about *tejo*? This is temperature. You can feel heat or cold. How about *vāyo*? This is pressure, pushing, moving or motion. We can feel this too.

Tangible objects are just these three material qualities.

12) *dhammāyatanaṃ*

This is cognizable object. These are objects we take with our mind, right? We don't take them by our eyes, ears, nose, tongue or body. Collectively, we can call the 7th through the 12th *āyatana* the six sense-objects, though.

The reality here is *cetasika*, *sukhuma-rūpa*, and *nibbāna*. So what does *dhammāyatanaṃ* take? The 52 *cetasika*, the 16 types of subtle matter, and *nibbāna*. We have no concepts here, right? This is because concepts don't belong to reality. We're talking about realities, right? Concepts are not realities. This is why we exclude *paññatti* here.

If we're talking about *dhamma* objects, or *dhammārammaṇa*—which we studied in the third chapter of the first book—then *paññatti* is included. But we're not talking about *dhamma* objects here. Instead, we're talking about *dhammāyatanaṃ*, which is different.

We have six *dhammārammaṇa*. Do you remember these from the third chapter of the first book?

a) all 89 types of *citta*
b) all 52 types of *cetasika*
c) the five sensitivities (i.e., eye-sensitivity, ear-sensitivity, nose-sensitivity, tongue-sensitivity, and body-sensitivity)
d) the 16 kinds of subtle matter
e) *nibbāna*
f) *paññatti*

In contrast, *dhammāyatana* take just three:

a) *cetasika*
b) *sukhuma-rūpa*
c) *nibbāna*

Please remember the difference between these two.

So how many entities do we have here? We have 52 *cetasika*, 16 subtle matters, and *nibbāna*. These 69 total entities are regarded as the sphere of cognizable objects. We can't see *nibbāna* with our eyes. We're talking about *dhammāyatanaṃ*, right? So how can we see *nibbāna*? With the mind. This is because it's a cognizable object. If someone says they practice meditation and can go to heaven to see *nibbāna*, it's not correct. We can only see *nibbāna* with the wisdom-eye—not the physical eye.

So, how many *āyatana* are there altogether? There are twelve. Why did the Buddha talk about these 12 *āyatana*? So that we could see the absence of an ego or entity. He wanted us to see that there is no ego, no person, no man, no woman. There is just these 12 *āyatana*. When we understand that there is no ego—rather, there is just these 12 *āyatana*—this very understanding may lead us to liberation.

These *āyatana* are especially suitable for those meditators who are deluded by *rūpa*, or materiality. Among the 12 *āyatana*, the Buddha talked a lot about *rūpa*, didn't he? But when he talked about *khandhas*, he talked about just one *rūpa*, right?

How many *rūpa* did he talk about in the context of *āyatana*? He talked about *cakkhāyatanaṃ*, *sotāyatanaṃ* and *ghāṇāyatanaṃ*, as well as *jivhāyatanaṃ* and *kāyāyatanaṃ*. He also talked about *rūpāyatanaṃ*, *saddāyatanaṃ* and *gandhāyatanaṃ*, as well as *rasāyatanaṃ* and *phoṭṭhabbāyatanaṃ*. See that? All of these are *rūpa*. As for mind, he just talked about *manāyatanaṃ* and *dhammāyatanaṃ*. The Buddha mostly talked about *āyatana* as an analysis of *rūpa*. This is why those deluded by *rūpa* will understand easily. This is especially suitable for those deluded by materiality. When we practice meditation, we will clearly understand what these realities really are.

Where does *āyatana* come from? Briefly, *nāma-rūpa*. Just *nāma* and *rūpa*. What about the five aggregates? Four of them are *nāma*. In total, they are just *nāma* and *rūpa*.

<u>*The 18 Dhātu*</u>

Now, we go to *dhātu*, or elements. We have 18 elements.

Dhātu means that which bears its own characteristics. It doesn't follow anyone's power. No one can control it because it bears its own characteristics. That's why we call them *dhātu*.

What are they?

1) *Cakkhudhātu*
2) *Sotadhātu*
3) *Ghāṇadhātu*
4) *Jivhādhātu*
5) *Kāyadhātu*
6) *Rūpadhātu*
7) *Saddadhātu*
8) *Gandhadhātu*

9) *Rasadhātu*
10) *Phoṭṭhabbadhātu*
11) *Cakkhuviññāṇadhātu*
12) *Sotaviññāṇadhātu*
13) *Ghāṇaviññāṇadhātu*
14) *Jivhāviññāṇadhātu*
15) *Kāyaviññāṇadhātu*
16) *Manodhātu*
17) *Manoviññāṇadhātu*
18) *Dhammadhātu*

What's the reality of *cakkhudhātu*, or eye-element? The reality is *cakkhu-pasāda*, or eye-sensitivity. That is *cakkhudhātu*. What is an element? That which bears its own characteristics. So what's the characteristic of *cakkhudhātu*? Just seeing. It's for seeing, right? If you want to see something, you can't use your ear or your nose. You use your eye. This supports seeing, but eye-sensitivity cannot see. What sees? Eye-consciousness, right? But this is supported by eye-sensitivity.

What about *sotadhātu*? This is ear-element. Its reality is *sota-pasāda*, or ear-sensitivity. *Ghāṇadhātu* is nose-element. Its reality is *ghāna-pasāda*, or nose-sensitivity. *Jivhādhātu* is tongue-element. Its reality is *jivhā-pasāda*, or tongue-sensitivity. *Kāyadhātu* is body-element. Its reality is *kaya-pasāda*, or body-sensitivity.

Rūpadhātu is visible object, *saddadhātu* is sound, *gandhadhātu* is smell or odor, *rasadhātu* is taste, and *phoṭṭhabbadhātu* is *pathavī, tejo* and *vāyo*.

Next, we have *cakkhuviññāṇadhātu* (which is what we call eye-consciousness-element), *sotaviññāṇadhātu* (ear-consciousness-element), *ghāṇaviññāṇadhātu* (nose-consciousness-element), *jivhāviññāṇadhātu* (tongue-consciousness-element), and then, *kāyaviññāṇadhātu* (body-consciousness-element).

For the last three, we start with *manodhātu*, which is mind-element. Do you remember when we studied the reality of this in the first chapter of the first book? What is the reality? *Pañcadvārāvajjana*, or the one type of five-sense-door adverting consciousness, and the two types of *sampaṭicchana* (receiving consciousness). These three types of consciousness are called *manodhātu*.

Manoviññāṇadhātu is mind-consciousness-element. *Mano* means mind, *viññāṇa* means consciousness, and *dhātu* means element. How many? It is 76 types of *citta*. Excluding the 10 types of five-sense-impressions (which is the two types of *cakkhuviññāṇa*, the two types of *sotaviññāṇa*, the two types of *ghaṇaviññāṇa*, the two types of *jivhāviññāṇa*, and the two types of *kāyaviññāṇa*) and the three types of *manodhātu*, the remaining 76 types of consciousness are called *manoviññāṇadhātu*. We have 89 total types of *citta*, right? So we subtract the 13 types I just mentioned to get 76 types that are called *manoviññāṇadhātu*. When we do *Paṭṭhāna* chanting, we see that word, right? We will study it more soon.

The last one is *dhammadhātu*, or cognizable-element. This means the same thing as *dhammāyatana*, which is the following 69 entities: 52 *cetasikas*, 16 subtle matters, and *nibbāna*.

How many of these are what we can call subjective elements? Six. What are they? They are the first five elements (i.e., *cakkhudhātu, sotadhātu, ghāṇadhātu, jivhādhātu* and *kāyadhātu*) and *manodhātu*. These six elements are called subjective elements.

What about six objective elements? These are *rūpadhātu, saddadhātu, gandhadhātu, rasadhātu* and *phoṭṭhabbadhātu*, as well as *dhammadhātu*. These are called objective elements.

The remaining six elements are called intellectual elements. They are concerned with mind, or consciousness. What are they? They include *cakkhuviññāṇadhātu, sotaviññāṇadhātu* and *ghāṇaviññāṇadhātu*, as well as *jivhāviññāṇadhātu* and *kāyaviññāṇadhātu*, plus *manoviññāṇadhātu*. These are the six intellectual elements.

Altogether, that's 18 elements.

When we study these 18 elements, we won't see an ego or a person. We see their nature as just elements performing their duty. In every moment, there is just *dhātu* arising and disappearing.

So among the *dhātu*, how many are *nāma* and how many are *rūpa*? The first through the tenth are just *rūpa*, right? And the 11th through the 17th are just mind. But the 18th is *nāma* and *rūpa*.

When we studied the first chapter of the first book, we learned about how many types of *viññāṇa* (consciousness) there are, right? We have *cakkhuviññāṇadhātu, sotaviññāṇadhātu* and *ghāṇaviññāṇadhātu*, as well as *jivhāviññāṇadhātu* and *kāyaviññāṇadhātu*. Plus, we have *manodhātu* and *manoviññāṇadhātu*. In other words, all types of consciousness can be classified into seven *dhātu*.

We should understand that because of *cakkhudhātu* and *rūpadhātu*, there arises *cakkhuviññāṇadhātu*. This means that because of the contact between eye-sensitivity and a visible object, eye-consciousness arises.

In the same way, because of the contact between *sotadhātu* and *saddadhātu*, there arises *sotaviññāṇadhātu*. Because of the contact between *ghāṇadhātu* and *gandhadhātu*, there arises *ghāṇaviññāṇadhātu*. Because of the contact between *jivhādhātu* and *rasadhātu*, there arises *jivhāviññāṇadhātu*. Because of the contact between *kāyadhātu* and *phoṭṭhabbadhātu*, there arises *kāyaviññāṇadhātu*. And lastly, because of the contact between *manodhātu* and *dhammadhātu*, there arises *manoviññāṇadhātu*.

...

So, the manner of teaching depends on the audience and their mental faculties. The Buddha considered the nature of the person he was teaching. He knew that if he explained impermanence in terms of the five aggregates, there would be people who would understand right away. Other people needed to hear impermanence taught in terms of the 12 bases for them to understand. "Oh, I see. There's no person, no personality, no man, no woman. There's just *nāma* and *rūpa*." In still other cases, the Buddha needed to explain impermanence in terms of the 18 *dhātu* for his audience to understand.

For meditators, the main point is to understand that no matter what you contemplate on—whether your meditation object is the five aggregates, the 12 bases or the 18 elements—you need to come to realize their nature of impermanence, arising and disappearing, and so on.

The Four Sacca

Now we go to *sacca*. This is very important too. Now, all mind and matter—all *paramattha dhamma* (realities)—will be explained in terms of the four *sacca*, or truths.

1) *Dukkha ariyasacca*

You already know what *sacca* means. *Dukkha* means suffering. You already know this too. You experience it every day. In *Pāli*, *dukkha* consists of *du* and *kha*. *Du* means contemptible, and *kha* means emptiness or void. Therefore, *dukkha* is a contemptible void. Another meaning is "difficult to endure." If you understand *dukkha* as suffering, that's okay too.

Why *ariya*? This means pure, or noble. We should know why this *dukkha* is *ariyasacca*. So what's the reality of *dukkha ariyasacca*? It is the 81 types of *lokiya* (mundane) *citta*, the 52 *cetasika*, and the 28 *rūpa*.

Why do we call this *ariyasacca*, or a noble truth? This is the noble truth of suffering, right? In terms of a noble truth, noble doesn't mean high or lofty. The truth isn't necessarily high or lofty, wholesome or unwholesome. What is true is called *sacca*.

Dukkha ariyasacca is the noble truth of suffering. It exists in the three planes of suffering, but not in supramundane *citta*.

2) *Dukkhasamudayo ariyasacca*

This is the noble truth of the cause of suffering. Its reality is *lobha cetasika*. This craving, this *lobha* is the cause of suffering.

3) *Dukkhanirodho ariyasacca*

This is the noble truth of the cessation of suffering. Its reality is *nibbāna*.

4) *Dukkhanirodhagāminīpaṭipadā ariyasacca*

This is the noble truth of the path leading to the cessation of suffering. Its reality is the eight factors of the Noble Path. We studied the eight *magganga* already, didn't we? Indeed, these eight *magganga* are the *dukkhanirodhagāminīpaṭipadā*, or the Noble Eightfold Path.

I'd like to talk a bit more about why we call these *ariyasacca*.

Ariya means pure or noble, right? *Dukkha, samudaya, nirodha* and *magga*—these Four Noble Truths—are understood by the noble ones. Not everyone knows *dukkha*, right? Sure, perhaps everyone understands *dukkha-dukkha*. But maybe only meditators understand *saṅkhāra-dukkha* and *vipariṇāma-dukkha*. So these truths are understood or penetrated by the noble ones. That's why they're called *ariyasacca*.

Another meaning is that the truths were taught by the greatest noble one. Who started teaching these Four Noble Truths? The Buddha, who was the noblest of the nobles. So, truths taught by the greatest noble one are called *ariyasacca*.

Another meaning is that these are truths that will make you a noble one. In other words, if you understand the Four Noble Truths, you will become a noble one. You can't gain enlightenment and become a noble one without knowing or understanding the Four Noble Truths.

Still another meaning is that they are real truth. The Buddha said that birth is suffering, decay is suffering, disease is suffering, and death is suffering. Who can go against that? Right? This is real truth. Where's it come from? Craving, or attachment. Who can reject this? No one. You have to accept it because it's correct. If there is no craving, then there is no suffering, which means there is *nirodha* (*nibbāna*). This is supreme bliss. Who can reject that? No one. What do those who would like to gain enlightenment have to do? Try to follow the Noble Eightfold Path leading to *nibbāna*. No one can reject that either. These Four Noble Truths can't be rejected because they are actual truths.

So why do we call these *ariyasacca*? Because of these four meanings.

The Buddha taught about the five aggregates (*khandhā*), bases (*āyatana*), and elements (*dhātu*), right? He also taught about *sacca* because after you know *ariyasacca*, you gain enlightenment. As such, this teaching is very useful for people. See that, right?

Some people have said that there's nothing in the Buddha's teachings that lies outside of the Four Noble Truths. The Buddha taught every day for 45 years. In the whole of his teachings, there is nothing outside of the Four Noble Truths. Everything is included in them.

What do we see with these Noble Truths? With *dukkha ariyasacca*, the reality is *lokiya citta*. There's no *lokuttara citta*, right? With *samudaya*, the reality is *lobha cetasika*. With *nirodha*, the reality is *nibbāna*. And with *magga*, there is just the eight *maggaṅga*.

Where are the eight types of supramundane *citta*? They're not included here, right? See that? Where are they? After all, there is nothing within the Buddha's teachings that lies outside of the Noble Truths.

We take off the eight types of supramundane consciousness and their specific *cetasika* because we already took off the eight *maggaṅga*, right? In other words, they are part of *magga sacca. Lokuttara citta* associates with 36 kinds of mental factors, so when we take off the eight *maggaṅga*, that leaves 28 mental factors. These leftover 28 *cetasika* from the eight types of supramundane consciousness can just be put into suffering because their characteristics are the same as *saṅkhāra-dukkha*.

The four *phala citta* associate with 36 kinds of *cetasika* since they are part of *lokuttara citta*. In the context of *phala citta*, we can still put the eight *maggaṅga* into *dukkhanirodhagāminīpaṭipadā* because they are the results of *magga citta*. See that?

I would like all of you to try to understand and practice to see these realities in order to gain enlightenment. Now, time's up. Thank you.

Q: What about an arahant? What kind of vedanā do they have when they're not in nibbāna?

Sometimes, *sukha vedanā*. Since they have bodies, they have *dukkha vedanā* too. They can also have *upekkhā vedanā*, but they don't have *domanassa vedanā*. The eight types of *mahākiriyā citta* are accompanied by either *somanassa* or *upekkhā*, right? They have two. So, some have two *vedanā*, but not *domanassa* because that's only found in unwholesome consciousness, which they already eradicated.

Arahants can only have *dukkha vedanā*, *sukha vedanā*, *somanassa vedanā*, and *upekkhā vedanā*.

Q: What about plants and rocks and things like that, do they have mind and matter interaction?

No, just matter.

...

Today is April 11, 1999. I would like to continue talking about *sacca*—the Four Noble Truths. As you've all learned here, we can briefly call the Four Noble Truths by the names *dukkha*, *samudaya*, *nirodha* and *magga*. The full names are long, right? But please try to remember these four short names.

What is the reality of *dukkha* (suffering)? The reality is all existence in the sensuous-sphere, the form-sphere and the formless-sphere. *Lokiya* (mundane) consciousness, *cetasika* and *rūpa* are called *dukkha*.

What do we see when we practice meditation? Just the mundane, right? We may see our mind, mental factors or material properties. We see *dukkha*, right? Why do we see *dukkha*? We already studied this. It is because all of these *citta*, *cetasika* and *rūpa* are being oppressed by arising and disappearing. This is why we call them *dukkha*. So, lacking the supramundane, all mundane phenomena are suffering.

With *samudaya*, the reality is *lobha*, or craving. Craving is the cause of suffering.

And what is the reality of *nirodha*? It is *nibbāna*, or the cessation of suffering. Many people say that Buddhists just talk about suffering. But there's not only suffering being talked about here, right? The Buddha also taught the cessation of suffering, or supreme bliss. This isn't talking about suffering. *Nirodha* is *nibbāna*.

Magga is the cause in order to reach the cessation of suffering. The cause is the eight factors of the Noble Path. It's not the cause of cessation, mind you. Rather, it's the cause in order to reach the cessation of suffering.

So we can see here that the first and second Noble Truths—*dukkha* and *samudaya*—are mundane. The third and the fourth—*nirodha* and *magga*—are supramundane. See that, right? Mundane and supramundane. Suffering and craving are mundane, and *nibbāna* and the Noble Eightfold Path are supramundane.

How about cause and effect? What's the cause here? The second Noble Truth (*samudaya*) is the cause of the first Noble Truth (*dukkha*). The fourth Noble Truth (*magga*) is the cause in order to reach the third Noble Truth (*nibbāna*). The second and fourth Noble Truths are causes, and the first and third Noble Truths are effects. See that? Just cause and effect.

As I said, there is nothing in the Buddha's teachings that lie outside of the Four Noble Truths, but the Noble Truths just have cause and effect. Buddhism is about cause and effect.

Now, with respect to noble truth and ultimate truth, what is ultimate truth? *Citta*, *cetasika*, *rūpa* and *nibbāna*. These are ultimate truths. The Four Noble Truths are ultimate truths. See that?

What should meditators follow, do or avoid if they really want to gain enlightenment? We should know this. Every meditation center, including this one, has rules written down. Maybe you can't read the ones we have written on our walls here because they're in Thai. But those who come to practice meditation here should follow certain rules that prevent us from declining in our practice. They are designed to help us improve our concentration and grow our knowledge until we reach our destination. This is very important too.

So, there are seven things that I would like you to remember. These seven things will help prevent you from declining in your practice. These are especially useful for meditators.

The Seven Rules for Meditators

1) Not to be fond of busyness

What does this mean? Some people like to do this or do that. They have many, many things to do. They enjoy staying busy. They have so many things they want to do. But that type of person cannot improve their concentration and wisdom. We should not be fond of busyness.

Some people like to entertain themselves by drawing or playing games. This isn't good for meditators trying to gain concentration. When you come to practice meditation at a retreat, you don't have to do anything else. Don't do anything else.

2) Not to be fond of gossip

As all of you know, most people like to talk and talk. They love to talk non-stop for hours. Right? Meditators should not be fond of doing this. We need a silent retreat with no talking.

3) Not to be fond of sleeping

Some people sleep more than 10 hours. How can you gain enlightenment that way? Meditators coming to a meditation center like this one for a silent retreat should sleep no more than four hours. That's enough sleep for a meditator. In daily life, though, six hours is sufficient.

Some people sleep for six or eight hours during the night but then take a nap during the day too, right? We shouldn't do this, especially as meditators. Don't be fond of sleeping.

4) Not to be fond of society

Some people are always going to birthday parties, this thing or that thing, chasing after their social life. When they do, they neglect their spiritual life. As such, they can't improve their concentration or their wisdom. They cannot reach their liberation.

Don't be fond of society. Instead, reduce society. Many people go to weekly parties and out to restaurants but this isn't good behavior for meditators.

5) Not to fall under the influence of evil desire

Even when we're at home or spending time at a temple or meditation center, we can get lost in evil desire. "I want to see this...hear that...smell this..." or "I want to eat...I want to wear that..." We get lost in thinking about colors, smells, sounds, tastes and touches. This is evil desire. We get lost in thinking about getting our hands on things we want.

Meditators should not do this.

Instead, what should we do? Just concentrate. When we concentrate our mind on our primary object, evil desire has no opportunity to arise. The only opportunity we have to control our desire is when we're practicing meditation. Even if we close our eyes and try to shut out the world of visual objects, evil desire constantly arises anyway.

6) Not to have evil friends

Friends are very important. If we associate with evil friends, they will induce us to do like them. Maybe we won't follow their ways at first, but given enough time and influence, we likely will. They will give us bad ideas and guide us in unskillful directions.

Don't have evil friends. This is very important. By this, I mean don't have evil teachers either. Some teachers expect things from you. That's not a good friend. A good friend and a good teacher will not expect anything from you.

7) Not to stop halfway

This refers to practicing meditation and gaining some concentration but then stopping. It's not good to do this. Keep trying until you reach your goal. Don't stop halfway.

These seven things are very important to understand. Please follow this guidance. As all of us would like to realize the Four Noble Truths, we study and understand them intellectually. But we have not yet experienced them by path-knowledge. Perhaps we understand suffering and the cause of suffering, right? But we don't really know the cessation of suffering yet, right? We just know through inferential knowledge at this point. It's not yet intuitive knowledge.

To help us realize the Four Noble Truths, the Buddha offered some discourses of guidance. He gave us four factors to help us become a stream-enterer, to gain the first stage of enlightenment. What do we need? Please remember these four things, as they are the four essentials for becoming a stream-enterer:

The Four Essentials for Stream-entry

1) Association with the virtuous

This means good friends and a good teacher. We need these, right? Good people.

2) Listening to good doctrine

Good doctrine means that it should be concerned with realities that lead us toward enlightenment.

3) Giving proper attention to the Dhamma

This means that we should have proper attention with anything that comes across our eyes, ears, nose, tongue, body and mind. If we still see a man, a woman, a permanent thing, mine or yours, these are concepts—not realities. When we're not seeing realties, it's wrong view. When we have wrong view, mental defilements can arise. It could be craving, hatred, anger, conceit, or perhaps jealousy. This is because we are still seeing concepts and not realities.

When we see just mind and matter in everything—just five aggregates—we don't see mine or me or I or you. There's no personal belief and no ego delusion. No mental defilements arise. This is proper attention. Just mind and matter. Seeing is just seeing-consciousness. It's not me.

When we see mind and matter, we don't see some sustained thing that persists. One moment at a time, there is arising and disappearing. We see these realities, these characteristics. This is proper attention. Impermanence, unsatisfactoriness, uncontrollability. Not ego; rather, non-self. If we see this, it's proper attention.

We should have proper attention. With whatever we see, hear, smell, taste or touch, those who really want to gain enlightenment should have proper attention.

4) Conducting oneself in conformity with the Dhamma

If we would like to become a stream-enterer in this life, we should conduct ourselves in conformity with the Dhamma. So what do we have to do? In brief, the Dhamma is concerned with morality, concentration and wisdom. When we fulfill these three things, we gain enlightenment.

Conforming with the Dhamma means that we need good virtue, or morality. At minimum, our five precepts should be firm and pure. Without pure precepts, we can't gain enlightenment. If we can't fulfill our precepts, we can't gain concentration. We can't gain enlightenment without concentration. We need to practice meditation every day to train the mind to gain concentration.

Some people have good virtue and good concentration but practice only *samatha* (tranquility) meditation. They may gain concentration but it doesn't conform with the Dhamma. So what do they still need? Wisdom. They need to improve their wisdom, step by step. I'm talking about *vipassanā* knowledge. Try to practice meditation to gain knowledge.

So this is what it means to conduct ourselves in conformity with the Dhamma. If we really want to gain enlightenment, we need morality, concentration and wisdom.

So, four kinds of things. What numbers do we need? What numbers do we already have?

1) Associate with the virtuous
2) Listen to good doctrine

Don't listen to stories. Listen to doctrines about the five aggregates, the 12 bases, the 18 elements, the Four Noble Truths, the factors of enlightenment, and so on.

3) Give proper attention

We already study and know. How about your attention? We have to train the mind.

4) Have morality, concentration and wisdom

If these four kinds of things are fulfilled in this present life, you will become a stream-enterer. These are the four factors to gain the first stage of enlightenment.

The Four Kinds of Meditators

For the most part, if we lack proper attention, our actions, speech and thoughts will go in the wrong direction. But when we have proper attention, it leads to moral consciousness. Consequently, we will have wholesome thoughts, speech and behaviors.

Among meditators, there are four kinds of persons:

1) In the old days, the Buddha or the *arahants* would teach a few words or a couple of sentences and the student would gain enlightenment right away. The discourses talk about this. After just a few words, the student would realize the Noble Truths and become a noble person.

2) In the old days, the Buddha or the *arahants* would take an hour or so to explain something in detail. The student, in turn, would understand the reality of impermanence (and so on) and then gain enlightenment.

Nowadays, we can't find these two kinds of people. Today, there's no way for students to simply listen to the Dhamma and gain enlightenment, even if we listen for hours. These two kinds of people existed only in the time of the Buddha. We know about these people because their enlightenment stories are in the discourses.

3) The person has to study and practice and then gains enlightenment. We call this person 'guidable'. This is people like us. We need to study first and then practice. After that, we can gain enlightenment.

4) Even if the person practices meditation every day, there is no way for him to gain enlightenment in this life. However, this practice of meditation can be the cause for enlightenment in the next life.

So we have these four kinds of meditators. We're the third type, right? We study and practice, and can then gain enlightenment. We can't just listen briefly or in detail. We can't gain enlightenment that way.

The Four Modes of Progress to Deliverance

Some people ask, "Why do people who practice meditation have different experiences? Some don't have to practice for long before they gain enlightenment, while others practice for a long time before they see results. And some people suffer in their practice, while others have it very easy. Why?"

We have four kinds of deliverance. I'd like you to keep this in mind. What number might we be? These are the four modes of progress to deliverance:

1) Painful progress with slow insight

Insight means knowledge, right? In this case, practicing meditation is very hard. The person suffers a lot while sitting in meditation. The insight is slow too. It takes a long time for them to gain knowledge.

Why is the progress painful? Because they have so much mental defilement. We studied the 10 kinds of mental defilement, right? They have a lot of greed, hatred and delusion.

Why is there slow insight? Because their five mental faculties are very weak. This is why it's slow. Remember the five mental faculties? They are faith, effort, mindfulness, concentration and wisdom. These are very weak, so insight is very slow.

2) Painful progress with quick insight

In this case, painful feelings keep arising and arising when meditation is practiced. There is a lot of suffering. But the realities and the characteristics are soon realized. As such, enlightenment can happen quickly. Even though the person has to suffer, he might practice meditation for just a couple of weeks or a month and gain enlightenment.

3) Pleasant progress with slow insight

In this case, there's not much suffering to be endured while practicing meditation. Sitting or walking meditation is very pleasant, with little or no painful feelings. However, gaining knowledge is very slow and attaining enlightenment takes time.

4) Pleasant progress with quick insight

In this case, there's little suffering when practicing meditation. The meditation is pleasant, with insight coming quickly. The person understands and realizes realities and the characteristics of mind and body. In not so long, they gain enlightenment.

So, after you gain enlightenment, what kind of person were you? You will know for yourself.

How about you, Marjorie? Painful or pleasant?

Q: I think I'm number 1.

That's okay, right? You'll gain enlightenment eventually.

Some people cry because the pain is so bad. Others sit in meditation for a week and feel rapture and happiness. When they go to the meditation master to report their experiences, they're very happy to tell about it. Sometimes it doesn't take so long for people to gain enlightenment.

So, why painful progress? Many mental defilements. Why slow? Mental faculties are weak. Quick? Mental faculties are strong.

We need to understand these things.

So now we know the conditions to become a stream-enterer, the different types of meditators, and what we have to do as a meditator to make progress in our development of concentration and wisdom. We should follow this guidance. Don't worry. You can gain enlightenment in this life.

Q: When you talked about ultimate truth, where is vedanā in that?

Look at suffering. It includes mundane *citta* and the 52 *cetasika*. *Vedanā* is part of *dukkha*. *Vedanā* is *saṅkhāra-dukkha*. Why is it *dukkha*? Because it is just arising and disappearing too. It's changing all the time. This is *vipariṇāma-dukkha*. Pain feelings are suffering as well. This is *dukkha-dukkha*.

Do you remember when we studied the three kind of *dukkha*?

Let's look at *lobha*. This craving is the cause of suffering, but it too is just arising and disappearing. This too is *dukkha*. It is *saṅkhāra-dukkha*. Craving doesn't last long before it changes too. This is suffering in change, or *vipariṇāma-dukkha*. However, *lobha* is not *dukkha-dukkha*. Craving is not painful.

In talking about the Four Noble Truths, we learned that *lobha* is the cause of suffering. We call it *samudaya*. *Samudaya* means cause or condition. Soon, we will study dependent origination, which is about cause and effect. All causes are *samudaya*. But we should understand the context. Are we talking about the Four Noble Truths, about dependent origination, or something else? If we're talking about dependent origination, craving itself is the cause or the effect. We will study this very soon. For now, though, we know the Four Noble Truths: *dukkha*, *samudaya*, *nirodha* and *magga*.

Q: If the fourth Noble Truth is dukkhanirodhagāminīpaṭipadā ariyasacca, why are we calling it magga? Where does it say magga?

Even though the name doesn't say *maggaṅga*, the reality is the eight factors of the Noble Path. This is *maggaṅga*. We just call it *magga*, or the way.

Any more questions about the Four Noble Truths?

If you have no questions, we'll start the next section. It's a profound teaching of the Buddha.

The printing of this book was generously sponsored by:

Las Vegas Sayādaw - $500
Nun Medhāvī & Rita Chanvisanuruk - $500
Nun Sandra Than Pe (Sandapuññamī) - $500
Daw Shoke Chain & Myo Win (Wendy Zhuang) - $300
Darin Zimmerman - $200
Saisuda Saedan - $100
Anintita Sivara - $100
Douen Peterson - $50
U Sann Tun Ni & Khin May Oo - $700
Daw Kyin Sar Yi Family - $200
Rose Lu Family - $200
Daw Kyin Yi Family - $100
Sopranee Singralavanich - $100
Suda Thongnoi & Family - $100
Supreeda Dispun & Family - $100
Sompis R Bhukeaw - $200
Supatra Dibona Numthong - $100
Good Thai Spa Massage: Kantamanee, Rattawipat Wanporn Prasert - $100
Samruay Chaisiri - $100
Pramong Pellerin - $100
Jumnian Noppagit & Family - $100
Bounlom Outtha - $40
Wimon Thompson - $20
Naruemon Swann - $60
Kunnika Albertson - $20
Wanphen McIntosh - $20
Prasert & Karatai - $20
Somporn Santago - $40
Pui – Piyawan Phillips - $100
Sandar Chen - $100
Pavinee (Mam) Chen - $100
Jintana & Jimmy Coe - $100
Khun Wan - $50
Khun Watsana - $20
Sirinart Butrpho - $100
Merrylou & Geno Lonardo - $20
Ping Kumpanon Family - $300
Gin Yu - $200

Made in the USA
Columbia, SC
21 October 2024

44488943R00115